GANDHIAN MODEL OF DEVELOPMENT AND WORLD PEACE

Gandhian Studies and Peace Research Series

1. Gandhian Model of Development and World Peace/ R.P. Misra (Ed.)
2. Conflict Resolution Through Non-Violence : Role of the Universities (in two Vols.)/ K.D. Gangrade and R.P. Misra (Eds.)
3. Vol. 1 : Science and Ethics/ K.D. Gangrade and R.P. Misra
   Vol. 2 : Development without Destruction/ K.D. Gangrade and R.P. Misra
4. The Social Philosophy of Mahatma Gandhi/ K.S. Bharathi
5. Gandhian Humanism/ Mohit Chakrabarti
6. Gandhian Holistic Economics/ Shashi Prabha Sharma
7. Gandhian Spiritualism : A Quest for Essence of Excellence/ Mohit Chakrabarti
8. Gandhian Perspective on Population and Development/ A.K. Sharma
9. Thoughts of Gandhi and Vinoba : A Comparative Study/ K.S. Bharathi
10. Economic Philosophy of Mahatma Gandhi/ Shanti Swarup Gupta
11. Political Thought of Mahatma Gandhi (The)/ K.S. Bharathi
12. Gandhi and 21st Century/ Janardhan Pandey (Ed.)
13. Gandhian Philosophy of the Spinning Wheel/ Mohit Chakrabarti
14. Gandhian Satyagraha : An Analytical and Critical Approach/ Ajay Shanker Rai
15. Gandhi and His Religion/ (Lt. Col.)/ P.A. Raju
16. महात्मा गाँधी विचार वीथिका/ एस.पी. अग्रवाल
17. Poverty of Gandhian Philosophy/ Himansu Roy
18. Right to Equality in the Indian Constitution : A Gandhian Perspective/ Shashi Nath Saraswati
19. Meditations on Gandhi : A Ravindra Varma Festschrift/ M.P. Mathai, M.S. John and Siby K. Joseph (Eds.)
20. Politico-Economic Ideas of Mahatma Gandhi : Their Relevance in the Present-Day/ Sukhendu Mazumdar
21. Moral Lessons from Gandhi's Autobiography and Other Essays/ K.D. Gangrade
22. Fire Sans Ire : A Critical Study of Gandhian Nonviolence/ Mohit Chakrabarti
23. Gandhian Alternative (Volume 1 : Towards a Gandhian World Order)/ Suresh Misra (Ed.)
24. Gandhian Alternative (Volume 2 : Nonviolence in Action)/ Savita Singh and Bharati Misra (Eds.)
25. Gandhian Alternative (Volume 3 : Socio-Political Thoughts)/ Anil Dutta Mishra and Sushma Yadav (Eds.)
26. Gandhian Alternative (Volume 4 : Economics Where People Matter)/ V.K. Natraj Kamlesh Misra and Neeru Kapoor (Eds.)
27. Gandhian Alternative (Volume 5 : Education for Human Development)/ Suresh Misra (Ed.)
28. Gandhian Approach to Development Planning/ Ram Binod Singh

Gandhian Studies and Peace Research Series—1

GANDHIAN MODEL OF DEVELOPMENT AND WORLD PEACE

R.P. MISRA
Editor

CONCEPT PUBLISHING COMPANY, NEW DELHI-110 059

ISBN 81-7022-227-3

First Published 1989
Second Edition 1990
Reprinted 2006

R.P. Misra (*b.* 1930)

Published and Printed by
Ashok Kumar Mittal
Concept Publishing Company
A/15-16, Commercial Block, Mohan Garden,
New Delhi-110 059 (India)

Phones : 25351460, 25351794
Fax : 091-11-25357103
Email : publishing@conceptpub.com

Preface to the Second Edition

This book, being reprinted within a short period of six months, is indicative of the growing interest in Gandhi and his philosophy. There is violence, conflict, insecurity and debasement of eternal human values all over the world. While clouds of thermo-nuclear war are still hovering, newer dangers posed by the annihilation of life on the earth through environmental pollution, over-warming of the earth and attack of ultra-violet rays resulting from widening ozone hole loom large before us. The lopsided development that started with the industrial revolution in Europe has now engulfed the whole world. This book gives a glimpse of the Gandhian way to rectify the situation.

As the proposal for a second print came up for discussion, a set of two volumes entitled *Conflict Resolution through Non-Violence: Role of Universities* on related themes was ready for the press. Suggestions for new studies and publications also came up for deliberations. It was decided to incorporate all these and also future publications in a series called *Gandhian Studies and Peace Research Series*. This volume is the first in this series.

I am confident that the series will be as popular as its first volume and the efforts that we are making in Gandhi Bhawan, University of Delhi, to contribute to the creation of better and more livable world will make further headway through the medium of these publications.

R.P. MISRA

Preface to the First Edition

As the twentyfirst century draws closure, the human race faces unprecedented challenges for its survival and development. The Third Wave is surging and tommorow's technologies are already outdating todays. But in terms of human values, we still live in yester years. Our capacity to destroy has vastly increased but our willingness to temper this capacity with humility and wisdom has not changed for the better. As such the stabilities of the past are being replaced by the uncertainties of the future.

New technologies offer opportunities to do more for more people now, and in the future. But the rat race for acquisition and personal agrandizement has left millions of people of the world poor and destitute. Billions of dollars are being spend on weapons of destruction, but we have paltry little to quench the thirst and hunger of millions.

Gandhiji said that the earth had enough to satisfy everyone's need but not everyone's greed. We must periodically examine the economic, social, and technological policies we persue globally nationally, and locally so that the needs get precedence over the greeds. We must also have fresh looks at the concepts, theories, and models which are foundations of policies pursued by different nations and peoples. We should not be swayed by what is popular and widely accepted. What is good in the long run, is often unpalatable in the short run. The survival and development of man in future will depend on our willingness to use the unprecedented opportunities offered by the ever expanding knowledge and fast changing technology for constructive rather than destructive purpose which in turn depends on our capacity to re-establish a more humane social order.

Mahatma Gandhi offered a model of such an order. His philosophy of history; his experiments with what he said TRUTH, and his vision of a future wherein human life will be valued as an end rather than as a resource, were concretized in this model. It was a model of resonant humanity at peace. The economic relations which bind the people together and keep the system dynamically creative, progressive and peaceful constitute the core of the Gandhian Model.

The Gandhi Bhavan, University of Delhi, has launched a series of studies and conferences to examine and analyse Gandhi's ideas, thoughts, and concepts in a common frame of reference, distill his principles of action, and discover the structural details of his model of a new and peaceful world order. This is to be achieved in four stages.

As a first step in this direction, a national conference on Gandhian Model of Development and World Peace was held on 29-31 January 1988. This volume is the by-product of that conference. The next step includes holding of an international conference on Theory and Practice of Conflict Resolution with particular reference to Gandhian ideology. Research involving the following aspects will constitute the third stage:

1. Collection, collation and analysis of Gandhian literature on development, peace and harmony;

2. Case studies of selected experiments in India and abroad on peaceful conflict resolution at local, regional or national/international levels; and

3. Preparation of research reports and training documents using the above materials

Publication of the materials so produced for wider distribution and utilization of the same in training of the youth and community leaders, will be the final stage of the programme.

This volume contains a set of papers discussed in the conference on Gandhian Model of Development and World Peace. A few papers have been drawn from outside the conference proceedings to fill important gaps. The book has been published with a view to carry the message of Gandhi and the views of the participants of the conference to a much wider circle of people having interest in Gandhian ideology.

I am grateful to the contributors for participation in the conference and writing the papers at a rather short notice. We do hope that their support to Gandhi Bhavan will continue in future and that the book will add a new dimension to the work being done in India and abroad on Gandhi and his means to establish peace and harmony in the world.

R.P. MISRA

Contents

List of Contributors

Lata Chatterjee: Boston University, Boston, U.S.A.

Sandhya Chaudhri: Department of Gandhian Studies, Panjab University, Chandigarh

Clark D. Cunningham: Wayne State University, Detroit Michigan, U.S.A.

R.R. Diwakar: Chairman, Gandhi Peace Foundation, New Delhi

Marjarie Fernandes: Sr. Lecturer in Economics, Janki Devi Mahavidyalaya, Delhi University, New Delhi

K.D. Gangrade: Pro-Vice Chancellor, Delhi University, Delhi

Om Prakash Gupta: Gandhi-Kasturba Seva Sangham, Aman Basera, Uppal, Hyderabad-500039

D.B. Kerur: Member Secretary, Gandhi Darshan Academy, Kothrud, Pune

R.P. Misra: Director, Gandhi Bhawan, University of Delhi, Delhi

Suresh Misra: ICSSR Doctoral Fellow, G.B. Pant Social Science Institute, Allahabad

K.M. Muniandi: Gandhi Niketan Ashram, Kallupatti, Tamil Nadu

Jai Narain: Lecturer, Department of Gandhian Studies, Punjab University, Chandigarh

Robert T. Norman: Urban and Regional Planning Programme, Graduate School of Public and International Affairs, University of Pittsburgh U.S.A.

Kamalakant Panda: Motilal Nehru College, Delhi University, Delhi

B.P. Pandey: Gandhian Institute of Studies, Rajghat, Varanasi

M.L. Sharma: Department of Gandhian Studies, Panjab University, Chandigarh

Shashi Sharma: Lecturer in Economics, Daulat Ram College, Delhi University, Delhi

M. Subrahamanyam: Reader, Department of Political Science, Aligarh Muslim University, Aligarh

S. Vardarajan: Department of Geology, University of Delhi, Delhi

1

INTRODUCTION

R.P. MISRA and T.R. LAKSHAMANAN

Perspectives on Peace

Human survival and development depends on world peace - on whether we can prevent nuclear war; on whether we can harness modern science and technology to the betterment of human welfare; on whether we can forestall serious natural resource and environmental damages; on whether we develop the appropriate adjustments and institutions to share the fruits of technical change equitably enough to ward off hunger, malnutrition and the conflicts generated by the disadvantaged. While impressive advances have been made in raising the consciousness of people about the dangers of war in general and nuclear war in particular, much remains to be done on increasing the awareness of the generic nature of local conflicts and threats to peace originating from the massive modernization processes underway in the Third World.

The question of peace and international cooperation has to be addressed from two complementary perspectives. One derives from a perspective of peaceful coexistence among nations and states. It focuses on avoidance of war and includes strategies, processes and instrumentalities that minimize tensions, augment the balance of power, attempt to reduce arms and armed forces, and promote negotiated settlement of international problems. It builds on the large corpus of research on international relations, superpower rivalries, regional conflicts and security, and the technological and organizational innovations that may help manage arms control negotiations and peacetime cross-national links between military and civilian groups.

The second perspective is 'bottom up' and stems from a view of local conflicts among groups of peoples and subnational units that often spill over into the rest of the nation, neighbouring nations and have the potential to threaten regional and international peace. Indeed, many major conflicts have been rooted in small scale conflicts resulting from real or perceived ethnic, political, social and economic deprivation of one group or the other. Frequently, such local conflicts derive from the change processes underway in the developing regions of Latin America, Africa, and Asia, where the pace of technology change and economic development is very brisk; where the adverse impact of man on certain elements of the environment are already severe and where social injustice resulting from the vastly unequal relations between groups and regions within and among countries have tended to get accentuated. While the seeds of many of these conflicts lie in the colonial experience, they have been exacerbated greatly in the post colonial period by the choices of development technologies, by strategies of natural resource management, styles of institutional development and the nature of insertion of these countries in the World Economic Order. (See Fig. 1)

A deeper analysis of these two dimensions of the problem of peace suggests considerable correlation between them. International conflicts generate their impacts on peoples everywhere often affecting their occupational structure, earning capacities, social relations, and lifestyles in general. On the other hand, local conflicts originating in some form of socioeconomic injustice, often spill over into the larger world region in terms of contagious conflicts, involuntary migration, etc., and where superpower involvement occurs, they become major threats to peace. Further, local conflicts, given their frequent and widespread occurrence can cause cumulatively enormous

Figure 1

Nearly all the 25 big wars going on in the world this week are in third world countries. They have killed about 3m people so far—four-fifth of them civilians.

THE WORLD'S WARS

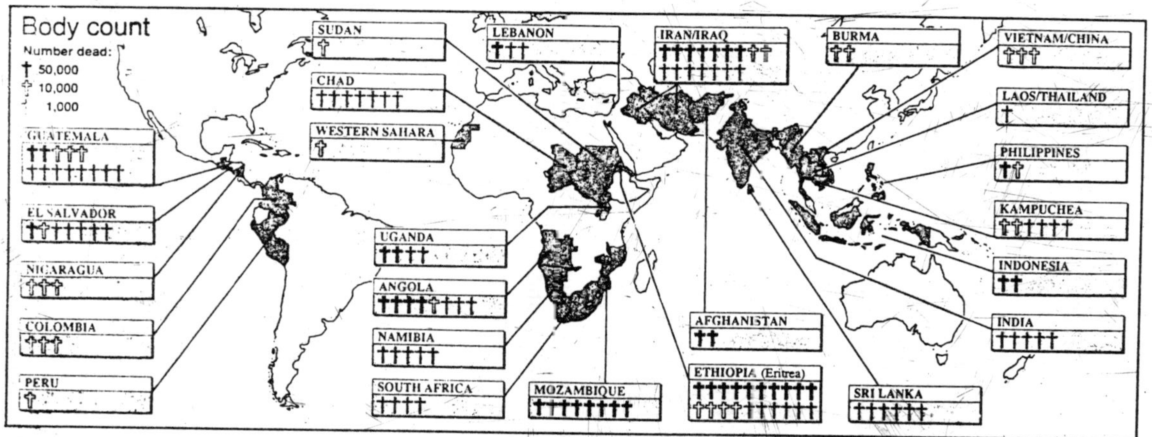

Source: "The Economist", March 12, 1988

Turn south for the killing fields

suffering and loss of human life, even without international spil-lovers. Again, when one contemplates the destructive power of emerging armament technologies, the potential that local conflicts hold for widespread regional and even global devastation is non-trivial. Consequently, these conflicts have to be managed at both the international and local levels.

A survey of the literature and works in progress concerned with peace and conflict resolution suggests however, the dominance of the first perspective of avoidance of major conflicts resulting from superpower and large regional power rivalries. Little, if any, attention seems to have been devoted to local conflicts among groups of people that have considerable potential for international repercussions. Greater attention to the latter problem would require a broader approach. Wherein the analysis of apparent and immediate causes of conflicts in these Third World societies is matched by a simultaneous inquiry into the conflicts inherent in the ongoing complex process of transformation - the wrenching process of formation of nation states out of highly heterogeneous ethnic and social groups, the massive dislocations associated with sweeping technological and economic changes, and the processes of changes in attitudes and life-styles associated with modernization.

A number of approaches to address this problem do exist and range all the way from liberal to the Marxist positions. These approaches are not only partial but incorporate fundamental notions of competition and confrontation that limit their capacity to ameliorate conflicts. An approach that has been inadequately emphasized, but holds out considerable potential in this area is the Gandhian model of conflict resolution. The Gandhian approach emphasizes individual development in a cooperative modality. This communitarian approach to tackling change in a number of dimensions that Gandhi advocated appears to embody elements which could greatly reduce a variety of conflicts at source, and thus strengthen the efforts at global peace.

The Gandhian Approach

The roots of a significant number of local conflicts and threats to peace appear to lie in the inequities and deprivations which derive from history and the processes of socioeconomic and political transformation underway in the developing world. Consequently, efforts to alleviate local conflicts must be build on our understanding of the complex links between change processes and types of conflicts.

Such a broad understanding of the conflicts inherent to the social structure and institutions is the province of the "grand systems" of political economy. Two of the better known grand systems are the liberal and Marxist. We suggest here that the Gandhian model of conflict resolution and peace is another grand system whose ideology and operational logic, though less well known, hold out great potential for our purpose.

Each grand system has a set of basic assumptions and 'ethic' that constitute a matrix of ideas for validating that system's notion of social progress. This reciprocal relationship between ideology and operational analysis typifies all grand systems. A comparison of these three alternative grand systems can be provided by the way they would conceptualize the fundamental unit of decision and action in the realm of political economy. The liberal system focuses on the atomistic individual as the relevant unit; on the description of economic behaviour in terms of subjective choices among alternatives; on the notion of social welfare as the maximization of individual utility sums. The socialist system views the entire economic system as the basic unit, views economic progress in terms of the growth of the forces of production and focuses on 'relations of production', 'surplus value' and the rapid increase of social product.

By contrast, the Gandhian system eschews both the notions of the atomistic autonomous individual maximizing his utility in a self-regulating economy, and the notion of processes of production autonomously effecting changes in the organization of production, class relationships,. and the magnitude and distribution of social product. Instead, the Gandhian model suggests that the fundamental attribute of human economic behaviour lies in the relationship of the individual to socioeconomic microgroups and the relationship of microgroups to society. The basic economic act is neither the choice between economic alternatives nor the social division of natural product, but the adjustment between individual and the microgroups to which they belong, and of those microgroups to society. It is this *collaboration* which is the basic theme of the Gandhian system of political economy.

The Gandhian system is viewed as organized in microgroups that are viewed as fundamental constituents of the economic system and given full scope to develop their potential in the context of noncoercive forms of political control. Social welfare is defined in terms of the functioning of the collaborative microgroup vis-a-vis its members. There remains the problem of violence (i.e. selfish/non-collaborative/exploitative behaviour) by one microgroup against another or by a combination of microgroups against others. This is tackled by organizing the economic system as a whole as an interlocking hierarchy of microgroups. The economy as a whole is organized as expanding circles or 'oceanic circles', with mutually reinforcing links. Gandhi visualized also large scale economic organizations whose efficient operation requires both hierarchical discipline and some components of a centralized management subsystem. To deal with problems of avoiding coercive or exploitative (violent) behaviour, Gandhi suggested the principle of trusteeship that encouraged an active participatory decision framework. In addition, his system calls for profit making institutions which are subject to social control by being structured as decentralized institutions. Thus the entire structure of Gandhian economy is visualized as a collaborative enterprise whose major priority is the full utilization of manpower. Gandhi believed that the introduction of technology and patterns of development must be consistent with the full employment objective.

Gandhi expands this notion of a progressive, collaborative and non-coercive economy into ecological, social, institutional and ethical dimensions of the social system. Thus his ideas on the need for harmony between man and natural environment anticipated by decades much of the recent concerns regarding natural resource exhaustion and environmental damages, even in the advanced countries. Gandhi, noting the tendency in both capitalist and Marxian systems to increase rapidly the per worker resource consumption, suggested that in the absence of appropriate correctives, long before 'everyone' comes to reach a state of material affluence, modern economic growth will be brought to a halt by resource limitations - a prediction that the MIT (Forrester Meadows) World Models also made four decades later. While technical improvements in resource saving and resource substitution have reduced the danger of resource exhaustion, Gandhi's notions of changing the system of social incentives for resource use are the same sort that current advocates of environment quality and resource conservation in 'Spaceship Earth' believe in.

The broader Gandhian system which includes ideas on the choice of technology, economic growth with equity, and man as the 'end' of development is less well understood and articulated. These ideas have their foundations in Buddhist, Hindu and Christian Philosophies. Gandhi secularized these ideas and used them to attack the very cause of conflict in human society. Indeed the Gandhian system of interrelationships between the realm of political economy, ecology, social institutions, ethics and the humanized development, the causation is nonlinear and peace or conflict prevention are endogenized. Conflict is expected to be controlled at source.

Gandhi's ideas have been used to resolve a variety of problems. He could mobilize millions of illiterate people to wage a non-violent 'war' against the British to independence for India; Bahuguna a frail man from the mountains of Himalaya could follow Gandhi's footsteps to stop the destruction of forests by mobilizing the people for the Chipko movement; Vinoba Bhave, a disciple of Gandhi could secure thousands of acres of land for the landless through voluntary donations; Aryaratne in Sri Lanka could launch Sarvodya social order, based on mutual help and self-reliance; Fukuoka in Japan could experiment with natural agriculture; and Martin Luther King in the United States could win civil rights for the minorities. One can relate many cases and examples of successful experimentations. Cases of failure are not rare either.

Gandhi was neither a theorist, nor a philosopher. He was a man of action - an activist. One has to piece together many of his writings and actions to understand him and his concepts. It involves penetrating beyond the concrete Gandhian programmes and uncovering the analytical foundations on which they were based. Only then can we hope to rationally infer how, starting from Gandhian foundations, we can tackle the contemporary problems of development and peace.

Such an approach will require two things. First, it will require selectivity. From the corpus of Gandhi's pronouncements on various issues, which run into 100 volumes, we must select those which concern peace and conflict resolution. Second, it will require reinterpretation. The Gandhian concepts and analysis will require to be translated into the vocabulary of contemporary conflict resolution analysis and put into a relationship with the conceptual analytic framework of the modern approaches to peace.

Gandhi developed non-violence from a general formal ethical imperative to a concept of growing socioeconomic and political content. As he inveighed heavily against the oppression and violence in social life resulting from competitive and militaristic society, he wrote extensively on social, economic, political and ecological aspects. We have to assess these documents, some of which are perhaps fugitive, for review and interpretation in a systematic way. We must note that some of Gandhi's writings are often characterized by a paradox, if not by contradiction. Gandhi claimed to be a type of socialist, while at the same time believing in the Jeffersonian notion that a government governs best when it governs least. As one examines these hard to reconcile notions, two things are to be kept in mind. First, all these individual pronouncements have to be reconciled in the broader framework of his ideas. Second, when that is difficult, Gandhi's notions must be viewed not as fixed, but evolutionary and reinterpreted in the contemporary context. It is to this broader contemporary interpretation of the Gandhian Model, that we must direct our attention.

We must note that this is not a straightforward task. Over the last six decades or more, the Gandhian notions have attracted quite a bit of sentimental and mystical baggage. A considerable degree of demystification is necessary. We have (a) to develop a systematic interpretation of the Gandhian Model of development and conflict resolution, (b) to translate its contents into the vocabulary of contemporary literature on peace and conflict resolution, (c) to report on our research to the scholarly community in the peace and international cooperation area on the one hand and common people on the other and (d) to develop, deliver and evaluate training on the Gandhian approach to conflict prevention to opinion leaders the world over.

The Seminar

A comprehensive exploration of Gandhian literature and thoughts on development and peace requires collaborative efforts by a wide variety of experts ranging from traditional Gandhians adhering to the letter of what Gandhi said and wrote to modern social analysists who look into the spirit underlying his words and actions. Of course, there are those who reject Gandhi and his approach as irrelevant to their model of the emerging world. We must respect their privilege to hold their opinion and must try to understand the frame of reference of their thinking, for the divergence in conclusions often result from differences in perspectives.

As a first step in this direction, Gandhi Bhavan, University of Delhi, has decided to organize a series of seminars, symposia, Round Tables, and conferences involving researchers, thinkers, activists in the field of Gandhian studies, conflict resolution and international peace. The seminar on Gandhian Model of Development and World Peace held on 29-31 January 1988 is the first activity in this series.

The seminar attracted a large number of potential participants. Due to logistic limitations only thirty of them were invited to present papers. Since the meeting was exploratory in nature, the discussions extended far beyond its scope. Not all the papers, therefore, could be accommodated in this volume. Moreover, the papers written in Hindi were set aside for publication in a separate volume. To fill a few significant gaps, some papers not discussed in the seminar were also included. Thus the book now contains twentytwo papers, a short review of which is given below.

The present paper introduces the theme and thrust of the book and gives a summary view of its contents. The next two papers contributed by Kamalakant Panda and O.P. Gupta focus on Arms Race in the world and its implications for human welfare. Panda sees a conscious racial design. "It cannot be characterized merely as a symptom of underlying structural maladjustments... It could also be seen as a socio-cultural hegemonistic design meant for creating a situation of cumulative inequality". He reminds that the military expenditure minus R & D investments, in 1987 was $ 930 billion registering a 600 per cent increase since 1960. The two super powers accounted for 59 per cent of the total.

The implications of these expenditures have their ramifications all over the world. The national economies of the two superpowers are unable to cope with the emerging socio-economic realities. Structural maladjustments including unemployment are on the increase. Part of the problem is being diverted to the newly emerging nations which have become the centres of proxy wars. Expenditure on armament in the Third World Countries in 1981 was $ 81 billion which was 15-20 times more than the Official Development Assistance given to them by the developed countries. Panda concludes that poverty precedes political instability. Hunger cannot be tolerated any longer and concurs with Amartyasen's Theory of Entitlement as the basis for a new social order. There is need of weaponless deterence policy.

Gupta carries these reasonings further and concludes that "man has become a wrecked ship on the high seas". Mutual fear and distrust have clouded his thinking. It is this distorted thinking and contorted image of the world, which is the root cause of war. The problem lies in the man himself and hence the present attempts at disarmament and peace at the international level must be backed by simultaneous efforts at the local, regional and national levels to create and sustain an environment in which compassion, fellow-feeling, tolerance etc. grow. He calls this approach as basic to Gandhian philosophy.

Social Dynamics of Marx and Gandhi is the theme of the paper contributed by D.B. Kerur. Marx was a realist, saw the world as it had emerged through time and evolved the concept of class conflict. Gandhi saw not only the evolution of the society but also the evolution of man and projected both in the future. He was a visionary. He could not accept determinism. Gandhi's man was to act not on the dictates of the predetermined trend; he was to create a trend. "Gandhi raised politics to the level of religion. Truth and non-violence were the new secrets of political action. Gandhi resisted economic inequality but did not approve class war," for he knew that wars cannot be eliminated by wars nor injustice by injustice in reverse. That is why he never approved the inhuman aspects of either capitalism or socialism, and opposed industrialization, urbanization and mechanization short of human touch.

Gangrade's paper is a critique of the current economic and social development theories, approaches and practices and concludes that the struggle for development and eradication of poverty has to be conducted without sacrificing values and ethics that are cherished most. The symbiotic relationships between means and the end cannot and should not be broken. That alone can establish lasting equality and development.

The next three papers dwell on technology and development. In her paper on *Technology and Man: Gandhian Perspectives*, Shashi Sharma looks into the real meaning of human life - its purpose and mission. Man is a potentially Divine Entity; he is a part of whole and has the wholeness enfolded within him. As such she sees with Gandhi the man as the whole universe in a capsule form. It has vast potentialities. Its purpose is the realization of truth. Economics must be subservient to the basic goal of human life. When labour is treated as a means, it leads to exploitation, unemployment, inhuman living conditions, etc. Man becomes a machine to be oiled and fuelled. Purpose of development is to help man unfold his personality, his inner strength and develop his potentialities to the fullest extent.

Jai Narain interprets Gandhi in matters of technology as non-dogmatic and, humanist. In his scheme of things man is the centre piece. Nothing should come in the way of his freedom, self-expression and self-reliant development. No psychological, social or mechanical system should bind him to slavery. If man remains free; if he is not enslaved, Gandhi has no objection to sophisticated technology. Bullock cart for him is as meaningful and important as aeroplane. Both are important and relevant but only if they keep man human.

Lata Chatterjee's paper on *Women and the Promotion of Technological Development in Society* brings to our attention that technology is not neutral to sex, economic status, regional setting etc. True, technology has benefitted all but researches lead to the conclusion that the women are assigned to the lower technology end of production and therefore they have been paid less even for the same job. With further advances in labour substituting technologies, the demand for labour is declining affecting the women more than the men. This trend is likely to be further accentuated in future. In this context the Gandhian approach to technological development acquires added importance.

Public Health, Poverty and Empowerment written by David Werner warns us that in today's world the biggest obstacles to health for all are not technical, but rather social and political. Widespread hunger and poor health do not result from total scarcity of resources, or from overpopulation, as was once thought. Rather, they result from unfair distribution of land, resources, knowledge, and power - too much in the hands of too few. Or, as Mahatma Gandhi put it: "There is enough to meet everyone's need but not everyone's greed."

Referring to health care, he says, it "can be either people empowering in the sense that it gives people greater control over the factors that influence their health and their lives, as well as greater leverage over public institutions and leaders. Or it can be people disempowering, insofar as it is used by the authorities as an instrument of social control. People empowering health care utilizes health education, *not* to change people's attitudes and behaviour, but rather to help people to change their situation or, as Pablo Freire would say it, to change their world."

The tenth chapter covers Cunninghams paper on Legal Ethics. The concept of rule of law is one of the greatest contributions of modern civilization. Theoretically speaking, it has a great equalizing power for it applies to all irrespectives of ones status or background. It has, however, become an instrument to maintain inequality in the society. The growing complexity of laws and unequal access to institutions of justice resulting from unequal distribution of wealth and power, have made the concept of rule of law irrelevant in many societies.

Gandhi's objection to our legal system was not based on the above two considerations alone. He was against institutionalized legal system *per se*. He did not want the man to feel dependent on others for resolution of his problems with fellow beings or the society as a whole. Everyone must feel obliged to settle his or her problems amicably with others. One should not look outside for help and watch helplessly the decision to be given by others. This is possible if spiritual toleration is built in the human *Samskara*. It will not only help settle issues peacefully but will also minimize the emergence of conflicts and confrontations.

This concept is applied by M.L. Sharma to the problem of communal harmony in his paper on *Relevance of Mahatma Gandhi's Approach to Communal Harmony*. If violence cannot be stopped by violence the only way to bring communal harmony is to create a situation in which liberal attitude, truthfulness, humility, compassion, and tolerance become the bed rock of social relations. His eighteen point constructive programme was to generate such a situation.

Education was considered by Gandhi to be one of the main instruments to rebuild a non-violent society. Gandhi's life and work was an incessant search of truth leading to pathways of humanistic development. Varadarajan's paper elaborates this point under the title *Search for Unity in Diversity*. Diversity does not mean difference. Difference emphasises distance; diversity emphasises uniqueness. Live and let live principle is built in the concept of diversity. What unites the unique is a set of commonalities. When applied to society of different religions, colours, races, castes etc, it means a common set of *samsakaras*, common culture, common nationhood. This is what Subramanyam in his paper on Gandhian model of communal unity tells.

Lata Chatterjee takes us to Ghana in West Africa to prove that the Gandhian approach to development alone can solve the problems of the developing countries. The paper is divided into three parts; (1) organisation of production in Ghana (2) Regional impacts of production processes, and (3) Gandhian Alternative. She demonstrates with facts and figures that the poor have benefitted least from development planning in that country. Only collaborative and cooperative approach at the grassroots level involving the people can help empower the poor. Local level planning using the local resources and managed by the people themselves is needed.

Towards a Gandhian approach to planning is the title of paper by

B.P. Pandey. Best planning utilized the entire man power. Life should not be pyramid with apex sustained by the bottom. It should be an ever widening never ascending circle in which everyone has a place of honour; everyone is productive; and everyone is self-reliant; is the Gandhian view. He worked for decentralized economic order, and considered peoples participation as the most basic essence of planning. Suresh Misra calls for a realistic assessment of Gandhian thinking on Indian village. According to him, the Gandhian philosophy offers a practical way to a peaceful social revolution; to improve the quality of life of the people; and to ensure a self-reliant rural economy. His message was more for the future. And more and more of us now realize that the man who was treated as irrelevant once, is becoming more relevant than ever before. R.R. Diwakar has explained in a very succinct manner the meaning of Sarvodaya - which can be said to contain the essence of Gandhian model of development. Sarvodaya consisted of the observance of *Satya* (Truth), *Ahimsa* (non-violence), *Asteya* (abstinence), *Brahmacharya* (celibacy, chastity), *and Asangraha* (not to treasure or store).

R.T. Norman's paper entitled empowering cities and citizens enunciates a community based theory of power wherein individual needs and aspirations are met and served by the community through collaborative efforts. As Gandhi propounded, for such a planning, practice of non-violence was essential. He raises problems and questions which beg response. But pleads 'let us start'.

Education for Integrated Development (Muniandi), *National Integration and Education* (Sandhya Chowduri) and *Some Reflections on Development, Peace and Education: Gandhian Perspective* (Fernandes) conclude that education must be the concern of the community and not of the government. School should be the nerve centre of the community. If we can teach our children not only the three Rs but also truth, tolerance, brotherhood, non-violence, manual work, etc. through examples of our own, we can create a peaceful and progressive society. Learning by doing was the essence of Basic Education. They plead for return to the Gandhian approach to education and training.

Gandhiji's contributions to the perennial principles and eternal elements of Indian tradition by Kerur constitutes the last chapter of the book. The paper calls for the spiritualization of every aspect of life particularly politics to ensure the emergence of a peaceful social order.

On the whole, the papers, despite wide coverage, offer a central message which is summed up in the last para of Suresh Misra's paper which we quote below:

> What, therefore, is needed today is to work with true dedication for the principles that he (Gandhi) cherished and always valued. It is a pity that just within 40 years of Independence, the Father of the Nation has become a mere ceremonial figure; the Great has become a dwarf among his own followers. Today the country needs to develop and propagate the ideals of this Great Man *more than even before*.

Let us hope that we will move in this direction fast and make our own contributions to creation of a just and peaceful world using Gandhian approaches detailed in various chapters of this volume.

2

ARMS RACE, POVERTY AND POLITICAL INSTABILITY

KAMALAKANT PANDA

Any comprehensive and perspective oriented analysis of the issues of arms race, poverty and political instability would have to take into account, besides the Manichaean projection of both national and international "intersubjectivity", a broad and complex question of socio-economic and politico-strategic dimensions of both the developed and develoing economies. It cannot be visualized merely as a symptom of underlying structural maladjustments often characterized by increasing imbalances and inequities that operate inexorably to the detriment of the developing countries. It could also be seen as a socio-cultural hegemonistic design meant for creating a situation of cumulative inequity. As both strategy and ideology, it is not only subscribed to by both left and right developed economies, it is deliberately substantiated by policy projections of the ruling elites of the developing economies. The situation is, as usual, further aggravated by the structural and management deficiencies of the developed market economies that have resulted in the continuing trends of a high level of inflation, monetary disorders, chronic balance of payments imbalances, and unemployment crisis. This situation has been exploited by the developed economies as a pretext for postponing the adoption of measures necessary to attain structural changes in the international economy that are bound to affect the developing economies resulting in the sharpening of the contradictions throughout the international economic interactions. Not surprisingly the developed economies get these measures legitimized in the name of improving and expanding domestic psychological parameters as well as areas of national bargaining process for having an easy access to the international resources structures. The growth of science and technology, mutually stimulating action-reaction-over-reaction patterns created out of excessive militarization of political processes, increased involvement of internal military-industrial-bureaucratic complexs and external multinational industrial corporations in providing legitimizations and interactions between a domestic monopoly structure and its external counterparts, and multiple sectoral adjustments between divergent social, economic, cultural and political components of the systems, have often necessitated the creation of a new correlation between economic power and political power. This post-war development can never be understood by a Marxist perspective that provides a misleading and dangerous framework that considers all political disagreements to be caused simply by socio-economic structures of a system. It often ignores the role of a minority within the dominant class that controls the State apparatus. It also neglects the psychoanalysis of political conflicts that is bound to result in a clash between the citizens and the State, particularly in a society where needs outstrip goods available.

Since the Second World War, an evidence of an aggressive armamentism, its camouflaged form of exploitation, could primarily be seen in the militarization programme of the superpower economies, their desire to dominate and share various regions of the world. Since 1960, the military expenditure all over the world has gone up by 600 per cent. This amount does not include armaments oriented R&D programmes in the defence establishments and civilian research programmes of allied nature. In 1987, out of the total annual global military expenditure of $ 930 billion, the USA spent $ 293 billion on its military and the Soviet Union, $ 260 billion. Both represented more than 59 per cent of the world's military expenditure. There was an increase of $ 13 billion in US military spending and $ 15 billion in the Soviet spending from 1986. During 1987, the developed countries spent $ 790 billion on the military, a boost of $ 76 billion. Twentytwo wars were under way in 1987. This huge expenditure on armament programmes has adversely affected the economies of the developed countries. The sluggish growth rate of only 2 per cent in the US economy has forced the Wall Street experts to be pessimistic about the overall economy's future. Since February 1985, the value of dollar has fallen by almost 50 per cent, with an unemployment figure at 5.9 per cent in 1987, prediction of an inflation rate to rise by 4.3 per cent in 1988, and a foreign trade deficit of $ 156.2 billion in 1986, and a federal budget deficit dipping to $ 148 billion in the fiscal year ending on September 30, 1987, the US economy would be in a recession before the end of 1988. This economic crisis is bound to affect the economies of the developing countries that are linked to the US economy, and would definitely put them out of gear leading towards an increasing authoritarian structure.

The proliferation of the arms trade has adversely affected the balance of trade and terms of exchange. This situation is an important element of coercion that affects developing countries in any negotiations. The debt burdens of developing countries have given birth to infrastructural inhibitions that affect the incentive structure of decision-making process, the savings and capital formation methods, issues of national integration and regional growth, and social and political stability. It breeds an on-going armament culture and provides an alibi as well as justification for State repression of non-State institutions.

During 1986, despite a little decline in the ratio of debt to GNP, debt service as a proportion of exports of goods and services increased. The ratio of debt to GNP went on increasing from 20.6 in 1980 to 35.8 in 1985. The real interest rate for developing countries decreased from 12.1 per cent in 1985 to 8.1 per cent in 1986. Although many debtor countries expanded their exports during 1983-84, "for several of the highly indebted countries low commodity prices, high real interest rates, sluggish growth in the industrial countries, and in some cases their own macro-economic and trade policies" meant that the present levels of debt could not be reconciled with the present levels of growth leading to a peculiar situation often referred to as "the debt overhang".

The International Financial Corporation in its latest annual report mentions that there is a continuing stagnation of capital flows to developing countries which has resulted in a net transfer of resources from them to the tune of $ 30 billion in fiscal 1980. Since 1981, there is a steady decline in new commercial lendings. Foreign direct investment flows to capital importing developing countries has not increased since 1983, and has remained at around $ 10 billion in 1986. The 109 developing countries reporting to the World Bank debtor reporting system paid out $ 30 billion more in interest service than they received in the form of net disbursements of long-term loans from both private and official sources. During 1986 the gross domestic product of the developing countries, as a group, deteriorated, coming down to 3.6 per cent from 4.2 per cent in 1985. According to the IMF reports, the Third World debtors in 1987 paid back $ 5.9 billion more than they borrowed from it. New loans amounted to $ 4.3 billion and repayments to $ 10.2 billion. Loans outstanding from the fund amounted to $ 36.6 billion at the end of 1987. It is estimated that the Third World debt would stand at $ 1,085 billion by the middle of 1987.

Besides, the Third World capital flight of $ 300 billion to the United States and Western Europe, during 1974-85 from the residents of the developing countries, has definitely contributed towards declining growth tendency in the developing countries. More than half of this "flight capital" came from Latin American countries, the heaviest Third World debtors. This could definitely have been used to build infrastructural frameworks so as to tackle, say, for example, the global unemployment which has increased 800 per cent since 1960. "Evidently, much more must be done by the major debtors generally to create the environment and build the private-sector confidence that will attract large inflow of foreign investment and encourage return of significant amounts."[1] According to the UN Economic Commission for Africa (ECA) annual report, the African foreign debt burden grew to over $ 200 billion in 1987. "With the continuing sluggish performance in overall output and the high levels of unemployment and population growth, there were hardly any improvements to be expected in the incomes of the majority of African population".[2] Notwithstanding the role of a favourable climate, and pursuit of sound economic policies and domestic democratic reforms by the African governments, a meaningful global economic measure and a positive commitment by the international community to come to the rescue of the continent is the dying need of the hour. And this is perhaps the only way to stop the tendency towards growing political instability among the developing countries.

Poverty precedes political instability. It creates a climate of hunger, hunger for militarization of social process, politicization of outlook, and an authoritarian political structure. Referring to hunger, Professor Amartya Sen in his study for a World Institute for Development Economics Research (WIDER) is of the opinion that hunger in the modern world is more intolerable than past hunger not because it is typically more intense but because it is now so unnecessary. Hunger, according to his "entitlement" approach, could be combated both by a better functioning economic system to provide people with regular means of the income and survival, and a social security scheme to provide compensatory entitlements when employment rewards are inadequate or absent.[3] In a motivated and willing political structure of a developing economy, resulting out of an interaction between domestic monopoly structure and their external counterparts, areas of priority, both in the economic infrastructural framework and in domestic political process, are for the creation of a psyche of acquiescence, not of acquirement. Such a state is not for, and definitely not capable of the expansion of a productive political process as that often leads to an intellectual questioning of the very nature of the ruling elites in a developing economy.

By the mid-1970s, the global military expenditure was estimated to beat the level of $ 400 billion a year. Since 1945 some 100 conventional conflicts have occurred particularly on the territories of the developing world. Since 1966 about 100 military satellites per year have been launched. Some 40 per cent of these are photographic reconnaissance spacecraft. In mid-1983, a plan to develop and build an electronic reconnaissance satellite called Zircon with an estimated cost of $ 750 million was approved by the British Government. Besides, a lot of expenditure is involved in the production of ASAT weapons and ballistic defence weapons (BMD). The Soviet Union conducted some 20 ASAT weapon-related tests between October 1968 and June 1982. The Soviet leader Yuri Andropov declared in August, 1982 that "the Soviet Union assumes the commitments not to be the first to put into outer space any type of antisatellite weapon". Since 1983, the United States has been developing its SDI programmes. Notwithstanding the signing of the historic INF treaty in Washington in December 1987 between the USA and the USSR to eliminate their intermediate-range nuclear missile forces, the SDI programme is being continued.

Coming to the armament culture, and its impacts on the socio-cultural and economic life of the developing countries, it has been documented that between 1968 and 1978, military expenditure of NATO declined from 56.2 per cent to 42.8 per cent whereas the military expenditure of the Warsaw powers increased from 25.3 per cent to 28.6 per cent. During this period, the Third World expenditure on armaments increased from 6.02 per cent to 13.7 per cent.[4] In 1981, the world military expenditure touched £ 500 billion while less than £ 15 billion was spent on international development cooperation. During 1978-81, world military expenditure was at 3 per cent a year after discounting inflation. According to the Palme Commission reports, the developing countries accounted for one-fourth of the total arms expenditure. The report estimated that the total military spending in 1982 was over £ 600 billion - more than the entire income of 1,900 million people living in the 50 poorest countries.[5] Referring to the armament programmes of India and Pakistan the Palme Commission Report said: "Of particular concern is the trend in both States towards more advanced weapons, particularly aircraft. There is also a danger that the military competition in Asia as a whole may turn into a nuclear arms race." During 1961-79 India was the leading importer of armaments in South Asia amounting to £ 4.3 billion worth whereas both Pakistan and Afghanistan accounted for imports of armaments worth £ 1.9 billion each.

It has also been documented by Ms. Sivard that the weapon build-up in the developing countries created new areas of tensions. It exacerbated conflicts among the LDC neighbours. Of the 125 or more conflicts which have occurred since World War II, 95 per cent have been in developing countries. In most cases, foreign forces have been involved, Western powers accounting for 79 per cent of the interventions, communists for 6 per cent, other developing nations for the remainder."[6] Out of 141 countries surveyed 54 countries imported £ 64 million worth of arms during 1961-79. This was almost three-fifths of the total armament imports by LDCs. The USSR supplied 47 per cent of the total armaments, the USA 39 per cent and China a little above 4 per cent. The biggest recipients of armaments were Vietnam, Pakistan, pre-Suharto Indonesia and North Korea in that order. Significantly these 54 countries were either directly controlled or dominated by military governments in 1978. Ms. Sivard established that "Approximately three-fourths of those trained by the superpowers (both US and USSR) came from countries now under military governments, half of them controlling countries in the low-income category. The military assistance provided by the superpowers and the raising of military budgets in the developing countries have, in most cases, led to the recurrence of military dominated regimes and militarization of their political process."

The increasing military expenditure in the developing countries to the tune of £ 81 billion in 1981 as compared to £ 33 billion in 1972, non-fulfilment of the original development assistance target of 0.7 per cent of their gross national product (GNP) by the developed nations as contemplated by the Development Assistance Committee (DAC) of OECD and its subsequent decline to 0.26 per cent in the late 1970s, destabilization of systemic power structures in the various developing countries, steady worsening of the balance-of-payment situation, inflation and budgetary deficits in the developed countries, fall in gross domestic products (GDP) from 0.6 per cent to -0.8 per cent in 1981, the emergence of what is known as underground economies, and the negative impact of the arms race on social welfare programmes have created such a situation of cumulative inequity that unless both the developing and developed countries adopt what the then World Bank president, Mr. A.W. Clausen called policies of expansion and growth – non-inflationary and sustainable growth – in order to pull the world out of its present recession,[7] we are destined to head for an impending international economic crisis. The increasing military assistance provided by the developed economies and middle powers and the increase in the defence budgets in the developing countries have led to the marginalization of society and militarization of their political process ultimately leading to the creation of a psyche of acquiescence. This provides a classic climate to the neo-colonialists to beef up their strangleholds.

Since 1950, the United Nations has adopted a number of resolutions requesting the developed countries to reduce their military budgets and to employ the released fund for the economic and social developments of the developing countries.[8] During the 1970s a number of studies have been conducted by the United Nations regarding the relationship between disarmament and development.[9] According to unofficial estimates, the world military expenditure at the early 1980s reached around £ 510-630 billion in current prices. This figure exceeded by a factor of 1.3 - 1.6 the total external debt of non-oil developing countries and is about 15 to 20 times greater than the amount of official assistance to the developing countries in 1980.[10] Also, between 1972 and 1982, the developed market economy countries' share of total world military expenditure practically doubled.[11] The increased military spending in the absence of an increase in national savings that can be effected through a decrease in other budget expenditure or increase in budget revenue is likely to intensify inflationary pressures. This was the main philosophy of the resolutions and studies prepared by the UN during the 1970s and early 1980s. The rate of growth of saving as a percentage of national income does not automatically lead to a situation when the national economy would take off and the process of growth would automatically be accelerated. Unless growth-with-equity oriented priorities are nationally determined the gross domestic saving is not likely to create a climate conducive to high rate of growth in national income.

Despite detente, and a relative relaxation of international tensions, and despite a number of arms control agreements – limited ban on testings, prohibition of nuclear weapons in the outer space and agreements on the nuclear weapons free zones in different parts of the world – the nuclear arms race has continued unabated.

The International Conference on the Relationship between Disarmament and Development held under the aegis of the United Nations in September, 1987 in New York has emphasized the central role of the United Nations in searching for a common interest in seeking security at lower levels of armaments and finding ways of reducing these expenditures. The continuing arms race has hindered the process of confidence-building among States. Disarmament and Development constitute priority concerns of the international community as a whole.[12] The Conference emphasized that "the real economic growth as well as just and equitable development, and particularly the elimination of poverty, are necessary for a secure and stable environment at the national, regional and international levels. They can reduce tensions and conflicts and the need for armaments."[13] Growing interdependence among nations, inter-relationship among global issues and mutuality of interests call for approaches which respond to the needs of humanity as a whole. Multilateralism provides an international framework within which the economic and security interactions between developing and developed economies have to be understood, analysed, and answered. "Non-military threats to security have moved to the forefront global concern." Polarization of wealth and poverty at the national and international levels results in the gross and systematic violation of human rights. Mass poverty, unemployment, illiteracy and malnutrition often predate political instability. There is need for an effective and mutually reinforcing relationship now than ever before. "Poverty", said Rajiv Gandhi, Prime Minister of India, in his address to the International Seminar on Non-Alignment and World Peace, New Delhi, on August 7, 1987, "is perhaps the greatest threat to our security... No prosperity can be there for the North if there is instability, if there are cyclical ups and downs and structural mal-functioning in the present economic system as .... today. For our prosperity and that of the North, we need steady sustained development. It is for this reason that we seek a mutually reinforcing symbiosis of stable prosperity in the North and sustained development in the South."[14]

In academic debates three theories regarding the contemporary nuclear armaments dynamics have been advocated. It seems that defensive approach, through the use of domestic variables model, systemic model and nationalistic model, has gained much momentum among the academic circles to explain the structural realities of the arms race. Under the domestic variables model, emphasis has been put on various deterrent strategies, role of military-industrial bureaucratic complex and socio-economic structures of the society. The systemic model looks at the arms race as the result of international structural issues; the nationalist model is animated by a aggressive defensive psychology. It is both misleading and dangerous to treat the arms race framework as a product of mere power policy of expansion. If the arms race is the result of a power policy doctrine alone, then, it could easily be changed through the introduction of a new policy pattern. The concept of arms race could only be understood as a system of relations of exploitations – cultural, economic, political, ideological, juridical and military and the like.

In these later years of the 1980s, it is, perhaps, not very difficult to identify the two most dangerous developments in the nuclear arms race: first, the rapid change in the nuclear arms technology has led to changes in the nuclear armaments doctrines, war strategies and strategic environments; second, the risk of ever increasing vertical and horizontal proliferations. It is widely believed that the ongoing technological developments in the nuclear weapon systems are necessitated by threats to national security, and as a corollary to the evolution of nuclear weapons. However, it is a fact that new weapon systems emerge not because of any military or security considerations but because technology by its own impetus often takes the lead over policies, creating weapons for which needs have to be invented and deployment theories have to be adjusted.

Indeed, in the new strategic environment there seems to be an inverse relationship between security and pervasive militarization. A channelization of armament expenditure to non-military expenditure would help accelerate development in developing countries and would negate a perpetual crisis-type atmosphere and would strengthen a just economic structure. Disarmament-development dichotomy has to be seen not from a bureaucratic MILEX/GNP angle, but as a strategy to accelerate nation-building process. Security-disarmament linkages, therefore, have to be comprehended not simply by reorienting national security policies to international security framework but by linking domestic security perspectives to infrastructural considerations, incentive structures of decision-making process, taxation system, inflationary trends, savings and capital formation methods, and questions of national reorganization interactions. What we need today is a different logic, approach and mind that can transcend narrow politico-security considerations. As the Thorsson Report put it: "The world can either continue to pursue the arms race with characteristic vigour or it can move consciously and with deliberate speed towards a more sustainable international economic and political order. It cannot do both." There is a need for converting an increasingly militarized global culture into a culture of peace or, as Jonathan Schell proposes, a deliberate policy of 'weaponless deterrence'. What we need today is a comprehensive alternative understanding, an integrated vision of the world without nuclear weapons.

REFERENCES

1. *Indian Express*, New Delhi, September 3, 1987.
2. *Times of India*, New Delhi, January 6, 1988.
3. *Times of India*, New Delhi, February 22, 1988.
4. World Armaments and Disarmaments, *SIPRI Year Book 1979*, London, 1979, pp.1-17. R.L. Sivard, 1978 , *World Military and Social Expenditures*,Virginia, pp.5-9. *Report of the Preparatory Committee for the Special Sessions of the General Assembly Devoted to Disarmament*, Vol.IV, General Assembly Official Records, Tenth Special Sessions, Supplement No. 1/(A) 5-10(1), p.110.
5. Common Security: A Programme for Disarmament, *The Report of the Independent Commission on Disarmament and Security Issues*, London, 1982.
6. R.L. Sivard, 1981, *World Military and Social Expenditures*, Virginia, 1981.
7. *Times of India*, New Delhi, April 18, 1983.
8. General Assembly Resolution 35/142 of December 12, 1980, on the reduction of military budget.
9. *Reduction of the Military Budgets of Permanent Members of the Security Council by 10 per cent and Utilisation of Part of the Funds Thus Saved to Provide Assistance to Developing Countries* (A/9770 Rev. 1), UN Publications, Sales No. E 75.1.10. *Economic and Social Consequences of the Arms Race and of Military Expenditure* (A/32/88/Rev.1), UN Publications, Sales No. E.78 IX.1; and the most recent and most comprehensive *Study on the Relationship between Disarmament and Development* by a group of governmental experts (A/36/356. Annex).
10. *Development Cooperation: 1981 Review*, Paris, OECD, 1981, Review Table A-1. See also, *Study on the Relationship between Disarmament and Development* (A/36/256, Annex), pp.46, 52, 58, and 61.
11. World Armaments and Disarmament, *SIPRI Yearbook 1982*, London, 1982, p. 140.
12. K.K. Panda, "Disarmament and Development - An Indian Perspective" in *International Spectator*, Netherlands, Special issue on Disarmament and Development, June, 1983.
13. *Document on International Conference on the Relationship between Disarmament and Development*,, New York, September 9, 1987.
14. Press Information Bureau, Government of India, Prime Minister's Address to the International Seminar on Non-Aligned and World Peace, New Delhi, August 7, 1987.

3

GANDHIAN APPROACH TO DISARMAMENT AND PEACE

OM PRAKASH GUPTA

The problem of disarmament and peace is not in fact, as it appears to be merely a problem of disarmament and peace. The greatest problem of *Man* today is *Man* himself. Humanity can survive and fulfil its high purpose only if it understands the Human being. Man is of the Reality and Reality is of the man. All thought and knowledge, all philosophy and religion, ideologies and theories, concepts and values, purposes and programmes have their root in *man's* understanding of Reality, not in Reality as it appears, but in Reality as it is apprehended. Reality, as it is, is inconsistent, but Reality, as it is apprehended, is steady and whole. To understand and experience Reality we have to dive through diversity to the depths of the basic unity. In all affairs, personal, social, national or International, success is possible, only if, in spite of all social or political dissimilarities and differences in ideologies and religious beliefs, we sacredly and unreservedly stick to the principles of peaceful co-existence and friendly cooperation. Mr. Khrushchev, in his speech to the General Assembly of the United Nations on September 19, 1959, very rightly said that "in the 20th century one cannot undertake crusades to wipe out unbelievers with fire and sword as the fanatics of the Middle Ages did, without running the risk of confronting humanity with the greatest calamity in its History".

Man is not a meaningless, purposeless, accidental phenomenon. Man, as is said in the Gita, the Bible and the Koran, is made in His image. "In him lie millions and millions of years of cosmic evolutions. All the stages and forms and qualities are synthetically combined in him." Man is, therefore, of the inorganic elements of the plant, of the animal, and yet in the totality is unique from and superior to all the previous forms. He is the Cosmic Crystal.

Julian Huxley, the great scientist, has said that according to biology the superiority of man over other animals is because of his intellect and not because of his body. The principle of survival of the fittest in his case, therefore, applies to the fitness of his intellect and not body. Again because man is not merely a mentalized animal, he is the bridge to the Divine Being. The principle of live and let live also falls short of his stature. The only test of the fitness of man to survive is, therefore, in his letting others live or in his fitting the unfit to survive. The peaceful co-existence of which there is so much talk in the political circles all over the world would become meaningless if it is based *only* on the principle of live and let live. Live and let live is the negative aspect of co-existence.

The real, the positive and the peaceful co-existence has to be in the pattern of the co-existence of a mother and her newly born child lying on the same bed. Just imagine what would happen to the child and also to the mother ultimately if they decide to co-exist simply on the principle of "live and let live". When the child cries, in spite of all the personal ailments and discomforts the mother pats and feeds the child. She does not say, well! my child, you live where you are and let me live where I am. The mother and the child co-exist only because the mother takes over the responsibility to fit the otherwise 'unfit' child to survive. The peaceful co-existence between man and man and also between nation and nation is possible only on the principle of "fitting the unfit to survive".

The physical aspect of man is common with plants and animals. His mind being in the rudimentary stage his physical nature dominated and therefore animal-living became the purpose of his existence. All his vital forces of mind and even of the spirit he has harnessed to serve this purpose. Religion and morals are being adopted and utilized. Convenient philosophies and theories have been manufactured; policies, plans and programmes are all drawn up to fulfil that purpose. In short the purpose of man's life has become today more satisfaction of the instincts and impulses. His body, mind and the spirit are all harnessed towards the gluttonous pursuit of instinctive needs and desires.

Man: A Wrecked Ship on the High Seas

Man has become today like a wrecked ship on the high seas of time, being tossed up and down by the stormy waves and hurricane winds. Life to him has become purposeless. He is living because he is not dead, otherwise he has lost all meaning of life. This absence of a purpose has broken the harmony of his nature, disintegrated his personality both in the individual and in the collective. Selfish pettiness, unsocial desire, ugly competition, unbecoming conflicts, base understanding and callous values resulting in hatred, suspicion, distrust and violence rule the individual and social existence. Even the noble ideas and sentiments of love and brotherhood are being utilized for the base selfish interests. Man has become the killer instead of being the keeper of his brother.

This continued state of mutual suspicion, fear and distrust brought in the law that "might is right". Violent means and violent sanctions thus became the solver of all disputes. This is how war and violence were recognized as instruments to establish peace in society. Nobody ever wanted war and yet the history of human society is full of the records of battles and wars. Small strifes are being swollen into big riots, battles into wars and wars into world wars, and total wars. From arrows we have reached the Atom Bomb.

We are living in a very anxious and tragic world today. The knotty international problems of poverty, unemployment, starvation, disease and death are staring at us. There is fear, suspicion, mistrust and distrust everywhere and as a result there is a mad race to build newer and more destructive armaments. The annual military expenditures of all the countries today total approximately 1,00,000 million dollars and much more.

In the six years of the World War Two, about three million tons of TNT were used. The heaviest bomb in normal use was the one-ton "block-buster". Towards the end of the war the USA had, on August 6, 1945, dropped one atom bomb on Hiroshima and, three days later, another on Nagasaki. These two bombs killed nearly 10,000 times as many people as the average "block-buster" had done up to then. But in 1952 they created the thermonuclear bomb. The Nobel prize-winning American scientist, Linus Pauling, writes about this "fission-fusion":

> "Such a bomb is not much greater in weight than a one-ton TNT block-buster of the good old days of molecular explosives, but it has the explosive energy of ten million or twenty million times that of the one-ton block-buster, one thousand times as great as a Hiroshima or Nagasaki bomb....each one of them equivalent to twice or three times all the bombs exploded in the Second World War."

In 1954 came the superbomb. Its triple process of "fission-fusion-fission" produced unlimited explosive energy. Besides this there is another horrifying effect. "All nuclear weapons bring an additional hazard unknown to 'conventional' weapons - radioactivity. Each explosion charges the atmosphere with radioactive materials, some of which fall in the target area and the rest of which float in the upper atmosphere for years and are gradually distributed around the earth."

Two American experts testifying before a Congressional Committee said that "the casualties in the USA consequential on a 2,500 megaton attack carried out in twentyfour hours would be about eightytwo million dead, between blast, burns and radiation". General Gavin says that if both sides used thermonuclear weapons a world war might involve eight hundred million casualties.

Besides the dreadfulness of these weapons, the strategy of the most modern warfare has suffocatingly frightened man. Mr. Khrushchev, in his speech on September 19, 1959, to the General Assembly of the United Nations had said, "today atomic and hydrogen bombs are not only stored at ultra secret depots. They are carried by bombers that make flights over the territory of many West European countries. The situation is developing in such a way that superpowerful and super-long-range weapons could be discharged not only on the orders of Governments, but at the will of the individuals at the control panel of those weapons. But a State on whose territory a nuclear load is dropped whether by evil intent or owing to a technical fault or other accident, is hardly going to investigate how it happened, but will be obliged to react to it as to a military attack, as to the unleashing of war."

The root cause of all violence and, therefore, of all arms, conventional or nuclear, and of all wars, big or small, hot or cold, is the disorder and disharmony that man has, in self-ignorance, created in life. The human society today has tragically laid overemphasis on and given quite an undue importance to the physical aspect of life so much so that the mind of man is reduced to the state of a slave, which not only obeys the physical dictates but also obliterates the spiritual urges and makes it dance to the tune of the material nature and creates and constructs artificial justifications for them. The ego which is the basic life urge has become the individual ego, group ego, nation-ego, in the evolutionary development of humanity. But the only way to lasting peace and progress is the transformation and evolution of this very ego into conscious Human-self, Nation-self and Universal-self.

There are people, you may very well call them fanatics, who think that to shake the mind of man, who has so much enslaved himself in the ruts of routine and rigid thinking that even the two world wars were not enough to arouse him to action, perhaps an atomic catastrophe may be necessary. There are still others who would plead that since devolution has also a purpose in evolution, wars are not altogether out of place. They think there could be just wars and just wars must be retained. Theologians and ecclesiastics are deeply divided even on the issue of the morality of nuclear warfare. "The church as such refuses to give affirmative approval to the proposition that nuclear warfare is intrinsically immoral."

Symptoms, not the Cause

The main question before the war-resisters and peace marchers, before the heads of Government of all the States, before the

U.N.and before the peoples of the world in general is whether we want peace, real, lasting and positive peace or merely a ban on the nuclear tests, complete disarmament and abolition of war. Since peace is not mere absence of war or strife, all efforts to ban nuclear tests to enforce disarmament or to ask to abolish war would amount to a egative approach to peace. In fact all our efforts for peace so far recorded in human history have been like the Red Cross service. The aim of the Red Cross is to serve and bring peace to the wounded and never to work for eradicating the cause of wounds. Gandhi makes a distinction between the cause and symptoms of a disease. May be nuclear weapons or the conventional, may be hot war or cold, they are symptoms of the disease and not the cause. The cause or causes of the disease are in not understanding the human being.

Having put a tragic overemphasis on and given undue importance to the material aspects of life and existence and, therefore, to self-defence, security has become the top priority in all that man does. Peace to him is just absence of the possibility of any direct or indirect danger to his physical existence. The Upanishads say the feeling of otherness creates fear and danger but, at the same time, to be all alone is not pleasant. He wants others to accompany him but strictly on his terms. He builds up his physical strength as a deterrent to his neighbour. From whatever quarter he suspects any danger, he wants to bring it under his control.

The Rishi of the Vedas prayed to be blessed with peace upon earth below, peace in the middle air, peace in the heaven, peace upon the waters, peace upon herbs and trees, but what did the man do? He planned to bring under his control the earth, the winds, the space and the nature. The late Sir James Alfred Ewing had sounded a note of warning as early as 1932 by saying "Is man ethically fit for the bounties of science?... Control over nature's force has been placed in the hands of man before he is able to control himself." Sir Josiah Stamp has very carefully analysed the causes of this all-pervading disease and has drawn the following most important conclusions:

1. That hitherto too much attention was paid to researches on the Science of Matter and too little on the Science of Man.

2. That the material and the physical sciences have far outstripped the social sciences and the gap between the scientific discoveries and their sociological applications is tending to increase.

3. That progress in man's moral and spiritual nature has not kept pace with his intellectual progress.

4. That man has conquered the external world and obtained control ever nature's forces but he has still to conquer the inner world and gain control over the forces of his inner nature.

Let us remember if just out of fear and disgust of complete annihilation of mankind and total destruction of the world we turn away from violence "it would be," as says Mahatma Gandhi "like a man glutting himself with dainties to the point of nausea and turning away from them only to return with redoubled zeal after the effect of nausea is well over. Precisely in the same manner will the world return to violence with renewed zeal after the effect of disgust is worn out."

Peace is a positive phenomenon. It is a way of life, life based on the values of truth and non-violence, love and compassion. Multiplication of material wealth alone will not and cannot bring peace. Advances in science and engineering have almost solved the question of production and also of transportation and yet we find millions starving, not getting even one full meal a day and millions again going without sufficient clothing. America burns her surplus wheat. Why this poverty in the midst of plenty? Well, science can help in multiplying the material wealth but it cannot create in man the will to share and distribute. Along with material wealth unless we learn to limit our desires and universalize our thoughts there would not be peace on earth.

Mr. Khrushchev during his American visit once said "man is not made to kill man" and in support of his statement he quoted from the Bible, "Thou shalt not kill." In fact in saying this he did not quote the Bible but challenged it. As a hard realist he had discovered the truth that there will not be peace unless man learns that he is not made to kill man. He will not accept any religion unless it is made to rest on the support of scientific thought. Mere oral faith in the Book will not satisfy him. He wants religion, like the sugar which sweetens your mouth when you eat it, to produce its cash value.

To change man, attempts have to be made simultaneously on all the three levels - personal, national and international - where he influences and gets influenced. We may divide our plans and programmes for peace into immediate, middle range and long range. These, however, are not three stages of our programme. They have to be organically correlated and worked out simultaneously.

Since the nuclear situation is very nearly out of control and since there is danger, even without a third world war, of poisoning mankind if nuclear test explosions are continued, probably by more and more Governments, and since without stopping the nuclear tests there is little chance of stopping their manufacture and stockpiling, the immediate task before us is to fight this nuclear menace first.

Fear the Cause of War

In the 20th century at least, it needs little to prove that fear more than anything else is the cause of war. To fight this fear we need the twin tool of fearlessness and love. When on January 30, 1948, just a few hours before his assassination Margoret Bourke-White, an American correspondent, asked Gandhiji, how would he meet the Atom Bomb with non-violence, he replied, "I will not go underground, I will not go into a shelter. I will come out in the open and let the pilot see I have not a trace of ill-will against him. The pilot will not see our faces from his great height, I know. But the longing in our hearts that he will not come to harm would reach up to him and his eyes would be opened. Let us therefore appeal to the peoples of the world that in millions and billions they should deliberately but prayerfully expose or get ready to expose themselves to the direct danger of the nuclear tests. Like Bertrand Russel in the U.K. and A.J. Muste in the U.S.A. and many others in other countries we should prepare ourselves for direct non-violent action against these tests.

The U.N. is committed to save the succeeding generations from the scourge of war and to reaffirm their faith in fundamental human rights, in the dignity and worth of the human person, in the equal rights of men, women and nations, large and small. This great organization can be of great use only if it could be re-organized on the following basis:

1. It will be called a global or supernational organization with its doors wide open to all nations of the world.
2. There shall be equal status and equal representation of all the member nations.
3. There will be no vetoing power to any nation.
4. No member state would ever invade any country within or without this organization.
5. All member states must disarm themselves or at least surrender, for the time being, all their arms to this global organization.
6. All the member states should work in the spirit and with the belief that the peace and welfare of one is contained in the peace and welfare of all.
7. There should be very well coordinated effort to develop every country with the determination to fit the unfit to survive morally, socially and economically on the basis of voluntary, free and most liberal mutual aid.
8. All colonization and all exploitation should be tabooed.
9. As this organization has to be fully representative in the world context, all the member States must be fully representative in the context of their respective countries.

All non-nuclear powers be persuaded to sign peace pacts for non-violent aids as between themselves. Peace armies be raised both on national and international levels. To speak in the terminology of war let us develop non-violent moral deterrents instead of depending on violent and immoral nuclear deterrents. But it cannot be done, said Gandhiji, "unless big nations shed their desire of exploitation and the spirit of violence of which war is the natural expression and the atom bomb the inevitable consequence...". Unless this is done, "there is no hope for peace in the world".

Gandhi was a man of action. He wanted action here and now. We remember him today not because he said, "mankind has to get out of violence only through non-violence. Hatred can be overcome only by love. Counter-hatred only increases the surface as well as the depth of hatred" but because he found out the technology of non-violence and developed the tool of love. For non-violence he was prepared even to forgo the freedom of his country. His dream was to establish a just and peaceful order of human society. He made India his laboratory for his experiments in the non-violent techniques and tools.

He envisaged a three-pronged programme for the complete transformation of Human Society. The struggle for Indian independence was his immediate concern. To find out non-violent ways of solving all problems personal, national or international was his middle-term plan and to train people for the acceptance of new values was his long-range programme.

For the implementation of his immediate plan he used discussions, persuasion, non-cooperation and non-violent resistance as his tools and techniques. Political and economic decentralization backed up by his scheme of constructive work was the means to devise non-violent means for the solution of all social problems and lastly his scheme of Basic Education was his long-range programme to create from below all the sanctions for peace.

In the present context of world peace also let us make a three-pronged programme, the global, the national and that of the peoples. The same tools and techniques with some moderation and modification, I believe, can be employed in our present pursuit of world peace.

Let me say a word about disarmament also. All armes are the tools of war and violence. War and violence have been hitherto accepted as solvers of problems. But now, as said Mr. Khrushchev, "who can honestly say that the arms race has helped to solve a single, even the simplest international problem; on the contrary it only complicates and tangles the solution of all issues in dispute." It has become as clear as daylight that we have to find out some non-violent means to solve our problems. The question of disarmament is, therefore, a question of evolving and developing non-violent tools and techniques to solve our problems, whether personal, social, national or international.

There is again a difference between replacement and displacement. One is a positive action, the other is only a negative approach. Violent arms are to be replaced by non-violent ones or the very need of arms has to be eradicated. The process of disarmament has, therefore, to be in proportion and in consonance with the development of non-violent forces and sanctions such as peace brigades, and the raising of national and international morality.

Lastly, let me say a word about unilateral disarmament. Since the development of all arms is unilateral, to talk of unilateral disarmament is not without meaning. If any great country decides to disarm herself unilaterally, I am sure, it will be an example of non-violence of the brave and would certainly cut short the distance to world peace.

Let me sum up by saying that Humanity needs today a deep, comprehensive and total revolution, objective and subjective, in man and material, aiding a growing change of all the aspects of Human nature in harmonious relation to world peace.

4

SOCIAL DYNAMICS OF MARX AND GANDHI

D. B. KERUR

Society is a moving phenomenon. It holds a changing scene, presents a human drama enacted continuously. Master minds are busy in understanding the logic of this Social Drama. Often an endeavour is made to create a Science of Society. Natural Science has indeed succeeded in establishing the lawfulness of natural phenomenon. The stage was set for a similar exercise in the study of society. And we now have Social Dynamics. Society is a dynamic phenomenon--with growth and change as basic characteristics. This change is often not smooth. Differences and disputes, clashes and conflicts punctuate the process. Sometimes battles are fought, wars are waged.

At any point in time inequalities do exist in any society. These may refer to property, power, status, race, educational attainment or mere physical strength. With the passage of time, development of science and technology tend to perpetuate, even accentuate these inequalities. This is so, for the simple reason that fruits of development and accruing benefits remain confined to those who already hold the position and enjoy the privileges. With inequalities going deeper and getting harder,. the social structure groans under strain and tension. Solution is sought either through peaceful reforms and/or violent revolutions. Society moves on evolving a new structure relevant to the new needs.

Master minds are busy in examining this process, are busy in exploring the laws of social change and are busy in providing models that ensure order and progress, stability and change. Marx and Gandhi were such master minds, great seers in the human history.

Marx was a historian, a philosopher, an economist, a sociologist, a social scientist and above all a revolutionary. He was at once an analyst and a prophet--a prophet with positive message. Marx viewed society as a moving entity and developed a sharp theory of social change, a theory of conflict and a theory of conflict-resolution.

Mahatma Gandhi was at once a leader, a reformer, a missionary, a revolutionary and above all a Messiah. Gandhi was the architect of India's freedom. He has been held as the Father of the Nation. Yet Gandhian thought transcends the context of India. He viewed India's struggle for freedom in a universal frame of reference. The mankind was the context of Gandhian philosophy. Gandhi stood for a social change, fought for a new society and experimented in new ways of life.

Shaping of Gandhian Philosophy

Gandhi's Social Philosophy took shape over the years through continuous "experiments with truth". It was in South Africa that he developed his philosophy and technique of *Satyagraha*–an instrument for redressing the grievances of the immigrant Indian minority in Africa. On his return to India in 1915, he established an *Ashram*. It was not until 1919 that he began to play an influential role in the Indian National Congress.

The Congress had been in existence since 1885. For the first two decades Moderates--westernized intellectuals and professionals--led the Congress. Later, early in the 20th century, Radicals seeking inspiration in the ancient glory began to make a mark on the national organization. Swami Vivekananda descended as the apostle of Indian Nationalism. Yogi Arvinda, Lokmanya Tilak stood for Nationalism which originated in the sacred tradition of the land.

Gandhi took it over from Tilak and began to lead the Congress. The Rowlatt Act, Amritsar Massacre shook the country deeply. The days of cooperation advocated by the moderates and liberals were gone. Even responsive cooperation of Tilak was now a policy of the past. Gandhi advocated non-violent non-cooperation and a new phase in the history of Indian Nationalism was ushered in.

Under Gandhi the Congress soon got transformed into a disciplined mass movement. It was now a broad-based people's coalition--where the educated elite, sophisticated lawyers, prosperous businessmen, rich landlords and simple peasants all stood shoulder to shoulder.

Gandhi raised politics to the level of religion. Truth and Non-violence were now the secrets of political action. The unarmed illiterate common man was now fearless. Gandhi's life was an open book--an experiment with Truth. He led vast hordes of men along the path of danger with remarkable discipline and unity. Satyagraha in South Africa, all-India *Hartals* in 1919, 1920 and the famous *Dandi Yatra* were unprecedented events in the human history. Gandhi infused enthusiasm into millions; moulded heroes out of common clay and made them act with astonishing singleness of purpose and spirit of sacrifice.

Equally significant was Gandhi's constructive programme. Removal of untouchability, elevation of the status of women, protection of village industries constituted the social and economic content of this constructive programme. Craft education, cultivation of mother tongue and a common national language made up the core of his educational programme. A comprehensive constructive programme ensured sound foundation for the superstructure of the Nation. Besides, it provided an opportunity to the rich and the elite for a fruitful positive participation in the social work.

Gandhi's social programme was the legacy of Swami Vivekananda. In matters religious and spiritual he was Ramakrishna Paramhansa virtually reborn. While deeply dedicated to his own

Hindu faith, Gandhi recognized the unity of all religions. He brought social significance to virtues held supreme in personal life. Love and sympathy, devotion and dedication, suffering and sacrifice were now supreme social values. He preached the principles more through example than through precept. A great Karmayogi, modelled after the Gita. He influenced the people not so much by teaching, not even by his programme but by his character. To the masses Gandhi was not simply a political leader, a social reformer, a friend of the poor but a man of God, a Saint, an Apostle of Peace and Non-violence. A man with divine mission.

Gandhian Economic System formed an integral part of his Social Dynamics, a Corollary of his Social Philosophy.

British Conquest and Economic Stagnation

The village community combining agriculture and handicrafts was the basis of Indian economy. Production was primarily for consumption rather than exchange. Social life was governed not so much by the laws of the State but by caste codes.

The British conquest initiated a series of interrelated changes, which shattered, within the space of a few decades, the system that endured for wellnigh 3,000 years. A new land system, a new revenue system, a new system of administration came to be introduced. Railways were built, trade was encouraged, markets were widened. Transition to a money economy was speeded up. State law began to replace custom.

England by now was an industrial National State dominated by the capitalist class. The British rule in India was designed to increase the profitability to British Capital--resulting in the destruction of the pre-capitalist social and economic system in the country. It paved the way for the evolution of India on capitalist lines.

The British demolished the basis of the old order. However, they never allowed the rise of a fully developed capitalist industrial system. A retarded economic development, decay of peasant agriculture, general dislocation of social conditions simply accentuated the inequalities and hardships. Unemployment--open and disguised--and poverty were the two insoluble economic problems of the country. Gandhi's Khadi and Village Industries Programme provided a surviving support to the stagnant economy. Food and cloth, the basic necessities, agriculture and weaving, the basic occupations, should be, Gandhi insisted, within the control of the village. A self--supporting, self-reliant village community, a self-governing village was the vision of Gandhi.

Gandhi resisted economic inequalities. Yet he did not approve class war. To the rich, Gandhi advocated the Theory of Trusteeship. Beyond what one requires for personal needs, the remainder is to be held as a Trust for and on behalf of the society. In matters of industrial disputes, Gandhi pleaded reconciliation, mutual agreement and settlement. Be it political agitation, be it constructive social work, be it rebuilding of village economy, Gandhi ever insisted on Truth and Non-violence as the basic principles of action. His was an appeal to the inner conscience and inner instinct of love and sympathy.

Gandhi visualized an economic system–where each one without exception has an opportunity to work, where exploitation is totally eschewed, where almost all wants are met through local production, where exchange is resorted to in respect of commodities not locally produced. His was a Decentralized Economy.

Liberal Democracy and Socialism

Gandhi was in England for his higher studies when the modern era of scientific advance was making a headway. The West was witnessing unprecedented material development. Rise of liberal democracy, emergence of the National State were further attainments. However, economic slavery under the garb of political freedom was an evil concealed in the new development. Child employment was naked, and was defended on the plea of freedom of contract. Critics began to take cognizance of the ills of the Industrial Society. While the liberal rationalist saw the possibility of progress in the improvement of modes of production, the socialists repudiated the individual's right to profit at the cost of the community. These trends had an impact on Gandhi. In his own inimitable way, Gandhi attempted a synthesis. The backdrop of Indian history and Indian tradition was evident. Ruskin's *Unto This Last* was a major influence on Gandhi. The concept of *Antyodaya*, and later *Sarvodaya* had its origin here. In his *Hind Swaraj*, Gandhi has explained the concept of self-governing community.

The growth of capitalism in the early 18th century evoked two trends of criticism. One was backward looking - reactionary - described as romantic. The other was revolutionary known as Socialistic. Socialism began as a movement of revolt against the specific ills of capitalist industry--resulting in a theory of opposition to the system as a whole . Trade union movement imbued with socialist purpose began to grow.

Scientific Socialism of Marx

Soon the socialist criticism gained an ideological status. The history of socialism records the names of thinkers and pioneers. Saint Simon, Fourier, Sismodi, Proudhan and Robert Owen deserve attention. Yet Marx is the greatest among the Socialist critics. He claims his Socialism - and rightly - to be scientific socialism.

Marx lived at a time when Germany was just emerging as a Capitalist democracy. The entire experience of England in respect of industrial revolution and trade unionism and French experience of post-revolutionary struggle provided a fine perspective to interpret social conflict and social change. The dialectics of Hegel was the methodology. Yet unlike Hegel, for Marx economic factors rather than ideas and ideals were the determinants of social change. Individual ownership of the means of production and private entrepreneurship constitute basic features of capitalist economy. Profit is the principal incentive. However, in the course of competition, the rate of profit declines and crisis develops. We need not go into the detailed technical analysis. It is enough to note how unbridled competition results in excess production--excess in relation to demand–leading to a fall in the price and a decline in the rate of profit.

There is another aspect. Labour is primarily responsible for production. Capital indeed enhances productivity of labour. In the course of competition use of capital increases involving a relative fall in the employment of labour. This development has two consequences. One fall in employment leading to a fall in the income implying a fall in demand. Second, production is not commensurate with the enhanced productivity of the community. Both ways contradictions develop within the system - an increase in productivity and a fall in production, an increase in supply and a fall in demand. In such a situation, a fall in the rate of profit is simply inevitable.

The Capitalist tries to maintain and increase the profit rate. That further deepens the crisis. Profit simply understood is the excess of price over cost. For profit, we need to have either a price rise or a cost reduction. A general tendency of overproduction rules out any possibility of price rise. The other way open is through reduction in cost. Wages constitute a major element in the cost. Obviously, any measure to reduce cost simply leads to wage reduction and labour retrenchment. Anyway, the incidence is on the labour and finally a way out is sought through building combines, forming monopolies. This corners the consumer.

Thus unemployment, wastage of productive power, exploitation of the worker and the consumer constitute the inevitable consequences of the competitive system. Economic inequalities assume alarming proportions. Wasteful luxury consumption dictates the production programme.

Science and technology indeed enhance productive powers of the community. Growth and development rightly interpreted must ensure full utilization of productive capacity. With private property and private enterprise as essential tenets of the system, capitalism is bound to develop inherent contradictions. History demands, Marx rightly maintains, replacement of the system by socialism where social needs, rather than personal profit, planning in place of competition would be the main governing principles. This is a historical inevitable process. However, the propertied class, capitalists, may not--almost will not – accept the change. A class conflict, a political struggle becomes inevitable. And here, Marx urges and directs labour, the principal participant in the production process, to organize into a political power to seize the State and create conditions for the establishment of socialist economy.

Socialist Movement in India

Gandhi never approved the inhuman aspect of Capitalism. He was aware of the rise of labour and socialism in India. In 1908, Lenin referred to the emergence of the Indian Proletariat as matured sufficiently to wage a class conscious political mass struggle. Lenin based his judgement on the Bombay Mill Workers' political strike in protest against the imprisonment of Tilak. In 1920, the Indian Trade Union Congress was founded. Soon the Communist Party of India began to make its way. Gradually, the left elements in the Indian National Congress started mobilizing within the Congress fold itself. And in 1934 emerged the Congress Socialist Party.

Gandhi – essentially a man of the masses – had full sympathy with the new trend. Yet his adherence to nonviolence led many to regard Gandhi as a champion of the Capitalist, a Mascot of the bourgeoisie. This was far from the truth. Gandhi stood for socialist ideals as an end. All the same, he insisted on non-violence as a means. Socialism and non-violence were for him closely interrelated. "No man could be actively non-violent", Gandhi said, "and not rise against injustice no matter where it occurred."

Gandhi was fully aware of the impact of science and technology. He appreciated its contribution to the social progress. Total rejection of industrial and machine civilization, Gandhi conceded, was totally impossible. What he protested was the debasement of humanity. His views on machine deserve careful attention. To him, even his physical "body" was the most delicate piece of machinery. The spinning wheel and the oil press are also machines. When the machine is worked by human power, it is directly under human control. The possibility of its abuse is strictly limited. On the other hand, with the large-scale machinery man tends to become a cog in the machine. The process tends to become important than the producer and the produce. The situation turns out impersonal and machine dehumanizes man.

It was the craze for machinery, not mechinery as such, that Gandhi objected to. Machine indeed saves labour. Yet Gandhi wanted to save time and labour not for a fraction of mankind but for all. The supreme consideration for Gandhi was man. "The machine is like the body," he declared, "useful and only to the extent that it subserves the growth of the soul." He did recognize the importance of basic and key industries – which are bound to be highly mechanized and on a large scale. However, he wanted these to be nationalized and State controlled.

Autonomous Village Community – A Gandhian Vision

Gandhi conceived of the autonomous and self-contained village as the unit of society. As far as possible, every village, he said, should regulate its own economic and political life. A self-governed village would avoid the risks arising under either absolute dictatorship of the State or absolute anarchy of Statelessness.

Gandhi was aware of the defects inherent in the rural economy and urban civilization. The village is personal and intimate to the point of interference with one's private life. The urban city on the other hand is impersonal and indifferent to the point of callousness. Large-scale centralized mechanized production inevitably fosters the growth of cities and metropolitan centres. Cities do have a place in the Gandhian Scheme. But nothing will be allowed to be produced by cities which can be well produced by the villages. The proper function of cities – Gandhi argued – is to serve as clearing houses for village products.

Gandhi wants the bulk of India's population to get back to the land, stay in the land and live primarily off the produce of the land so that their families may be self-supporting, owning the implements they use, the soil they cultivate and the roof that shelters them. He did not want an uprooted class of factory workers, nor did he want a rapacious money lending business community to dominate. Gandhi visualized a responsible agrarian population, and the stable, and level headed people of small agricultural market towns dominating the cultural, social and political life of the country. This, of course, was not a plea for primitivity. It was a plea for a way of life that is instinctive to India, a way that provided a purpose, a faith and a meaning.

A village under the Gandhian Scheme would be self-supporting in respect of food and basic necessities. Requirements of food, cotton, grazing pasture, playground would have priority in the land use. Surplus land, if available, would be used for non-intoxicant commercial crops.

To the rich, to the landlords, to the businessmen and to the capitalists restraint and renunciation was Gandhi's advice. Wants by nature are limitless, and resources limited. The entire economic problem originates in this hard reality. Failure to discern between need and greed and reckless use of resources will soon lead society to the brink of ruin. Political ambition, power hunt and violence will only accentuate the process. Painful picture of the present environmental and ecological crisis simply confirms Gandhi's concern.

Historical Aspect of Gandhian Thought

A decentralized mixed economy with the State-controlled public sector, a network of enterprises ensuring productive employment to all the employables and a self-governing village community is the core of Gandhian Economic System. A stagnant economy groaning under poverty and deep inequalities was the immediate context of Gandhian Economic Thought. Traditional timeless ancient culture was the source of his social philosophy. His economic system evolved as a corollary of his philosophy. We are aware of the two-fold relativity of a thought. It is related to a situation and it is a reflection of an individual. An individual thinks and thinks about a situation. Gandhi, moulded in an ancient tradition, reacted to a historical condition.

Some elements in the Gandhian Thought need a little more critical analysis. Trusteeship concept is one such element. Gandhi appealed to the capitalists and landlords to hold the wealth as a trust on behalf of the workers and the peasants who produced that wealth. Capitalism and its political system provides opportunities and legal ways to acquire wealth without actually participating in the production process. It is simply unearned income morally indefensible. Yet the owner holds that, the legal sanction implies moral justification. In the circumstances, how can we ensure effectiveness of the Trusteeship concept as an instrument of social change. We have to resist unjust laws and organize a political struggle to take over the State for enacting morally justifiable legislation.

This is what Marx precisely advocated. Validity of eternal values like Truth and Non-violence, ethical and moral significance of social service and trusteeship are self-evident. Yet it is a hard task to ensure manifestation of these values and virtues in the day-to-day activity, much more difficult in the individual behaviour.The present rules and the laws that uphold the private interests and the social institutions that safeguard the class interest would always tempt the individual to protect and pursue self-interest. Class conflict and social discontent seem to be unavoidable.

Before we conclude, we may refer to the left reappraisal of Gandhi. E.M.S. Namboodripad writes, "Gandhi became the Father of the Nation precisely because the idealism to which he adhered in the years of anti-imperialist struggle became a practically useful political weapon in the hands of the bourgeoisie, ... he became more or less isolated from the bourgeoisie in the latter days of his life, because his idealism did in the post-independence years become a hindrance to the self-interest of the bourgeoisie".

The situation only calls for a Social Change, a change that will do away with the unjust laws, evolve new institutions, create conditions congenial for peace and prosperity for one and all without exception. This has to be the objective of a Social Revolutionary.

Marx the Realist and Gandhi the Visionary

Karl Marx built up his theory of Social Change almost with a mathematical precision. He gave a clarion call, "Workers of the World Unite. They have nothing to lose but their chains". Marx awaited the impending economic crisis and the consequent revolution. He passed away without the realization of this revolution in his own lifetime.

Mahatma Gandhi "experimented with truth". A pilgrim of peace, he was a freedom fighter, "Do or Die" was his call. Power to the grassroots was his message. In his search for communal harmony, Gandhi embraced martyrdom with a smile.

Humanity hopefully awaits a meeting of Marx and Gandhi to ensure a peaceful social change.

This is what Marx precisely advocated. [illegible] able man and [illegible] [illegible] [illegible] and the so-called upper [illegible] [illegible] [illegible] factories, which make it difficult for the individual to [illegible] of his [illegible] and the laws that uphold the private [illegible] and [illegible] institutions that safeguard the class interest would always drive the individual to [illegible] and [illegible] self-interest, this conflict and social discontent seem to be unavoidable.

Lenin, we conclude, we may refer to the [illegible] example of Gandhi. [illegible] writes, "Gandhi became the 'Father of the Nation' precisely because the idealism to which he adhered in the years of [illegible] imperialist struggle became a [illegible] political weapon in the hands of the bourgeoisie. If he became more or less isolated from the bourgeoisie in the latter days of his life, because he [illegible] [illegible] independence was [illegible] hindrance to the self-interest of the bourgeoisie."

The situation can [illegible] Social Change, a change that will do away with the unjust [illegible] [illegible] for peace and prosperity for one and all without exception. This has to be the objective of a Social Revolutionary.

Marx the Realist and Gandhi the Visionary

Karl Marx built up his doctrine of Social Change almost with a mathematical precision. [illegible] Workers of the World Unite. They have nothing to lose but their chains. [illegible] the impending [illegible] crisis and the [illegible] [illegible] without the [illegible] of this revolution in his life time.

Mahatma Gandhi [illegible] [illegible] His life was [illegible] [illegible] which the communal harmony [illegible] cemented [illegible]

Humanity hopes to achieve a blending of Marx and Gandhi to have a peaceful social change.

5

ECONOMIC AND SOCIAL DEVELOPMENT: A GANDHIAN PERSPECTIVE

K.D. GANGRADE

Development is neither a static nor a uniform concept. As a historical fact, the classical model remained the only model in the West until 1913. After World War I, especially after the Russian Revolution and the Great Depression, the classical model declined and alternative forms emerged. After World War II, the world entered another new stage of development. Development must be defined in each of these stages. Furthermore, development always varies widely in different countries. Yet there are important features of development common to all phases and to all types of modernization. The most important common feature is that of growth. To develop means to advance, to further, to evolve, or to expand by a process of growth. A modern society is one which is growing, expanding and advancing.

Development is a process of societal transformation from a traditional society to a modern society, and such a transformation is also known as modernization. A modern society is also a rational society. While all societies have rational and irrational elements, modern society is said to be rational that it is not dominated by super-natural factors or by tradition and that it assigns high value to making decisions on the basis of reason and performing tasks in accordance with rational methods and procedures. Another common feature is the building of Nation-State as the unit of development. This is why modern development is often known as national development. Development involves institutional changes. Institution is a significant element in the life of a culture which is persistent and enduring, which regulates pattern of behaviour; and which is widely tolerated, sanctioned or legitimized by society.[1]

Development is considered to be a process of improving the capability of a nation's institutions and value system to meet increasing and different demands social, political and economic.[2] Development has also been defined as economic growth plus social change as bread plus dignity;[3] as a technical solution to underdevelopment; as institutional building; human development, a more equitable spread of distribution and development resources. However, in the first UN Development Decade which began in 1961, development was almost equated with economic growth. During this Decade, the world's total Gross National Product increased by $ 1,000 billion. About 80 per cent of this increase went to countries with a per capita income of $ 1,000 with 25 per cent of the world population. Only 6 per cent of the increase went to countries where per capita yearly income average was 200 or less and areas comprised 60 per cent of the world population.

The second UN Development Decade, therefore, stated that Development for the developing countries is not simply an increase in productive capacity but a major transformation in their social and economic structures.[4] Economic growth and social progress are not mutually inter-dependent, but are organically related parts of a simple process of development.[5] And the third Development Decade launched in 1981, laid emphasis on Basic Minimum Needs.

The basic values underlying development are human dignity, equality and social justice. These three concepts are not separate and distinct but interrelated and dependent on each other. Another principle implied in social development is the emphasis on *cooperation* as against *competition*. It lays emphasis on the *collectivity* as against *rugged individualism*. It does not deny the right of full development and expression of the individual and his/her role in decision making that affects their lives. It lays greater emphasis on the well-being of the total society and all its individuals.[6]

Development based on the principles of human dignity, equality and social justice can be defined as a goal and process that aims to achieve an integrated, balanced and unified (social and economic) development of society. It is international in scope and has a holistic, interdisciplinary, inter-sectoral and inter-regional approach to societal issues and problems. It focuses on "qualitative" development as measured by (a) the participation of people in matters affecting their lives, (b) the nature of social and interpersonal relations and (c) the relationship of people to their environment. Quantitatively, social development aims at structural and institutional reforms to bring about changes in the distribution of income, wealth and services.[7]

In fact, social development means something more than merely economic, political, social and environmental development. It is not merely an effort to provide ad-hoc growth targets in each of the sectors of planning. Social development planning requires the perception and delineation of the nature of interrelationships between the different sectors. Social development is an integrative concept and this integration depends upon clear enunciation of the values and the type of society toward which planning is to be undertaken.[8]

Development Philosophy and Objectives

Development is a process by which one's overall personality is enhanced. This is so for a society as well as for an individual. For society the identity is collective. Thus development for society means development of the collective personality of society.

Development of collective personality requires physical, material and economic development, but it is above all the development and application of consciousness. A child may grow physically while his personality does not develop. So it is with society. Thus, "economic development", while it is vitally necessary, cannot be treated as an independent variable divorced from its social bearings. Development of a society is social development, a process in which "economic" and "non-economic" elements interact organically with each other. Attempts to isolate the "economic" elements and fit them into any hypothetical model of "economic development" are, therefore, unscientific. Development thus defined is a multi-variate quantitative and qualitative change. It would be futile to attempt to measure any country's social development quantitatively and expect consensus about it. The world's richest society may be considered to be its sickest, and hence not developed at all. Such positions can be understood but cannot be refuted, and yet scientific judgments may be given on such a basis. While scientific judgments about social development need to be reasoned, cardinal quantification has often served as a fetish that has detracted from rather than helped evaluate the more essential qualitative attributes.

The Individual and the Collective

The individual and the collective might be thought to have conflicting interests. Our concept of the collective rules this out. The collective exists to the extent that individuals acquiesce in its sovereignty, and develops as individuals acquire more of this collective spirit. Thus a nation of "self-seekers" may be a collective only in the sense that its members have agreed to hold a common passport; if there is no more of the "collective spirit" it would be a very weak collective indeed.

The "collective spirit" is not necessarily an abnegation of individual interest in favour of a mystified concept of "society". We view the collective as a method of serving individual interests while at the same time raising individual consciousness, so that one progressively aspires to fulfilment of higher orders including fulfilment in developing together.

Aspirations Frontier

Within the framework of the above philosophy, development has to have its operational objectives. One of these is growth of the collective spirit. Stimulating the spirit of cooperation is another, by means of which the collective consciousness may be promoted and the quantity of social good to be produced raised. Creativity and innovativeness, and a problem-solving approach to life, are essential attributes of a dynamic personality and have to be cultivated. Improvement of knowledge is a basic requirement. A will to develop and faith in the collective creative potential of man are fundamental prerequisites with which society must be equipped.

Somewhat more complex is the question of attaining an "aspirations frontier". At any point of time individuals in a society have certain natural aspirations, such as a minimum of nourishment, clothing and shelter, some leisure and opportunity for cultural-scientific pursuits. For India his may have to be set as a long-term objective, beyond the material possibilities in the short run. This leaves the problem of sustaining morale in the short run.

The solution lies in the direction of creating values that give a sense of fulfilment in the very austerity that is necessary in the short run. Such fulfilment is possible only if the austerity is shared in a framework of collective effort for progress.

Self-reliance

Of all the new values to be created, self-reliance is the single most important. India has depended too long on external masters. This is much more true of Rural India which has depended too long on the city. The rural poor have been subservient too long to the rural rich and to the "officer" sent from the city, a subservience that has been forced upon them; in the process their own initiative and vitality have been sapped. The result is a history of exploitation of the "dependant" by the "master". The dependant, appearing to have no self-respect, commands no respect from others. He is laughed at by the world and despised at the same time as he is squeezed.

India cannot develop unless it rejects the soft option and resolves to be self-reliant. This means building up a combination of material and mental reserves that enable one to choose one's own course of evolution, uninhibited by what others desire. It requires maximum mobilization of domestic resources, but above all it requires psychological, and institutional staying power to meet crisis situations when the supply of essential materials is too short. This staying power is best attained collectively. Individually a hungry man feels isolated and his mental reserve wanes; collectively this reserve is reinforced for each and collective resolve gives individuals strength to fight a calamity with their heads high.

Self-reliance does not necessarily mean self-sufficiency. With psychological staying power a self-reliant society can open up and negotiate from a position of strength. But some measure of self-sufficiency in strategic areas that are easily prone to manipulation by exploitative interests is desirable. Such vulnerable areas are staple food production, technology and spare parts and military resistance power.

All these make the development of appropriate technology indispensable. While development of a modern sector is imperative, the technological revolution has to be primarily internally achieved.

Participatory Democracy

The collective as we conceive it functions through the active participation of the people. Without this the individual would not belong organically to the collective and the collective itself would not to that extent be a reality. Hence the collective and participatory democracy are inseparable concepts. Participatory democracy is not the formal voting of leaders to power once every five years and passive obedience in between; it is not merely government of the people but also, and more fundamentally" by the people". Participatory democracy rules out the dominance of any minority group over the broad masses of people. In the Indian context it precludes, therefore, dictatorship of the "elite" over the masses, of the city over the countryside and of the modern sector over the traditional, and new forms of external control which would dilute the processes of democracy. Moreover, there is no room in this participatory system for power-wielding, though intelligent leadership, which is alien to the broad masses of the people and tends to strengthen its own position at the expense of the latter; nor is there a place for the unaccountable and unresponsive bureaucrat who considers it beneath his dignity to have any interaction with the masses.

Consciousness Gap

The problem of a "consciousness gap" between the leaders of a society and the masses of the people remains. In concrete historical conditions in any society some persons may be ahead of others in perceptions of the need for social change, in their ability to systematize ideas whose origins are in the masses themselves, in seeing through complex relationships and in relevant technical expertise. Such men are natural leaders of society, whom the masses of the people tend to follow without coercion. Participatory democracy in such situations would not yet be complete, nor would the leaders be fully accountable to the people in a real sense. Such a relationship may be formally 'democratic', but in the depth of the situation lies the seed of *leadership ego* which may grow and gradually alienate the leader from his people, so that finally he leads them to a vision that is more his than theirs. This would, in turn, alienate the people and inhibit the growth of their collective personality. The leadership and the masses must, therefore, move in a mutually interacting process that systematically reduces the consciousness gap. Democracy in this sense is not a system to be implanted, but an objective to be realized through a process.

De-alienation

Many of the above objectives imply a regeneration and development of values that man has lost or nearly lost through ages of subordination to exploitation, maladministration and misdirection Regressive social relations and cultural taboos have paved the way for such alienation from Man's original and inherent potentials.

In essence, the development philosophy and objectives which we have enunciated centre around five core concepts which stand inseparably together.

1. Man as the end of development which is, therefore, to be judged by what it does to him.
2. De-alienation of man, in the sense that he feels at home with the process of development in which he becomes the subject as well as the object.
3. Development of collective personality of man in which he finds his fullest expression.
4. Participation as the true form of democracy.
5. Self-reliance as the expression of man's faith in his own

abilities.

In India, whose situation we are reviewing, rural development is the key to its overall social development. The personality of India cannot be enhanced without raising the personality of rural India. This leads us to a strategy of development which points that the countryside should be the centre of activity for contemporary India. The inner-directed strategy that we are seeking encompasses the city, but the focus and driving spirit is the village where the new Indian Drama will inevitably have to be played.

Gandhi's Philosophy of Development

Gandhi's development philosophy revolves around man, his society and nature and their respective and simultaneous development. He had a philosophy of work, wealth and happiness in line with the religious and ethical philosophies of the East as well as the West. His philosophy was governed by two fundamental and interrelated principles: *truth and non-violence (ahimsa)*. In recent years, his vision of life, society and civilization has been increasingly shared and practised in various parts of the country and the world with reference to several basic and contingent problems, like poverty, violence, discrimination based on caste and religion, ecology, centralization of wealth and power. This has created a tremendous interest in the people to know and understand his philosophy of development.

Physical development depends basically on proper nutrition, treatment of ailments, healthy living surroundings, and enough clothing to protect the body from the ravages of nature. As long a minimum quantity of these are not made available to the individual, he remains much too preoccupied with the problems of survival. A person dependent on others for primary necessities of life can hardly declare that all men are equal and he is a part of a society of equals. The word "development", because of this emphasis on economic condition in the developing region particularly, has thus been regarded mainly *as an economic concept concerned with the increased production and distribution of goods and services* in a more or less integrated system controlled by various agencies as partners in the exercise of State power. It still means affluence and is growth-oriented. Its maturation logically aspires after affluence. This development is planned mostly by the State which, with the help of bureaucracy and technology, carries out development tasks and projects.

Affluence as a goal of development was not in Gandhi's mind. He believed that there is sufficient to meet the needs of the people, but not their greed. He, therefore, refused to accept any move towards affluence as the goal of Indian Society. He believed that the type of development that had been achieved in Europe was the result of a systematic colonization and exploitation of both the people and nature. He, therefore, rejected not only supportive mechanism of development such as bureaucracy, technology and elitist education, but also the whole idea of development as conceived by the builders of the industrial society.

His opposition to this approach should be understood in relation to his philosophy of development, which is closely linked with his life philosophy. As a great unifier not only of persons but of ideas - his social, economic and political ideas are all interrelated and interdependent.

Gandhi had a holistic view of life. Accordingly, his development philosophy revolved round man, his society and environment (nature) and their respective and simultaneous development. He believed that, instead of man exploiting the society and both exploiting nature, there is a symbolic way of life which is in harmony with each other. In his frame of reference for development, man is the centre of attention. The objective is the moral and spiritual development of man. Man is primarily his consciousness, his capacity to be self-conscious and his built-in-potentiality to judge between good and evil, between what will help him in his evolution to higher levels of being and what will obstruct his path. This gives him a leverage, not only to aspire after higher levels but to endeavours to attain the same. Gandhi believed in this self-effort and the path he outlined lay through ethical, moral and spiritual disciplines. The keynote of his ethics is love, which means near identity of interest with every sentiment. This love has to be expressed in the form of service and sacrifice. His ethics in relation to material things and property consisted in his concept of trusteeship. Every human being is a trustee not only of his faculties and attainments but of everything he comes by, and trusteeship consists not only in using his powers and goods property, but in using them selflessly and for the well-being of all others.

Purity of ends and of means formed an important aspect of his thinking. He believed that means must justify the ends and refused to accept the maxim that ends should justify the means. He stressed on means because he felt that it is within the individual's control and not the ends. It should, however, be remembered that there is no rigid dichotomy between the two; sometimes end is changed into means and means to another end. Ends and means are interrelated and interdependent. Means is the end in making, the "end in embryo". It is determined and conditioned by the end. As a man of action Gandhi, therefore, tried to work out the means to achieve his desired ends - Sarvodaya and Swaraj - the new society of his thinking. Gandhi was not only a man of ideas. He could not rest by merely enunciating his idea on development. He tried to practise it. Based on his own experiments, he then worked out the details regarding a wide variety of things which he named as "Constructive Programme" and which he considered as vital for building a new society.

Gandhi and Rural Development

It is difficult to make a precise and generally acceptable statement about Gandhian approach to rural development. Gandhi's basic ideas on rural development will need to be spelt out in detail before we attempt any evaluation. One must begin with defining Gandhi's concept of individual-in-society. He held freedom of the individual above every thing else; this, in effect, meant that "man is the measure". But one must willingly adjust his individualism to social requirements of progress. This is possible only in a non-exploitative, non-coercive social order, which is based on love, altruism, spirit of service, dignity of labour, non-violence and equality.

The premises that follow are, firstly, that the root of violence lay in exploitation. Structurally, industrialism and machine civilization of the West were powerful causes of exploitation. They caused concentration of economic power in a few hands and in the city centres and, consequently, led to the decay of the villages. The very forces also generated an infinite parabola of wants and also corruption, when these wants could not be satisfied through honest means. Therefore, there is a need for voluntary action to curb the hedonist harm, i.e., "limitation of wants".

His second premise was that private property and capital were the main sources of inequality and exploitation. Working for economic equality meant abolishing the eternal conflict between capital and labour. It meant the levelling down of the few rich in whose hands is concentrated the nation's luck and levelling up of the semi-starved millions.

Methods of Social Transformation

Gandhi was emphatic on this issue. "A non-violent system of government is clearly an impossibility so long as the wide gulf between the rich and the hungry millions persists. The contrast between the palaces of Delhi and miserable hovels of the poor labouring classes cannot last one day in free India, in which the poor will enjoy the same power as the rich of the land. Violent and bloody revolution is a certainty one day unless there is a voluntary abdication of riches and the power that riches give and sharing them for common good."[9] Apart from the faith that Gandhi seems to place on the power dynamics of universal adult suffrage, it is very clear that the eventual threat of a violent revolution is directed towards the rich. "As far as the present owners are concerned, they would have the choice between class war and voluntarily converting themselves into trustees of their wealth."[10]

Now, coming to Gandhi's approach to rural development, the city-village antagonism becomes the overriding issue – "exploiting the villages itself is organised violence". He dramatized the problems: The blood of the villages is the cement with which the edifice of the cities is built. I want this blood that is today inflating the arteries of the cities to run once again in the blood vessels of the villages".[11] His opposition to industrialism and his plea for radical decentralization, and village self-sufficiency were geared to the liberation of the villages from city exploitation.

But Gandhi did not talk simply in terms of city-village dichotomy. In addition to referring to the village-exploitation role of the city, he spoke of "alienation" of the city dweller. He referred to the village as a "community", rather than as a socially and culturally structured unit.

However, Gandhi clearly indicated his priority, which would closely resemble the "target group" approach that is coming into vogue. To repeat, he said, "if India is not to perish, we have to begin with the lowest rung of the ladder. If that was rotten, all work done at the top or at the intermediate rungs was bound ultimately to fail".[12]

Removal of Rural Poverty

Removal of rural poverty was Gandhi's most urgent concern and it appears to be his ultimate concern also. "If you went to the villages of India you would find utter despair in the eyes of the villagers, you would find half-starved skeletons; living corpses". He immediately diagnosed the cause of the disease as well: "If India could revive them by putting life and blood into them in the shape of work, India would help the world." The degradation is due to unemployment. "The reason of our poverty is the extinction of our industries and our consequent unemployment."[13] "There is no other country in the world with the possible exception of China that is potentially so rich as India with its inexhaustible resources of manpower. Tap these resources, and you at once banish poverty from the country."[14]

Finally, and most importantly, the role that Gandhi assigned to the people for their own development should be remembered. "I believe that real freedom can only be realised by the awakening of Lok Niti (the politics of the people), that is to make the people aware of their own inner strength and encourage them to solve problems for themselves. Swaraj is to be attained by educating the masses to a sense of their capacity to regulate and control authority."[15]

Rural Development in Post-Gandhi Era

With this in the background, we proceed to discuss the post-

Gandhi rural development movement. A three-fold categorization of the Gandhians will be useful in this context: (a) The political Gandhians mainly of the Congress syndrome, which spreads across all political parties; they who ruled the country for about four decades and many of whom were partners in the new ruling setup. Among them, the Lohia Socialists (their leader had styled himself as an outcaste Gandhian) may need a special mention mainly because of their strong advocacy of the use of non-cooperation and civil disobedience; (b) The institutional Gandhians, i.e. those who work through the constructive work agencies founded by Gandhi or, later, after his death; (c) The "revolutionary" Gandhians - the group that is pledged to carry out Gandhi's last will and testament, by awakening people's power. Organizationally, they would be identified with the Sarva Seva Sangh.

Here we are concerned mainly with the last mentioned stream of the Gandhian workers. It must, however, be added that there is a considerable overlapping among the three categories, and the Sarvodaya movement represented a large degree of cooperation among the three, particularly in the field of rural development. In fact, the Gandhian institutions provided the infrastructure, including workers for the agrarian reform campaigns and rural development projects led by the Sarvodaya movement.

It must be noted that, at least until 1970, that is, when Mrs. Indira Gandhi emerged at the top of the ruling Congress Party, there was a great deal of cooperation between the official Gandhians and the Gandhian voluntary movement. In fact, it was generally accepted that the rural development policy and programmes of the Indian Government carried a strong Gandhian imprint, as if the Government were entirely guided by the Gandhian prescriptions in that sector at least. The Community Development Programme began symbolically on Gandhi's birth anniversary, October 2, 1952, "as a programme of aided self-help to be planned and implemented by the villagers themselves, the Government only offering technical help and financial assistance. Its objectives are to develop initiative in the individual and self-reliance in the village community".

Five years later, when it was found that "the contact established by the government through its officials had not been with the communities but with a few families... and that the richer cultivators had benefited disproportionately, if not indeed at the expense of the poorer ones....and that Community Development had failed to become a people's movement", Panchayati Raj which evoked the Gandhian vision of an Indian polity based on village republics was sought to be introduced.[16]

The leaders of the voluntary Gandhian movement hailed the Panchayati Raj System. Sri Jayaprakash Narayan devoted a great deal of attention through bodies like the All India Panchayat Parishad to make the official programme a success. His plea for the Reconstruction of Indian Polity as a participatory communitarian democracy bears a close resemblance to the official Panchayati Raj structure, excepting that he wanted it to be extended to the State and Union levels as well. Most of Sarvodaya leaders reiterated that Panchayati Raj was a means of achieving the Sarvodaya Society. It was not only that government legislation was sought to formalize the land gifts transfer secured during the Bhoodan-Gramdan movement, but a formal arrangement was also made to bring about coordination between the official Community Development Programme and Sarvodaya agencies for development of Gramdan Villages.

The disillusionment like "rich getting richer and the poor poorer" came, but not before it had come in official circles themselves. It is difficult to say if the Gandhians had, and still have, any clear critique of their own in order to assess what others are doing. Gandhi is still the most powerful rhetoric of the professional politicians to fool the people; they put Gandhi on the high pedestal, and pursue the capitalist path of development. The Sarvodaya leaders were also carried away by verbal correspondence with Gandhi's ideas. If the disenchantment came with the ruling politicians in the early 70s, it was due to political factors.

As far as the institutional Gandhians were concerned, they continued to plod on with one or the other item of the Constructive Programme indifferently or with little success. Khadi, which still continues to be the most important item, survived as a heavily state-subsidized economic activity. In fact, the Sarvodaya leaders' insistence on giving a "village-orientation" to Khadi and Village Industry products, i.e. to make it a programme of village self-sufficiency, rather than for urban consumers, as it largely is, almost threw the entire institutional infrastructure into a deep turmoil. In short, constructive work presented the picture of a fragmented, norm-oriented programme, run through disparate Gandhian voluntary agencies which miserably failed to regenerate the Gandhian Constructive Work, even as a programme.

Emasculation of Gandhi

So, it may be pointless to say if the Gandhian programme for rural reconstruction (the term is significant) is revolutionary or reformist in its character. It is the process that matters. The message has to radiate through each individual call in society and does not easily yield the organizational techniques. Yet the Gandhians did pursue programmes of rural development.

Some would say that the Gandhians failed to discern the immediate, intermediate and ultimate stages in the evolution of the Gandhian revolution. There is an idea of transition underlying Gandhi's method of change. In the immediate stage, Gandhi emphasized struggle, albeit non-violent, to end injustice and exploitation in order to purge society of all "anachronisms". The Gandhism that followed him tried to telescope his ultimate picture within the existing frame; it attempted class reconciliation within a highly unequalitarian order. Gandhi himself was afraid of the violence that might arise in mass scale peasant mobilization. However, in Gandhi one does see an urgency to end injustice. But Gandhi was totally emasculated by his followers. To them it became a question of struggle for *change vs. non-violence*. They did not even concede that for victims of oppression the right is all on one side. Did not Vinoba say: "If our gentle Satyagraha does not yield the desired fruit, we must infer that there is something wanting in our gentleness itself and we must, therefore, render it finer, gentler?" The Bhoodan movement epitomized this approach. Yet, it failed to yield the desired fruit.

The motive of development was to "realise the latent creative capacity of the people and to harness it for village development". But how could this be realized under a highly authoritarian and unequalitarian community power structure through consensus by working with it rather than against it?

Inequality and poverty are both relative concepts and both are the formidable economic problems facing the country. Poverty refers to the inadequacy of income to meet the basic necessities of life. Some value judgments are involved in determining what is minimum and what is not. The basic minimum requirements for a minimum level of living may differ from place to place and group to group. Therefore, poverty is time-specific, place-specific and socio-cultural specific. Though the G.N.P. has increased, it has failed to "trickle down" and consequently most of the development activities have bypassed the real poor in the country.

Inequality and Poverty–Rural-Urban Dichotomy

According to a survey by the National Institute of Nutrition, Hyderabad, the average rural diet is inferior to that of slum dwellers in the cities, and is deficient in pulses by 29.9 per cent, in milk by 45.2 per cent, and in fats by 70 per cent and in sugar and jaggery by 34 per cent, as compared to the minimum suggested by the Indian Council of Medical Research in 1981. There has been no improvement in the per capita average consumption of cloth since 1960-61, though there has been some shift from natural to synthetic fabrics. Hundreds die every year, for want of adequate cover during brief cold waves in North India. Sixty per cent of rural families still live in houses made of mud, bamboo and grass, which do not provide adequate protection against heavy rain, moisture and fire. Only 12 per cent of the rural population have a protected water supply; environmental sanitation is almost non-existent. Consequently, 10 children die every minute in villages due to diarrhoea and other water-borne diseases. Lack of health care in rural India is evident from the fact that death and infant mortality rates are 75.6 and 94.3 per cent higher than in the cities. More than 70 per cent of the rural people are illiterate and 93 per cent have no skill to enable them to pursue any profession other than primitive farming or manual work. Between 1971 and 1981 the number of landless workers and marginal farmers increased by 3.3 per cent per annum. This is nearly 50 per cent higher than the growth rate of total population of the country, and is indicative of the increasing pressure on land.[17]

It is no doubt true, that India is now amongst the first 10 industrialized countries of the world. It has entered the very exclusive nuclear and space club on its own. It has increased its GNP in real terms by more than three times since 1950-51. All this is true, but that has not helped the rural poor to meet their minimum basic needs.

The incremental capital-output ratio of agriculture in India between the year 1950-51 and 1980-81 has been found to be nearly half as compared to investment made in manufacturing industries. Agriculture in India remains backward, mainly because it has been starved of capital and technological inputs.[18]

The new masters come from no more than one per cent of households in the country, but they are backed by power elite who constitute about four per cent of the households consisting of administrators, industrialists, big business and property holders. The bitter truth about the present politico-economic situation is that the aforesaid five per cent have succeeded in importing a new kind of colonial rule which can best be described as "intra-national colonialism". The other bitter truth is that most of our politicians, instead of being crusaders, have become courtiers of political bosses, who themselves are living in a state of symbiosis with black money barons. In such a situation, unless the rural masses themselves get organized to demand their share in the material cake, they will continue to be treated as vanquished people.

The Sixth Plan set out to reduce the number of people below the poverty line from the existing 47 per cent to 30 per cent or, in aggregate terms, from 316 million to 215 million, a reduction of 101 million to be achieved in five years. However, as the 1981 census results became available the base year 1979-80 figure itself was revised from 47 per cent to 51 per cent–the aggregate from 316 million to 339 million.[19] Subsequent surveys, evaluations and assessments have also shown similar results.

Relevance of Gandhi to Professional Social Workers

Gandhi has dominated the political and social scene of India since the 1930's. But professional social workers have discovered him only recently. During this short period there have been the doctoral dissertations on Gandhi by professional social workers; there is also a book which was the product of a long dialogue between professional and Gandhian social workers.[20] Belated though it is, this recent interest is a welcome development. There is a danger that like a recent convert to a new religion, we may be carried away by our emotions into overlooking some of the major differences that exist between Gandhian views and ours. The doctoral studies, for instance, ignore the differences.

Gandhi's emphasis on the dignity of man and self-reliance, his belief in bringing about change in human beings through persuasion rather than by imposition of one's own views, his stress on the individual's freedom to decide for himself, his commitment to social justice and equality, his fight against exploitation of man by man: all these are in harmony with the professional social workers' goals, values and approach. Most of us will, however, find it difficult to agree with Gandhi's view on restriction of wants, abstinence, and a classless self-sufficient village society. While Gandhi genuinely believed in change through persuasion and was opposed to any type of coercion, his technique of Satyagraha, as pointed out by Joan Bondurant, does contain an element of coercion. The dangerous potentialities of the Gandhian technique of fast unto death when resorted to by individuals at the dictates of their conscience have been brought home to us in recent years. Imagine a situation when a client goes on fast in protest against the decision of a social welfare agency not to give him the help he wants or against the inadequacy of help offered. Of course, Gandhians may point out that it is not Satyagraha but *Duragraha*. But how is this fine distinction to be brought home to him?

There can be no disagreement with the Gandhian values of truth and non-violence. For Gandhi, these were absolute principles. He did not accept some values as primary and others as secondary, as professional social workers do. In the practice of social work there are situations when one may have to make a choice in favour of a particular value when it is not possible to reconcile it with another value. For instance, it may do more harm than good to tell a patient in a critical condition that there is little hope of his survival.

The lesson to be learnt from the simple life of Gandhiji is that one should not be swept off his feet in the current of modern technology and become its slave. In fact, he should become its master and exploit it for his as well as for others' development and well-being. The success of Gandhiji lay in understanding the cultural, intellectual and emotional level of his people. His talks were almost tinged with humour. His jokes and his fun with the villagers were fully at the level of the villagers. This helped him considerably in reducing the distance between the villagers and himself. He identified himself completely with the people and lived like them. But what a contrast one finds in the people's representatives who are elected now to govern the country.

What is the relevance of Gandhi to the generation after him? One stand that can be taken is that since Gandhi merely did what he considered it to be his duty to the society around him, he is no more relevant to posterity than the dutiful man of all ages. Gandhi himself did not claim originality in whatever he propounded. He was, he said, simply applying to his times the truths that are as old as the hills. One need not be, as it were, a hypocrite to justify almost anything in terms of Gandhi: he was not against the machines as commonly believed. Did he not describe the sewing machine as among the noblest human inventions? Even a votary of violence can claim the support of Gandhi: did he not, after all, say that he would prefer violence to abject surrender by cowardice? Gandhi possessed that faith in the individual, and a true Gandhian mass movement is that of the sum total of individuals each inspired by duty and truth. There is no leader in the Gandhian movement. Each participant must submit himself to the touchstone of non-violence to be individually sure of the rightness of the course.

An individual oblivious of what he owes to his neighbours and neighbourhood cannot be serving a larger cause. Only in the context of the rights of those in close proximity can a Satyagrahi be so elevated in spirit as to be absolutely non-violent to the extent of welcoming death. Hence his espousal of a society of small communities, in which only would Satyagraha by the individual live as an unfailing weapon against all exploitation as long as exploitation in any form exists.

In Gandhian technique, change of heart is sought through strengthening the control of super-ego. The appeal is to the conscience. In Freudian psycho-analysis, normalization (change) is sought through lessening the control of a too severe unrealistic super-ego. The concept of empathy in the profession is similar to the Sarvodaya concept of total identification with the people. However, there is an important difference between these two concepts. The Sarvodaya workers generally believe that in order to understand what problems mean to people, it is necessary for a social worker to live among them under similar conditions. Professional social workers feel that this is neither necessary nor desirable. It is not necessary because it is possible to identify with the people and understand their point of view without living like them. It is not desirable because a social worker has not only to understand the people's point of view but also to maintain the objectivity essential for an accurate assessment of the situation.

However, Gandhi was an uncompromising crusader who strove to establish a society where justice and truth would prevail. If the values he stood for and which are also enshrined in our Constitution are relevant today, Gandhi is relevant.

Conclusion

The struggle for development and eradication of poverty has to be conducted without sacrificing values and ethics that are cherished most. The Congress culture under the leadership of Mahatma Gandhi believed in using good means to achieve good ends, in making the villages of India completely self-reliant in Gram Swaraj which meant planning from the grassroots level and in placing individuals at the centre of all developmental activities. It opposed centralization of economic and political power in the hands of the State. It believed in limited government. It believed that the State should give favoured treatment in the matter of education to the economically backward and socially oppressed people of India. It believed in value-based politics. It put more faith in persuasive power than in the coercive power of the State to bring about the necessary social change and reforms. It believed in safeguarding democratic institutions and in maintaining the sanctity, dignity and independence of judiciary. Above all, it believed that politicians are servants of the people and not their masters. The politicians and leaders have deviated from the path of vibrant humanism to impersonal station, from complete de-centralization of political and economic power to total centralization of all power in the hands of the State. What matters most to all politicians is the acquisition of power at any cost, by any means, fair or foul. This type of culture is not conducive for the well-being of the people. Unless the fruits of development reach the poor and unless they acquire a certain faith in the usefulness of education, it would be futile to motivate, say, the agricultural labourer to change his style of living.

REFERENCES

1. Chi-Yuen Wu, the "Nature of Modern Development" in Dynamics of Development (ed) by S.K. Sharma, Concept Publishing Company, New Delhi, 1977, pp. 1-33.
2. Dennis Goulet, The Third World, from *World Development: An Introductory Reader*, ed. by Helence Castel.
3. *Towards Accelerated Development Proposals for the Second United Nations Development Decade*, U.N., New York, 1920, p. 2.
4. U.N. Accelerated Development, op. cit., p. 5.
5. *International Social Development Review*, No. 3, Evolving of the United Nations Approach to Planning for Unified Socio-Economic Development. An Introduction, New York, U.N., 1971, p. 2.
6. Salima Omer, *Social Development, International Social Work*, Volume XXII, No. 3, ISSN 0020, -8728, pp. 11-26.
7. *Ibid.*, pp. 15-16.
8. M.S. Gore, *Some Aspects of Social Development*, Department of Social Work, University of Hongkong and Tata Institute of Social Sciences, Bombay, 1973, p. 11.
9. *Constructive Work*, Ahmedabad, Navjivan Press, 1941 (See the preamble).
10. *Ibid.*
11. *Harijan*, 23 April 1946, p. 198.
12. *Harijan*, 13 April 1935, p. 68.
13. *Harijan*, 11 May, 1935, p. 103.
14. *Harijan*, 21 September, 1934, p. 253.
15. *Young India*, 29 January, 1925, p. 41.
16. Planning Commission, Programme Evaluation Organization, *Report*, 1957.
17. Bhanu Pratap Singh, "Betrayal of Rural India", *Indian Express*, May 22, 1985, p. 6.
18. *Ibid.*, p. 7.
19. Bharat Dogra, *Poverty Development and Poverty—India 1947-84*, published by Bharat Dogra, New Delhi, 1984, [pp. 212-241.
20. Sugata Dasgupta (ed), *Towards A Philosophy of Social Work in India*, Popular Book Services New Delhi, 1967, pp. 196-240.

6

TECHNOLOGY AND MAN–GANDHIAN PERSPECTIVE

SHASHI SHARMA

Modern economics views technology as an important determinant of economic growth. Improvement in the means and methods of production have the effect of improving the efficiency with which inputs are converted into output, thus lowering the average cost of production. Technological progress thus helps in maximizing output now or in future with the help of limited available resources.

A philosophical analysis of economic thought shows that there is fragmentary paradigm underlying modern economics which accepts that there is a basic dichotomy between a part and the rest of the world, the "self" and the "non-self. The various constituents of the universe are supposed to be finite discrete and mechanistic moving under some kind of force. Accordingly man is taken as a limited, material, mechanistic being functioning under the force of wants. The satisfaction of wants through the consumption of goods gives "pleasure" which a rational man always seeks to maximize. Man is thus basically supposed to be a consumer having unlimited wants. The purpose of economics is, therefore, pursuit of materialism, "augmentation of wealth" or achievement of undifferentiated growth leading to higher and higher increase in the flow of goods and services for the happiness or well-being of man. Unlimited technical progress is thus favoured in order to maximize output because more is always better.

Gandhian perspective on technology and man diverges sharply from that of modern economics since it is based on a fundamentally different paradigm, an altogether different world-view. It is essential to be clear about the Gandhian concept of man and the foundations upon which Gandhian economics is based before an attempt can be made to examine Gandhiji's views on technology and man.

Mahatma Gandhi accepts a "holistic" world-view taking all life to be vertically and horizontally like one homogeneous whole. He had an immovable faith that "God alone is", that there is an absolute, unitary, changeless reality which is ever existing and all pervading. He preferred to call this reality which is beyond time, space and causation "Truth" since nothing is or exists in reality except Truth. The apparent diversity and separativeness is a delusion created by the mind and senses. The substratum, the essence underlying all diversity is unity. In his autobiography , Gandhiji writes, "Often in my progress, I have had faint glimpses of the Absolute Truth, God, and daily the conviction is growing upon me that He alone is real and all else is unreal." Everything living or non-living is a manifestation of the same reality, the Truth. The same pure being is enfolded, involved or implicated in all the worldly objects. In other words, every single particle contains and represents the whole or it may be said that God is everything. The various parts in nature, due to the inner thread of unity, are interconnected and are functioning to help each other for the common good of the whole. This is due to the law of love, according to Gandhiji. Life is thus not in parts, but it is one whole.

The view that there is an ultimate oneness in life is the core of the Indian Vedantic philosophy, Gandhiji was particularly fond of the opening verse of the Ishopnishad which says, "Whatever life exists in this world is the abode of the Lord." According to the Gita, "the Lord dwelleth in the hearts of all beings." The experiences of the saints like Nanak, Kabir, Tukaram and others also show that nothing exists except God. It is surprising that now the latest developments in science are also leading us to a holistic and ecological concept of the universe which is very much similar to the Gandhian concept of Truth. According to Fritjof Capra, "As we penetrate into mater, nature does not show us any isolated building blocks, but rather appears as a complicated web of relations between the various parts of a unified whole." David Bohm also holds the view that the universe is a hologram in which each part somehow involves all the others, contains them or enfolds them.

Man: A Potentially Divine Entity

A new concept of man emerges according to the Gandhian holistic world-view. Man is a part of the whole and has wholeness enfolded within him. He is not simply a material being having an existence limited to the physical level only, he has an unbound spiritual existence also. At the spiritual level, man has unity with all human beings, animals, plants and everything else that exists. Man does not live the totality of his being due to ignorance. However, Gandhiji considers man to be potentially divine. Man has the capacity to transcend his mechanistic structure, reach higher and higher levels of consciousness and, ultimately, realize the totality of his being. As Gandhiji says, "I believe it to be possible for every human being to attain that blessed and indescribable sinless state in which he feels within himself the presence of God to the exclusion of everything else."

The purpose of man's life is Truth realization, to attain the highest and purest state of existence. Since God is in everything and all life is essentially one, Truth realization requires an identification with all that exists. Gandhiji thus arrived at the principle of Love or non-violence to realize God, the absolute Truth. Non-violence is not a passive state, it is an active engagement in every field of life due to the dynamic force of love. Love in relationships is selfless service to mankind. Thus to Gandhiji man is the supreme consideration because he is a manifestation of God. The path of non-violence for the realization of Truth led Gandhiji to arrive at certain principles or norms counted as truth, non-violence, non-stealing, non-possession, fearlessness, control of the palate, bread-labour, Swadeshi and trusteeship, to guide individual as well as collective life.

Economics must also be subservient to the basic goal of human life, that is, Truth and be helpful in its realization through non-violent means. Gandhian economics, therefore, deeply rooted in the holistic paradigm, moves within the framework of the accompanying concepts and the values of life. Gandhiji defines the well-being of man in terms of moral or spiritual welfare. Material welfare, however, has its right place since body is the instrument for achieving moral welfare. The purpose of economics is, therefore, provisioning of optional amount of goods and services in order to keep the body in a fit condition so that, through service, the highest potentiality of man may be realized. Gandhian economics is thus need-oriented and not want-oriented. Besides fulfilment of needs, the other basic objectives of Gandhian holistic economics are employment for all, eradication of all deprivation and exploitation, equality and welfare of all.

As stated earlier, man is the supreme consideration for Gandhiji. He is opposed to the modern approach to technology since ultimately, it adversely affects the life of man, his relationships and the environment in which he lives. Using the term "machinery" for technology, he has spoken and written at length on the evils of machinery. In *Hind Swaraj* he wrote, "Machinery is like a snake-hole which may contain from one to hundred snakes."

Gandhiji's central point of opposition to machinery is that in a country abundant with labour, machinery inevitably leads to unemployment . Labour is looked upon simply as an item of cost by modern economics. In order to minimize costs, machinery, there fore, comes in displacing labour. Competition among the producers leads to more and more technological advancement resulting in concentration of Capital in the hands of a few. With each step in technological advancement, capital-labour ratio increases which accompanied by lack of inevitable resources swells the ranks of the unemployed. Now, unemployment is bound to occur if the incremental employment-capital ratio is lower than the ratio between the current increment of the work-force and the available supply of investible funds. Criticizing the craze for machinery which is introduced in the name of labour saving but which eventually leads to unemployment, Gandhiji had commented, "Men go on 'saving labour' till thousands are without work and thrown on the open streets to die of starvation.

Full employment is one of the basic objectives of Gandhian economics. Work is not only a source of livelihood, it is a source of self-expression, fulfilment and creativity. The principle of economic independence and human dignity requires that work must be ensured for all able-bodied individuals of a society. Gandhiji, therefore, wanted technological advancement to take place within limits. He was thus advocating for labour-intensive industries in labour-abundant under-developed countries.

Unemployment Problem still Unsolved

It is often argued that technological progress may result in temporary unemployment but it will ultimately lead to full employment as a result of its influence on output-maximization. Gandhiji, however, does not accept the logic and says, "In fifty years there may be enough to employ everyone with modern technology. But we must have employment for every body long before this. We can do so only by giving up the craze for modernity which is today creating unemployment and poverty. It may be pointed out here that it is more than 150 years ago that the industrial revolution took place and since then technological progress has been going on at a fast rate, yet the problem of unemployment has not been solved. As a matter of fact, there is enough data available which make it sufficiently evident that unemployment has been continuously rising not only in the under-developed countries but also in the developed countries like the USA, Australia, Canada, France, West Germany and Great Britain.

As technological innovations take place leading to capital-intensive, large-scale mechanised production, wealth and income get concentrated in the hands of a few leading to sharp inequalities of income and poverty. Society gets sharply polarized giving rise to a dualistic nature of economy. The concentration of economic power becomes a cumulative process due to more and more technological advancement. The process feeds upon exploitation, the "haves" exploiting the "have-nots" at various levels of life. Reacting sharply to the exploitative character of machinery Gandhiji once said, "I will not have the enrichment of a few at the expense of the community. At present, the machine is helping a small minority to live on the exploitation of the masses.' He considered exploitation to be the essence of all violence and, therefore, he emphatically declared, "I am a determined foe of all machinery that is designed for the exploitation of people." On being questioned whether he was opposed to machinery only because it concentrated production and distribution in the hands of a few, he had pointedly replied, "Whatever cannot be shared with the masses is taboo to me."

As technological development takes place and industrialization begins in an underdeveloped economy, the modern sector in the urban areas thrives but the rural sector in the rural areas decays. The traditional handicrafts and village small-scale industries perish because they are unable to stand the competition from large-scale capital-intensive industries. The "backwash" effects of development in urban sector tends to denude the countryside of its skill and vitality leading to forced idleness and poverty. Gandhiji was deeply pained by this process of impoverishing the villagers and enriching the moneyed man. He knew poverty leads to lack of purchasing power and, therefore, the village industries are further ruined because of a lack of local market for their products. Even the vital raw materials needed by them are sucked away by the modern sector. The entire process entails impoverishment of the masses, widespread unemployment, mass migration to cities on the one hand, and concentration of income and wealth leading to conspicuous consumption, malallocation of scarce economic resources and balance-of-payment difficulties on the other.

At the international level, technical progress results in the exploitation of the underdeveloped countries by the developed countries. The L.D.C.'s are dumped with costly manufactured goods in exchange for their important primary products and raw materials. The so-called transfer of technology these days has also become a source of exploitation. The rich countries get rid of their obsolete and harmful technologies by selling them to the poor countries. These technologies make the rich of the underdeveloped countries richer and the poor poorer.

Technological progress for the purpose of accelerating industrialization in order to achieve undifferentiated growth rates leads to fast depletion of the non-renewable world resources, pollution and problems of ecology. "Earth provides enough to satisfy every man's need but not every man's greed", observed Mahatma Gandhi long ago. It is being increasingly realized these days that a dangerous situation of exhausting our fixed resource base might soon arise, if present economic trends remain unaltered. The impact of the depleting world resources has already begun to be felt in the steep rise in the prices of some of the resources like petroleum, mercury and lead in the recent years. Natural processes can replenish themselves within certain limits only. Indiscriminate use of technology leads to an incursion upon our air, water and soil. Gandhian perspective suggests that industrialization and technological limits must be carried out within limits so that the environment of which man is a part is not disturbed.

Machine Kills Man's Creativity

Gandhiji was against machinery because it atrophies the limbs of man, causes dehumanization and moral degradation. It kills initiative, freedom and creativity of the individual. Men are turned into machine minders with little freedom to exercise their own creative faculties. Technology alienates man from his true self, his work and product, fellow-beings and nature. As Schumacher has rightly observed, "Our current methods of production are already eating into the very substance of industrial man." The application of indiscriminate technology has either turned man into an exploiter giving full vent to his selfishness, envy, violence, vanity and pride lying dormant within him or has led him to become the exploited always living in fear, insecurity, depression and frustration, resulting in moral degradation in both the cases. As a matter of fact, Gandhiji felt that the development of science and technology without spiritual advancement inevitably leads to dehumanization, degradation and destruction of man.

Though Gandhiji vehemently criticized machinery because of its evil effects, yet his opposition was not indiscriminate and total. He recognized the good influence of machinery on labour productivity and in reducing the burden of human drudgery. He welcomed machinery so long as it helped in saving individual labour and lightened the burden of man, but he strongly rejected it as soon as it became an instrument of greed and exploitation, killing the freedom and individuality of man. He favoured technology within limits ensuring full employment, freedom, equality, non-exploitation, decentralization and self-sufficiency. An important consideration is that the masses should be able to own the technology. Gandhiji had suggested production by the masses instead of mass production in order to avoid the problems of centralization, distribution and exploitation. Another condition for ensuring decentralization in underdeveloped countries with shortage of capital is that machinery should be simple, cheap, easy to handle and easy to repair. Gandhiji had strongly pleaded for the revival of handicrafts, village and small industries in the traditional sector. The existing local technologies, therefore, must be revived and improved upon in the Swadeshi spirit. The "Charkha" received the place of pride and honour only because it symbolized employment, freedom, equality, decentralization and self-sufficiency.

The Gandhian principle of bread-labour also requires that machinery must be kept within limits. Everybody must do some physical labour in order to deserve the food that he eats. This is the sacred law expounded in the Gita and the Bible. The breach of the principle amounts to theft, according to the Gita. If this principle of bread-labour is followed by all, the use of machinery would automatically fall within its proper limits.

The logic that technological progress must be favoured because it leads to output-maximization, is not valid from the Gandhian point of view because the aim of Gandhian economics is appropriate consumption and not unlimited consumption. Gandhiji was, however, willing to accept a few heavy and capital-intensive industries with high technology in the national interest provided they are under State control and are subservient to the needs of the village and small industries. It may thus be concluded that technology was acceptable to Gandhiji within the framework of the values and concepts arising out of a holistic paradigm so far as it catered to the needs of man.

7

TECHNOLOGY AND DISPERSAL OF ECONOMY : A GANDHIAN PERSPECTIVE

JAI NARAIN

Technology has changed the world in which we live. The landing on the moon and the transplant of human heart are only the more spectacular of them but in countless ways, advances have been made which are likely to have a tremendous impact on man's life in the decades to come. Dr. Radhakrishnan has described these achievements in these musical words: "We have learnt to ride the waves of the wind, to harness the rivers for watering deserts, to master the earth and the creatures thereof and with the earth as our footstool reach out to the stars."[1]

In fact the very success of modern science and technology has generated to some extent a backlash. There is a great debate in the West among the economists and technologists about the dangers of unlimited application of modern technology for accelerating industrialization leading to exploitation of natural resources and the anti-life impact of technology on human existence itself. There is a growing feeling amongst many that we are going too far and the vastly increased power that technology has placed in the hands of man has not been matched by his ability to use it wisely. The club of

Rome[2] Thesis on this is a product of such debate. The new technology-generated dangers on land, ocean and sky have added new dimensions to human life. Indeed it is now being suggested that the present rate of technological progress may mean the tragic end of technology itself, though, paradoxically, the solution is still being sought in technology itself.

Alvin Toffler, in his best seller *Future Shock*, has well described the inexorable price we are paying for the advanced technology which we are told is being developed for our benefit.

"Our technological powers increase but the side effects and potential hazards also escalate. We risk thermopollution of the oceans themselves, overheating them, destroying immeasurable quantities of marine life, perhaps even melting the ice caps. On land, we concentrate such large masses of population in such small urban–technological islands–that we threaten to use up air's oxygen faster than it can be replaced, conjuring up the possibility of the new Saharas where the cities are new. Through such distribution of natural ecology, we may literally, in the words of biologist Barry Commoner, be destroying this planet as a suitable place for human habitation."[3]

The social fragmentation and onslaught on the traditional value systems have also tended to threaten human existence due to the degradation of environment. One consequence of modern science and technology has been dichotomy between the elite and the masses. There is a future shock for a man overtaken by his own knowledge, the consequence of which he is unable to absorb and adjust himself to.

There is also a great fear that mankind might be wiped out from the face of the earth by the big bang of a nuclear explosion. The creeping paralysis of society is creating as much fear of a mankind destroyed by the whimper of a man turned against himself. A risk of war is lapsing in military preparation which may promote accident, misunderstanding or miscalculation if not the actual nuclear war. A simple mechanical error will not give time for repenting the mistake. Remember the midnight burst of "Enola Gay" and "Small Bay" completely wiped out "Hiroshima" and "Nagasaki" from the map of the world. Assumptions are that nations are more likely to act rationally than irrationally, but our knowledge of human beings convinces us that they do not always do so.

Straight-line Concept of Progress Questioned

Further the poignancy of socio-economic consequences of technology resulting from overconcentration of economy further heightened by the problem of mass unemployment and the tense global atmosphere charged with conflict and violence, have spurred a renewed interest in Gandhi and his ideas. The insight that science has given us into a symbiotic relationship of earth's natural resources, the living and non-living, has increasingly called into question the straight line concept of progress as a function of growth in the Gross National Product. Also the failures of foreign technologies to create the impulse for adequate growth among the Third World countries has created a backlash. Above all the energy crunch has favoured a decentralized economy on Swadeshi lines with decentralized renewable resources-based energy policy. If industry is dispersed in rural areas, if production technology could be so organized that the bulk of production could be carried on efficiently at cottage or tiny scale, these problems could perhaps be controlled and the quality of life improved for the masses in their existing homes. All these factors along with so many others necessitate the paramount need to create an equilibrium between political power, economic and cultural needs so that technology could play its significant role through a Gandhian ethos.

The basic question Gandhi posed was whether "technology would remain controlled and in the service of man to reduce his drudgery and to help solve man's material problems", or "whether man would become so subservient to technology that ultimately he would be forced to sell his soul to Mephistophelian materialism and become alienated both from his fellow beings and nature by plundering it". [4]

Even with the present level of technology, it is possible to wipe out poverty and misery in this world. In the past four decades, the world has manufactured goods and services many times more than it did during the previous two thousand years. And all the time the number and proportion of the people who live below the poverty line has vastly increased. Why is it so? One answer is unequal distribution of resources and the concentration of technology in a few hands. But there is little one can do about this situation; even the most generous offer by advanced countries amounts to half and one per cent of the GNP to be transferred from rich to poor countries. Unfortunately, even this strategy is designed to keep rich elites in the poor countries in power; the object is not to bring about any solution to the problem of poverty through technological transfer. Indeed there can be no solution through technology unless the social role of technology and the pre-conditions of an autonomous and self-reliant model of economic growth are satisfied.

The Mahatma called for a programme of Swadeshi precisely for this reason. Swadeshi may have started as the rejection of British goods and the imperial policy of creating a class which willingly allowed itself to be enslaved by Western technology and culture. But he never confined this concept to this limited objective, though he fully used it. He broadened the definition of Swadeshi. There is self-reliance, even self-sufficiency in his Swadeshi but no isolation. This relates to the most important question of the day, namely, the transfer of technology. The main contradiction in the world today is that whereas the economic and technological interdependence of countries is increasing, neither economic nor technological resources are global. They are strictly within the control of a few developed countries which maximize the gain for themselves. Therefore, not only the technological gap between nations is increasing but transfer of technology has become a source of exploitation of poor nations and, ironically, for perpetuating the technological gap.

According to one report there have been 13,000 foreign collaborations in India since independence. There must be something drastically wrong with our country because Japan with 25,000 collaborations has pushed its per capita income to $ 14,000 per year as compared to $ 200 in our country. Probably the collaboration to produce Maruti car tells us why this is so. Foreign exchange worth Rs. 13,000 crores has already been remitted to Japan, but the Maruti car is not even 75 per cent Indian. Foreign collaborations, multinationals in the name of transfer of technology are leaving India dry.[5] And this is true about all other Third World countries who have allowed foreign collaboration on their soil. But this implication was not clear three decades ago when the newly independent and developing countries allowed all kinds of technological inroads to be made into their economies from the developed world. These countries have now realized that what has come in the name of technology transfer is designed, to quote Prof. J.D. Sethi.[6] "(i) to exploit the resources of the poor countries for the benefit of developed countries; (ii) create a dualism by isolating the sectors depending on Western technology from those dependent on and emerging from endowment of national resources; (iii) widen the already technological gap; (iv) stunt the very process of growth by creating a new consumer oriented industry and a class which consumes valuable resources; and (v) create a kind of technological imperialism which demoralizes developing countries and makes them accept the superiority of Western civilization".

Swadeshi not a Cult of Hatred

Gandhi diagnosed these evils through Swadeshi. In his own words, "My definition of Swadeshi is well known. I must not serve my distant neighbour at the expense of the nearest. It is never vindictive or punitive. It is in no sense narrow, for I buy from every part of the world what is needed for my growth. I refuse to buy anything however nice or beautiful, if it interferes with my growth or injures those whom nature had made my first care.[7] He did not reject trade. He only rejected the determinism behind the so-called principle of comparative costs and division of labour, which could not be defined without taking into consideration the level of technology. These determinisms of economic links ultimately become instruments of exploitation of the poor by rich, of the weak by the strong. He clarified his position in *From Yervada Mandir*, "To reject foreign manufactures merely because they are foreign and go on wasting national time and money in the promotion in one's country of manufactures for which it is not suited would be criminal folly and a negation of the Swadeshi spirit. A votary of Swadeshi will never harbour ill-will towards the foreigners, he will not be activated by the antagonism towards any body on earth. Swadeshism is not a cult of hatred. It is a doctrine of selfless service that has its roots in the purest ahimsa, i.e. love."[8] Thus Gandhi certainly permitted international trade and exchange of technology if this meant an exchange of equal advantage and did not involve injustice.

However, if it was a question of choice, he would have preferred self-sufficiency. But as a matter of practical policy, he did not think that India should stand aloof in that matter. He defined a Swadeshi article as any article which "subserves the interest of the millions even though the capital and talent are foreign but under effective Indian control.[9] He defined effective Indian control as "An industry to be Indian must be demonstrably in the interest of the masses. It must be manned by Indians both skilled and unskilled. Its capital and machinery should be Indian and the labour employed should have a living wage and be comfortably housed, while the welfare of the children of the labourer should be guaranteed by the employer. This is an ideal definition."[10]

Thus Gandhi did not advocate an internally or externally closed system. His Swadeshi means a certain amount of self-reliance, independence and freedom both internally and externally; no matter what model of growth a poor country adopts, it must not be either trade or aid constrained. Gandhi not only emphasized economic self-reliance but also the cultural identity of the nation--identity which modern technology was destroying. He saw modern technology imposing a new kind of imperialism on poor nations irrespective of the ideologies of the donor nations.

At this point in history, we cannot of course start from scratch. Already modern technology, in the name of foreign collaboration, has made large inroads into our country. But the basic questions still remain unanswered. Why the growth rate, the rate of capital accumulation, the rates of saving and investment, etc., have all declined as more and more technology comes to be imported? Why are more and more people being pushed below the poverty line? These people live in areas which are far away from the islands of modern technology. Our starting points are, internally, (i) the existence of numerous technological islands based on imported technology and collaboration; and (ii) the vast areas of populace whose development has come to stop. Externally, production and technology are becoming increasingly global and there is growing emphasis on interdependence. The struggle for survival, economic growth and social justice for the developing world, thus has become more and more difficult in the face of internationalization of technology, most of which is inappropriate for the developing countries.[11]

Seeds of Our Own Destruction

It is generally accepted by all that the underdeveloped countries should evolve methods of adapting imported technology and that if they can do so they would make a breakthrough. Indeed this view has given adaptation the same supreme role as is given to technology. But this is easier said than done. In developed countries there are scientific infrastructures and applied scientific facilities to bring about such adaptation. If such facilities were available in poor countries, there would be no need to import and adapt technology; it could be autonomously created. Besides, if an economic system in general is based on imported techniques with product patterns more suited to the demands of an unequal distributive system, technological adaptation will not help much. That is why Gandhi wanted technological development from bottom upwards rather than from top downwards, which is what adaptation implies. Technological innovation must take place all along the line and be consistent with the most abundant supplies of factor available. For example, India is an overpopulated country. We have a vast reserve army of unemployed, semiemployed and seasonally employed people both skilled and unskilled. And if we import highly labour-saving automatic technology from the other countries, we are sowing the seeds of our own destruction. In India we need only that technology which can give honourable employment to our all working hands. Our major problems are poverty, unemployment and concentration of wealth in a few hands, of course along with other so many problems. But in developed countries, the technology is innovated keeping in view the scarcity of manpower and other difficulties of those countries. Thus that technology when brought here will have more side effects.

This again brings us to the Gandhian principle that technological development must be matched or balanced with appropriate human, organizational and cultural development. The gap between technological and social development exists in every society, developed and less developed, but more so in the latter. The very absence of socio-economic prerequisites of an imported technology creates all kinds of problems. The most important question is whether technological development through imported technology creates a more independent, autonomous and self-reliant structure of the economy and decision making, or does it make it difficult to be so? The current pattern threatens to widen the gap. The danger is that two cultures may be created. But the structural and organizational constraints noted in the developing countries made Gandhi put up stiff opposition to any technology which stultified organizational changes.

Gandhi, in answer to the question whether he saw Swaraj at the end of a Swadeshi movement said, "Why not, once I said in spinning wheel lies Swaraj, next I said in prohibition lies Swaraj. In the same way I would say in cent per cent Swadeshi lies Swaraj."[12] He added, "What we need to do is to add to our capacity for labour with our hands and feet the person's technical skills, so that we may devise our own technology suitable to our requirements." He further clarified, "I would prize every invention of science and technology made for the benefit of all. There is a difference between invention and invention. I should not care for the asphyxiating gases capable of killing masses of men at a time. The heavy machinery for work of public utility, which cannot be undertaken by human labour, has its inevitable place, but all that would be owned by the State and used entirely for the benefit of the people. I can have no consideration for machinery which meant either to enrich the few at the expense of the many, or without cause to displace the useful labour of many."[13]

It is often forgotten that Gandhi was a village man as well as a global man. For him neither the village nor the world was static. Both were dynamic. He refused to accept that parts of the whole remained static and the society became dynamic and stable. So technology for him was more than a techno-economic concept; it was a part of the whole which included values, institutions and indeed the whole culture. Gandhi was, thus, a forerunner of those who attached enormous importance to the cultural and value impact of technology and he linked it with society, economy, justice and positive decision making. In his own words, "I want to save time, and labour, not for a fraction of mankind, but for all. I want concentration of wealth not in the hands of a few, but in the hands of all. Today machinery helps (a few) to ride on the back of millions. The impetus behind it is not the philosophy to save labour, but greed. It is against this constitution of things that I am fighting with all my might."[14]

In the end we can conclude with Prof. J.D. Sethi,"Metaphorically and even otherwise, the Gandhian system includes both the aeroplane and the bullock-cart. In the society of his vision, traditional technologies go through continuous improvement, modification, etc., to reduce the burden and drudgery of the working people and help them to produce more, but without creating the enslavement of man....The Club of Rome Thesis or limit to growth, etc., are the problems of the highly developed countries of the world. But for India and other similarly poor nations, where more than 40 per cent of the population is living below poverty line, it is almost nonsense to talk about limiting growth. At the same time, it is necessary for these countries to debunk the illusion of unlimited growth. Gandhi's relevance lies in this."[15]

REFERENCES

1. Dr. S. Radhakrishnan, *Speeches and Writings*, Third Series, The Publications Division, New Delhi, July 1959, May 1962.
2. The Club of Rome has among its membership such economists of eminence as Aurelio Peccei, an Italian economist who heads the management firm of Itloconsult in Rome; Kogoro Vemura, President of the Japanese Federation of Economic Organizations; and Alexander King of Britain who is Director General for Scientific Affairs of the Office for Economic Cooperation and Development.
3 Alvin Toffler, *Future Shock* (New York: A National General Company, 1971), p. 430.
4. J.D. Sethi, *Gandhi Today* (New Delhi: Vikas Publishing House Pvt. Ltd., 1978), p. 49.
5. *The Tribune* dated 26-2-1987.
6. J.D. Sethi, op. cit., P. 112.
7. *Young India*, 12-3-1925, p. 88.
8. M.K. Gandhi, *From Yervada Mandir* (Ahmedabad. Navajivan Publishing House, 1957), p. 66.
9. *Harijan*, 25-2-1939, p. 25.
10. Ibid., 23-10-1937, p. 311.
11. J.D. Sethi, op. cit., p. 114.
12. *Harijan*, 28-9-1934, p. 259.
13 Ibid., 22-6-1935, p. 146.
14 Quoted in B.N. Ganguli, *Gandhi's Social Philosophy—Perspective and Relevance* (Delhi: Vikas Publishing House Pvt. Ltd, 1973), p. 314.
15. J.D. Sethi, op. cit., p. 116.

8

PUBLIC HEALTH, POVERTY AND EMPOWERMENT– A CHALLENGE[1]

DAVID WERNER

Those of you receiving a degree in public health are faced with an unusual - and in some ways paradoxical - challenge. For, as we all know, in today's world the biggest obstacles to 'health for all' are not technical, but rather social and political. Widespread hunger and poor health do not result from total scarcity of resources, or from overpopulation, as was once thought. Rather, they result from unfair distribution of land, resources, knowledge, and power - too much in the hands of too few. Or, as Mahatma Gandhi put it: There is enough for everyone's need but not for everyone's greed.

It is often argued that the major obstacles to health are economic. And true, for most of the world's people, the underlying cause of poor health is poverty - poverty and their powerlessness to

----

1. David Werner, is known the world over for his book *Where is no doctor,* has recently published another manual of immense practical value, *Disabled village children: A guide for community health workers*. This paper is the text of the convocation address he delivered in 1985 at the Johns Hopkins School of Public Health. (Cowrtesy IFDA Dossier 65, May/June 1988).

do anything about it. Yet, the economic resources to do something about it *do* exist. Unfortunately, control over those resources is in the hands of local, national and world leaders whose first priority, too often, is not the well-being of all the people, but rather the quest to stay in power.

We are all aware of the health-related inequities that result in millions of premature deaths every year. One in two of the world's people never in their lives see a trained health worker. One in three are without clean water to drink. One in four of the world's children are malnourished. It has been estimated that to provide adequate primary health care for all the world's people would cost an extra US $ 50 billion a year - an amount equal to three weeks of world military spending.

So we can see that the underlying obstacles to primary health care are not really economic, but rather political.

The politics of health and health care are fraught with contradic tions. Just as an example, look at smoking. The governments of industrialised countries now warn their people that "Cigarette smoking is dangerous to your health". Yet these same governments, while cutting back on health benefits to the poor, continue to subsidize the tobacco industry with millions of dollars. And since fewer people in the rich countries now smoke, the big tobacco companies have bolstered their sales campaigns in the Third World, where the growing epidemic of smoking now contributes to more deaths that do most tropical diseases.

The subsidizing of the tobacco industry is but one of many, many ways in which attempts at public health are dissipated by governments that try to stay in power by catering to the interests of the powerful. The United States of America, as one of the world's wealthiest and strongest countries, has consistently made international decisions which favour the rich and powerful at the expense of the health and well-being of the poor majority. Its opposition to the United Nations mandate opposing the unethical promotion of infant milk products is a good example. It is interesting to note that in the long run the grassroots popular boycott of Nestle's and other transnationals did more to bring the milk companies into line than did all the mandates from the United Nations.

An equally blatant example of how U.S. foreign policy is prepared to obstruct a poor country's health in order to protect powerful economic interests is seen by its reaction to the Bangladesh Health Ministry's new drug policy. As we all know, overuse and misuse of medications in the world today has reached epidemic proportions. In poor countries, up to 50% of the health budgets are spent on imported drugs. Of the 25,000 different medications now being promoted, only about 250 are ranked as essential by the World Health Organization. Yet the drug companies promote their products in the poor countries with a vengeance. The information they publish about their products in these countries is often dangerously falsified. In many poor countries, the drug companies spend more on brainwashing and misleading the doctors than the medical schools spend on educating them. The companies repeatedly and illegally pay Ministers of Health under the table to keep on utilizing pharmaceuticals that have been banned in industrialized countries and dumped on the Third World. All in all, the abuses and false promotion of needless, costly, and irrationally combined medications have reached alarming and health-threatening proportions, particularly in the Third World. When the Bangladeshi government, recognizing serious shortages in 150 essential drugs, passed a decree that banned the import of 1,700 non-essential preparations, the transnational drug companies did everything in their power to make the Bangladeshi government annul the decree. After all, if a poor country like Bangladesh can take a stand against the transnational in favour of its people's health, might not other nations follow the example? So the transnationals began to make threats. Factories would be closed. Foreign companies would pull out. Workers would be fired. Acute shortages of essential drugs would result. The future of foreign investment in Bangladesh would be in jeopardy. Representatives from the US Government not only refused to support Bangladesh's new drug policy, but also threatened to reduce or discontinue foreign aid if it were upheld.

As has been demonstrated in China, Cuba, Nicaragua, Kerala State in India, and elsewhere, the health of people has more to do with fair distribution of resources than with total wealth. Fair distribution, in turn, depends upon equalitarian government. What it comes down to is that the health of the poor in the world today is abysmal because too many governments are in the hands of powerful elite groups or military juntas that do not fairly represent their people. Clearly, what is needed is radical change of governments and social structures. Those who rule the world today will not bring about the changes that are needed for the well-being of the people. They have too much self-interest in maintaining the status quo. The changes can only come about through organized action of the people themselves. In most countries today, primary health care implies a very fundamental social evolution - if not revolution.

In several countries today, popular revolutions have recently taken place or are in process. New governments with wide popular support have gone about redistributing resources and extending primary health services fairly to all the people. However, the powerful countries of the world, for the same reasons they opposed the UN resolution on infant milk products, or the Bangladeshi government's new drug policy, consistenly violate international and humanitarian codes in order to try to destroy the revolutionary governments that have dared to side with the people.

Yet the peoples of the world, little by little, are beginning to awaken, to join together or protest the exploits of the powerful, and the injustice which damages their health.

We are on the edge of a worldwide movement, led by the poor and oppressed, in defense of their rights to a fair share of what the world provides. Health for all can only be achieved through a struggle for social equity - a struggle led, not by those on the top, but by those on the bottom, by the people themselves.

Health work is never a political

Given the fundamentally political nature of health, what are those of you graduating today going to do with your shining new degrees in public health?

If what you are looking for is simply a well-paid respectable job, with a certificate from Johns Hopkins in your pocket then you should have no problem. But if you honestly want to help those in greatest need, gain the strength and ability to improve their health and their lives in a lasting way, then your future is less certain, and - depending on which country you go to - perhaps unsafe.

You may try to stay out of politics, to work within the realm of public health in the narrower, more conventional sense. Baby weighing, latrines, dark green leafy vegetables, MCH, ORT, GOBI, and all that.

But be careful. Even with the best intentions, you can easily end up doing more harm than good. Health work is never apolitical. Either it is done in ways that help empower people so that they can take greater control over the factors that determine their health. Or it is done in ways that result in keeping people under control, organizationally disabled, overly dependent on centralized, institutionalized, overprofessionalized yet inadequate services.

Thus, health care can be either *people empowering* in the sense that it gives people greater control over the factors that influence their health and their lives, as well as greater leverage over public institutions and leaders. Or it can be *people disempowering,* insofar as it is used by the authorities as an instrument of social control. People empowering health care utilizes health education, *not*, to change people's attitudes and behaviour, but rather to help people to change their situation. Or, as Pablo Freire would say it, to change their world.

I could talk for a long time about people-supportive and people-oppressive approaches to health care. But a graduation speech is appreciated mostly for its brevity. Therefore I would like to look at just one issue, which will perhaps make you reflect on the political implications even in areas that at first glance seem non-political.

The area I refer to is ORT, Oral Rehydration Therapy. (Personally, I prefer to call it RLL or *Return-of-Liquid-Lost*. This is because most of the world's people have limited schooling and may not understand words like *oral*, or *rehydration*, or *therapy*. I think the first step towards putting health into people's hands is to simplify our language. Besides, RLL - the *Return-of-Liquid-Lost* sounds friendlier and more poetic.)

I am sure that, in your public health program you have studied the various alternative approaches to oral rehydration in depth, weighing their comparative advantages and disadvantages. I wonder, however, how much you have looked at the political implications of the different alternatives: which are people-empowering, and which are dependency-creating. For surely the *empowerment factor* should always be a key consideration when evaluating the long-term implications of any health care alternative.

As we all know, when a child has diarrhea, the Return-of-Liquid-Lost can be lifesaving. Insofar as diarrhea is the number one cause of death in children in the world today, oral rehydration is one of the most important health measures that mothers, fathers, children, school teachers, and health professionals can learn. Its potential impact on people's health - and on people's confidence to cope for themselves with one of the world's biggest killers - is tremendous. It is safe to say that if school children could learn how to prepare and give the "special drink" to their younger brothers and sisters with diarrhea, then the world's children could have a bigger impact on lowering child mortality than do all the doctors and nurses on earth.

As you are well aware, there are two main approaches to oral rehydration therapy: "packets" and "home-mix".

Packets - or "sachets" as they were called by the experts until somebody discovered that not even College graduates understood that word - are prepackaged envelopes of sugar and salts for mixing with a liter of water. Packets are mostly produced in millions by transnational companies under contract to organizations like WHO, UNICEF, and USAID. They are usually distributed through regional office to health ministries, clinics, ORT centres, and, finally, to mothers when their children get diarrhea.

The home-mix, on the other hand, is prepared completely in the home, using local ingredients and traditional measuring methods in order to mix water with the indicated amounts of sugar and salt. Or it can also be made building on local customs, by using rice water, soups, or mild herbal teas.

The relative advantages and disadvantages of packets versus home-mix have been much debated. Studies show that their safety and effectiveness is roughly the same - provided that the packets are available when needed, which often they are not.

Politically, however, the two methods are diametrically opposite. The use of packets keeps the control of diarrhea medicalized, institutionalized, mystified, and dependency-creating. In order to rehydrate a baby with diarrhea, the family has to depend on a magical, often imported, 'medicine' that involves a whole chain of commercial, international, governmental, bureaucratic, professional, and distributional links. If any link of the chain fails, the supply of packets stops. Or if people in the countryside begin to stand up for their rights, the supply of packets stops. Thus, control of the most common, most fatal, most easily treated health problem is taken out of the people's hands. Poor families are made to look to government for help, and be grateful for small, lifesaving handouts.

The use of the home-mix has just the opposite effect of the packet. It is a de-mystified and de-mystifying approach that is independent of outside resources, except for an initial educational component. It helps people realize that with a little knowledge and no magic medicine whatever, they can save their children from a powerful enemy, without being beholden to anyone. Thus the home-mix helps to liberate people from unnecessary dependency and to build people's self-confidence in their own ability to solve the problems that limit their well-being.

It is no surprise, then, that around the world small community-directed programs committed to basic rights consistently choose the home-mix. Nor is it a surprise that WHO, most health ministries, and other large national and international agencies are "packeteers".

At this point I want to put in a good word for UNICEF, which in many ways seems to be more in touch with the real needs of the people and more aware of their potential than is, for example, the World Health Organization. Although UNICEF started with a strong promotion of the packets, over the last two or three years, it has moved progressively toward promotion of the home-mix approach to oral rehydration. In some countries, in fact, UNICEF is now promoting primarily the home-mix. I think that UNICEF is to be applauded for this, and that WHO needs to be taken to task for the wide gap between its people-empowering rhetoric and its people-belittling policies at the field level.

Health professionals are part of the problem

Oral rehydration is but one of many hotly debated health issues, which will concern you in the practice of public health. When you are faced with making decisions or giving advice as to alternative approaches, always remember to look at the political implications. Approaches which are people-empowering, even if they seem to take longer or to involve a greater element of risk or uncertainty, in the long run may do more towards bringing about a healthier, more equitable society, than other methods which appear to be safer, more predictable, more measurable, or more easily administered.

One thing I think is clear: health for all will only come about through a restructuring of our social order so that there is a fairer distribution of wealth, resources, and power - a society where people can learn to live together in peace, where professionals and labourers and farmworkers can embrace each other as equals, share the same standard of living, the same wages, and watch out that no one takes more than his share at someone else's expense.

But, as I have already mentioned, such a restructuring for a healtheir social order is not likely to come about from those at the top. It can only come through the organized, united action of those at the bottom.

As health professionals, *we* are among the fat and fortunate few, the elite of society, the one per cent of the world's population with university degrees. Whether we like it or not, we are in some ways part of the problem - part of the inner circle of a social order that perpetrates poor health. Our challenge, then, is not to try to change the people, or to try to make them more healthy according to our mandates. It is rather to allow the people to change us, to make us less greedy, more humble, more able to serve the people on their terms. Our challenge is to help those on the bottom create a new economic and social order in which everyone can afford to be healthy.

The choice is yours

I would like to close with a quote from Zafrullah Chowdhury, a doctor who was a freedom fighter in the liberation of Bangladesh, and who subsequently founded Gonoshasthaya Kendra, a community-based health program that has taken many courageous and innovative steps to help empower farmworkers, women, and others who have long been treated unjustly. Zafrullah, incidently, was offered the post of Minister of Health of Bangladesh, but turned it down, saying that working within the government, his hands would be tied. He felt he could do more to change policy from the outside working directly for and with the people. And in fact, the creation of the Gonoshasthaya People's Pharmaceutical Company to produce low-cost, essential drugs, was a key factor in influencing the Bangladeshi Government to establish a daring drug policy. The following, then, is a quote from Zafrullah Chowdhury:

> Primary health care is generally only lacking when other rights are also being denied. Usually it is only lacking where the greed of some goes unchecked and unrecognized (or unacknowledged) as being the cause. Once primary health is accepted as a human right, then the primary health worker [and, we might say, the *public* health worker] becomes, first and foremost, a political figure, involved in the life of the community and its integrity. With a sensitivity to the villagers and the community as a whole, he will be better able to diagnose and prescribe. Basically, though, he will bring about the health that is the birthright of the community by facing the more comprehensive political problems of oppression and injustice ... apathy, and misguided goodwill.

On the road that lies ahead, each of you graduating today will be involved in the struggle for a healthier society. Whether we like to admit it or not, conflicts or interest do exist between those on the top of the social pyramid and those on the bottom. I hope that each of you finids the courage and commitment to side with those on the bottom.

What I have tried to say to you this evening with too many words has been summed up far more eloquently by the school-boys of Barbiana, Italy, poor farmboys who were expelled from school and then helped by a priest to teach each other. This quote is from their book, *Letter to a Teacher*, which might as fittingly be entitled, *Letter To a Public Health Worker*. They say: 'Whoever is fond of the comfortable and fortunate stays out of politics, he does not want anything to change'. But these schoolboys add that: 'To get to know the children of the poor, and to love politics, are one and the same things. You cannot love human beings who are marked by unjust laws, and not work for other laws.'

The choice is yours. Good luck.

9

WOMEN AND THE PROMOTION OF TECHNOLOGICAL DEVELOPMENT IN SOCIETY

LATA CHATTERJEE

Introduction

"The work of a woman is never complete" is a common folk saying in various cultures. While most of the early research on women's work focused on their work for household sustenance and reproduction, there is currently an increasing interest on the income generation activities of women. In the last decade there has been an outpouring of literature on the labour of women–for the household and for the market. This paper is in this genre and focuses on the association between technological developments in production processes and the paid and unpaid work of women. It argues that women have facilitated innovations in technology and that this aspect has been largely ignored in the literature. Most attention has been paid to the impacts of technology on women rather than on women's fostering of technological developments in production and consumption processes.

The relationship between technological change–as represented by newer or improved products, processes, production structures and organizations of production and consumption–and gender remains complicated. There are contradictory relations between gender and technology in that technological developments have had both negative and positive impacts on the labouring characteristics of women. The history of women and technology is a story of occupational readjustments that have helped women's emancipation from unpaid production and dependent relations at home to paid employment for the market. Yet this transformation has been accompanied by great hardships and onerous costs that have involved exploitative wages, tedious repetitive work on machines designed for the greatest productive efficiency, occupational health hazards and constant ideological struggles to justify the right of women to work in technologically improved work environments.

A major strand of research that has looked at the interface of women and technology has documented the negative impact of technology on women's employment, particularly the displacements caused by the introduction of new technology (Dauber and Cain 1981, Whitehead 1985, Knight and Wilmott 1986, Maillier and Rosser 1987). Technology, particularly machine technology, commonly decreases the labour component in any production process and this is followed by a decline of employment opportunities in the technologically obsolete sectors. Labour historians and labour market analysts have shown that women are often concentrated in sectors that are technologically weak (Berg, Hudson and Sorenschur 1983, Hanawalt 1986). Consequently, the introduction of technology in these sectors has had more than a proportionate impact on women–leading to the lowering of their wages through labour market imbalances. An oversupply of workers relative to shrinking demand has led to the impoverization of women workers and their households. In such cases technological developments have marginalized women.

The introduction of technology, however, has also opened up avenues for women's employment. On the aggregate, technology increases the demand for labour since new products are developed and new needs are created. In the past, new products have often freed women from labour intensive, unremunerated labour in the home and increased the range of possible employment opportunities in the market. Also working conditions and wages have improved with the increase in the range of work opportunities, at least relative to that existing for women in earlier historical periods. However, men have improved their working conditions and increased their wages more than women through these technologically induced advancements in the manufacturing and service sectors. There has been an unequal gender appropriation of the benefits of technological advancement, even as women have fought for and achieved greater emancipation through technological developments.

There is considerable empirical evidence from developing and advanced economies about these dual impacts of technology, though the primary research emphasis has been on documenting the negative impacts of technology on women's labour. Relatively little attention has been paid to the subject of the impacts that women have had on the development of technology. This paper briefly reviews the literature on impacts of technology on women and argues that the empirically observable impacts can be more usefully interpreted in the context of their functional relationship with the promotion of technological developments in society. This paper focuses on how women, through their adjustments to the positive and negative impacts, have furthered the development and incorporation of new technologies in the production process. That is, women have not been the passive recipients of negative impacts of new developments of technology, rather, through their active adjustments to technologically induced displacements in their activities, they have aided the progression of technological developments in society. In this facilitative role they have borne more than their "fair share" of the costs of wastage and breakage associated with technological progress.

This paper adopts the increasingly dominant feminist perspective that there is a close interaction between the two domains of women's work–their unpaid work for the sustenance and reproduction of the household and their income earning activities. Both these domains are linked through the time budget. An analytical separation between women's work for the market and women's work for the household is theoretically unwarranted, particularly in the analysis of women's role in facilitating technical change. Many technological advancements have been stimulated in order to increase the allocation of women's work time in favour of work for the market. Household labour-saving products have stimulated inventions and technological developments in infrastructure and appliance industries. Since women have had to combine the time demands of two work domains–income-earning work and household maintenance work-there are important ramifications of these in women's role in facilitating technical change. In the contemporary period new adjustments in women's production of services can be explained through the concept of coproduction. Coproduction and its relation to service production in the two work domains will be explored later in the paper. However, all along women have had to divide their labour time between the two productive spheres. This division is intricately related to technological developments in production and consumption in society.

The paper is divided into four sections. There is a conceptual overview that discusses and very briefly summarizes the findings of the rich literature on women and their labouring characteristics. The predominant attributes of female employment are linked to the progression of technology in various sectors of the economy. In the two following sections, the paper discusses the role of women in promoting technical change in the manufacturing and service sectors. In the concluding section, a framework for analysing the role of women in technical change is provided.

Conceptual Overview

In this section a general statement is made about the relation between technology and women's employment. The relationship between technological change and employment has received and continues to receive considerable analytical attention. In this literature, however, the issue of gender has received less attention. Yet, technological developments have increased and continue to increase women's employment opportunities; in most countries of the world the percentage of employed women has increased in the post-war years (ILO 1981, OECD 1984). For example, in the USA, women accounted for 16 per cent of the labour force in 1870; by 1986 their share had increased to 44 per cent (Bergman 1986). Urquhart (1984) has shown that the primary source of new employment in most advanced economies has been the employment of women who did not previously hold jobs. Indeed female employment has been increasing at a faster rate than that of males in most high income countries

(Chatterjee and Lakshmanan 1987, Maillier and Rosser 1987). This also holds for less developed countries. In the majority of the Third World countries, in the last two decades, the number of women in formal wage employment has increased more rapidly than that of men (UNIDO 1980). The industrial sector has absorbed a major segment of this formal labour force, particularly in the manufacture of textiles, clothing and electronics. Nevertheless, the issue of what role the market participation of women plays in technological change remains inadequately explored in the contemporary vast literature on technical change.

It must be evident, even to the casual observer, that women in all stages in the life cycle are drawn into the labour market in great numbers when major technological changes occur in the marketplace. The expansion of women's employment during periods of technological change is not only a contemporary phenomenon. There is considerable evidence that, even in the proto-industrial phase, emerging types of manufacturing production made special use of a female labour force, adapting types of technical change specially suited to the work patterns of a gender specific labour force. For example, economic historians have drawn attention to the fact that technical change in the textile industries in the years between pre-industrial and industrial 18th century Britain--required and adapted to the large-scale use of female labour (Berg, Hudson and Sonenscher 1983, Berg 1985).

Technical change meant not only mechanization, but also the use of intermediate techniques, changes in work organization, wider use of inexpensive labour, increasing division of labour, and variable industrial structures. What are the characteristics of a gender bias in technological development? What role did women's household production play in determining the structure of work organization and the response of women to the new technologies? An understanding of this complex women-market-household production nexus is crucial in unravelling the role women play in promoting technological change.

Three existing strands of research are relevant to the understanding of this nexus. These three research themes are:

1. Sex segregation in the workplace;
2. Wage inequalities between male and female workers;
3. Ideology of the supplementality/ marginality of women's work and its relation to patriarchal elements of society.

The division of labour based on gender has been and is still common in both advanced and developing economies. Reskin (1984) notes there are three expressions of this sex segregation. First, women are relegated to different spheres of activity–women to the home activities and men to market activities. Second, paid employees work in predominantly one-sex settings. In the USA in 1980, over 32 million workers were employed in industries where the workforce was at least 80 per cent male or female. Industries such as metal, construction, railroads are more than 90 per cent male. Women constitute more than 75 per cent of the workers in direct sales, apparel and fabricated textile manufacturing. Third, there is a functional segregation even in the integrated industries, that is men and women do different jobs within the same industry. In hospitals, for example, nurses and clerical workers are predominantly female and doctors and administrators are predominantly male. In spite of remarkable changes in the composition of the workforce and occupational structure, sex segregation levels have remained stable throughout the 19th and 20th centuries. While some gains have been made in the sexual integration of jobs, most men and women work in sex typical jobs (Reskin and Hartmann 1985). Women are concentrated in a small range of feminized jobs, most often in less skilled, lower paying jobs relative to their male counterparts with equivalent education and age.

In the developing countries the manufacturing sector is also divided between feminized industries and others where women are not employed in significant numbers. Aggregate statistics on occupational sex segregation have been documented by the ILO (1981). In addition several case studies have traced this for specific industries in a variety of countries in Asia, Africa and Latin America. For example, in Morocco in the three main industries that account for 75 per cent of the manufactured exports–carpets, clothing and food processing–women account for 70-100 per cent of the workforce (Joekes 1985). That women have been incorporated into the industrial workforce on the basis of sex segregation has been documented for the offshore multinational electronics factories in Malaysia and Singapore (Lim 1981), for textiles and assembly plants in Mexico (Srinivasan 1981), manual workers in Brazil (Humphrey 1985), and urban manual and clerical workers in India (Joshi and Joshi 1976). The adoption of technological inventions in the production process has been made possible due to sex segregation. The association between sex segregation and technological developments will be illustrated for the manufacturing and service sectors later in this paper.

Two of the most consistent descriptors of female employment are the segregation of the sexes in the workplace and the gap between men's and women's earnings, and the two variables are correlated. Sex segregation has aided the practice of paying low wages to women workers in the various stages of the production of final goods and services. A wage gap has persisted from the early industrial revolution in the U.K., when women in increasing numbers began to work for wages outside of their households. The wage gap has remained despite the extensive labour force participation of women and efforts of the women's movement. The "average" pay of females, whether manual or non-manual, is always lower than that of males at each age level (Maillier and Rosser 1987). For example, in the USA more than 25 years after the women's movement made the wage gap an issue, women were earning, compared to what men earned, 70 cents to the dollar in 1987 (Mann and Hellwig 1988). This can be compared to 60 cents to the dollar in the early sixties and 63 cents to the dollar in the late seventies. While the gap is being reduced at a slow rate, it is not primarily due to comparable wages for comparable jobs. Rather this minor reduction reflects the loss of higher wage blue-collar jobs by men and the selective migration of women into male preserves such as law, medicine, business and engineering. Treiman and Hartmann (1981) provide a comprehensive analysis of the characteristics of unequal wages. Roos and Reskin (1984) have focused on the separate job ladders and exclusionary practices that restrict mobility between male and female positions.

The wage gap exists in the developing countries as well (Dauber and Cain 1981, Ahmed 1985, Afshar 1985). This is true not only in the low technology traditional sectors. For example, Joekes (1985) shows that in Moroccan clothing factories using modern technology, producing for the European clothing market, women machinists earned about 70 per cent of the pay of male machinists performing identical tasks on the assembly line with similar age, experience and hours of work. This wage gap facilitates the incorporation of technology into production processes since women provide a low wage reserve labour force that is important in periods of technological transformation. There are structural parallels between the increasing part-time work of women in the service sectors, in the contemporary period, with its low wage character and the low wage incorporation of women in the manufacturing sector. The connections between low wages, sex segregation and technology development will be illustrated later.

Sex segregation and low wages for women, both of which are important for technological development, have been justified on ideological grounds. Matthaei (1982) discusses the undervaluation of women's work, particularly the concept of the gender hierarchy of value that has been used to justify women's lower wages. According to patriarchal ideology, women were expected to be temporary workers, gainfully employed in predetermined periods of their life cycle–between maturity and matrimony. Though the reality of women's participation in the labour force was quite different, this argument justified the lack of investment in and commitment for the skill development in women. Women learnt their skills in an informal manner through practical experience and a trial and error method. The lack of skill was used to justify lower wages, through a circular reasoning. In a sex segregated labour situation lower skill, lower productivity, lower technology jobs were available to women and adaptability of women provided a major source of energy for the recomposition of economic activities during periods of technical change.

The ideology of supplementary wages still exists in the Third World where industrial wages can be extremely low and insufficient for the subsistence needs of women. For example, Mather (1985) discusses women's low wages in West Java. Even though female wages provided a major source of money for food, clothing and shelter in working class families, there was a tacit agreement between parents and factory managers about the supplementarity of female wages. This permitted employers to pay below subsistence wages and kept the women dependent.

During periods of technical change it is necessary to have a pliant and efficient labour force that is willing to accept new work situations. In the next two sections documentary evidence will be provided about women's adaptability and efficiency, both in the experimental new technology end and the residual, obsolescent end of the technology spectrum in the manufacturing and service industries. There is a need for low wage labour since in the former there is the risk minimization logic of the entrepreneur and the latter there are in reality lower productivities.

Women's lower wages have been an issue for feminists for more than 100 years. Yet there has been resistance form union organizers as well. Feldberg (1983) has discussed the influential role of the union organizers in fighting for higher wages for men relative to women. The ideology of skill and family wages were used in this fight. The family wage confirmed the expectations of women as supplementary wage earners and extended the sexual division of labour in the household to the market. Ideological arguments were also used to justify the part-time status of women workers.

These three variables that reflect the conjunction of ideology and practice with respect to women in a patriarchal society can be directly linked to the role women have played in the incorporation of technology as innovations in the production process and their access to technological improvements. The differential pace of technological development and its adoption in production processes has been made possible through gender biases in the development and differential allocation of technological improvements. Commonly, technological advances are made earlier in sectors of production dominated by male workers, since their wages are higher and there is a greater incentive for capital labour substitutions in those sectors. When technological advances are made in the female dominated sectors this is commonly followed by displacement of female workers in favour of male workers. Higher wages are possible since productivity increases due to improvements in technology and male workers appropriate the higher wage jobs. Such jobs are reclassified as "skilled" through this process of technological improvements. However, displacement of women workers does not eliminate the need for women's employment. They shift to other low technology, low productivity sectors which then become sex segregated and have low wages attached to them. In fact, it can be argued that low wages of women and their consistent emplacement in low productive sectors has permitted the development of different production structures that maximize profits and returns to capital.

This pattern of displacement and emplacement of female workers and their unequal access to technological improvements can be found in all periods of history and in a wide range of countries of the developed and developing worlds. What explains this consistency and why have men and women accepted this unjust practice. The ideology of women's primary work as pertaining to household maintenance and reproduction and their work for the market as being supplementary has provided the rationale for this.

We can see this ideological debate with respect to women's employment in each cycle of technological development whether it is in agriculture, manufacturing or services. It is ironic that the clerical sector is dominated by women, yet three arguments were used against the entry of women into the clerical professions. It was argued that clerical work was not suited to women's nature, they lacked the capacity for physical endurance and that their entry would displace men. All three arguments were derived from patriarchal values that define femininity in terms of women's domestic role and the supplementarity of their incomes.

In the next two sections these concepts are explored with respect to the manufacturing and service sectors.

The Role of Women in the Development of Industrial Technologies

Women's role in the development of industrial technology results from the conjunction of the three factors mentioned earlier and the profit-making needs of entrepreneurs. Historical evidence will be used in this section to demonstrate that functional segregation of the sexes, and the low wages of women, have been used for the advancement of technology in society. Functional segregation, as noted earlier, results from the classification of specific jobs as male and female within integrated industries. While it is possible to document the existence of functional sex segregation in job tasks at any point in time, over time there is continuous reallocation of tasks between men and women. Technological change in industrial sector has been associated with the twin processes of dynamic incorporation of women in production processes that were male dominated and incorporation of males in tasks that were female dominated. For example, in the USA women were actually the first industrial workers (Glazer 1980). They were displaced by males, primarily immigrants. Since union organizers viewed women workers as threats, the ideology of female attributes and of supplementary wages were used to deny women access to industrial work after their displacement. Until the first world war blue-collar work, except in a few feminized industries, was considered to be a male activity. The enhanced demand for workers and restricted labour supply created by war-time needs allowed women to demonstrate that they were competent to work in engineering and other "male" jobs. Continuous reallocation of tasks between men and women implies that no task is intrinsically male or female. It is societal needs that determine what at any particular phase will be considered as specifically "women's tasks" and on occasion through redefinition, as predominantly "male tasks". If this observation is accurate then we need to explore the association between the varying expressions of functional segregation and technological change.

While the actual tasks women performed and the machines they operated varied in time, their role in the development of technology in the production process has remained constant. Functional sex segregation permitted them to be employed in tasks with lower levels of technology embedded in them and low wages allowed profit extraction from their labours even though overall productivity could be low in activities using obsolescent technologies. During periods of technological change women were involved in both the high risk experimental phase of new technology and in the high risk, unstable, obsolescent phase of old technologies. During the stable phase of any industry women worked in subsidiary and auxiliary jobs. They aided male operators of machines and made their use of new technological advancements more efficient–hence more productive. That is, through their performance of auxiliary tasks they not only facilitated the control of more productive technology by male workers, they allowed capital formation to proceed more efficiently–capital that could be reinvested as new technology. However when new technology was introduced into female dominated sectors and productivity increased, the benefits of higher productivity were appropriated by male workers. These tasks became reclassified as male preserves.

However, two aspects remained constant. First, women were paid lower wages than men, irrespective of whether they were in the experimental phase of new technology, stable phase of mature technology or declining phase of obsolescent technology. That is, women's wages were not commensurate with those of men in the different phases of technological development in a particular production process. Second, sex segregation remained as a characteristic of the male-female division of work. Through continuously readjusting in their work spheres, women facilitated the process of technological advancement. What guided this reallocation of tasks? Why was this reallocation necessary? How was this process of changing sexual division of labour related to the development of technology? In summary, maximum returns to capital from the existing technologies and investments of capital for new technology were facilitated through these apparently changing manifestations of functional sex segregation.

One consistent thread that ties together this shifting task responsibilities is the definition of what constitutes "skill". Skill, in the labour process, is not defined in terms of human attributes. The definition of skilled and unskilled has been based on productivity rather than on the true skills required for production. Since women have been primarily incorporated into sectors and tasks that had lower levels of technology embedded in them, or were technologically obsolete, they have had lower productivities. The use of lower technologies that caused "lower productivities" permitted women to be classified as unskilled and to receive lower wages. In many instances lower technologies required higher levels of skills. On the other hand, when male workers were reallocated to female tasks with new production processes and higher levels of technology, these tasks were reclassified as "skilled" since productivity was increased through the incorporation of new technology. Higher productivity permitted higher wages of which the men were beneficiaries.

It is short-sighted to concentrate on one phase of the cycle–the displacement of women by technology and/or male workers, without paying attention to the whole cycle and the role of technology in this. While such practices are clear examples of sexual discrimination and exploitation that can be traced to patriarchal relations in society, there has been a functional reason for this that is related to the way in which technology is developed and incorporated into production processes. Though this redefinition of tasks as male and female, society permitted the gradual development and incorporation of technology. Gradual incorporation of technology is necessary for two purposes. First, technological advancements are made in a piecemeal way due to the idiosyncratic nature of the development of inventions. Second, there are economic risks attached to the transition from inventions to innovations. Industrialists seek to minimize their risks by accepting innovations that have been tried and proven successful by a few entrepreneurs. The piecemeal introduction of technology into production processes has been possibly due to the adaptive role that women have played in accepting jobs and the lower wages provided to them in a society dominated by patriarchal values. Since the process of the invention of technology and the adoption of inventions into the production process as innovations is uneven, women through their acceptance of lower wages, residual employment and absorption of the negative impacts of technological development have permitted entrepreneurs to selectively adopt technological innovations into their production processes. Their lower wages have allowed entrepreneurs to experiment with technological developments and to continue with the replacement of obsolete technology at a pace suited to their profit making needs. The ideology of supplemental earnings, weaker physical stamina and like values that were used to justify the lower wages and sex segregations were external manifestations of deeper structural forces that relate to the relation between labour and capital defined in a patriarchal context.

These patriarchal ideologies facilitated the adoption of technological development even though male workers need not necessarily have been conscious of the expendable roles that fragmented social divisions of labour create. (Parallels can be drawn for other forms of division-race, ethnicity and the like.) What are the various mechanisms that have been used to exclude women from the technologically more productive and financially more lucrative occupations and job tasks within occupations? Since women have demonstrated time and again the capability to perform a wide range of tasks and to use complex machines, it will be interesting to analyse the various institutional and ideological mechanisms that have permitted the transformation of female into male and male into female specific tasks. The three most important mechanisms were and still are: the level of capitalization, access to training and continuity/periodicity of work.

While technology increases productivity it requires capital for its adoption. Capital has been used as a mechanism to transfer women from higher productivity and hence from higher wage to lower wage jobs. A few illustrations from the work of labour historians are provided. Bennett (1986) notes that women produced commercial ale, one of the two basic food items in medieval England, after the manufacture of bread, the other basic food item, became professionalized. baking required ovens and equipment that was relatively expensive and professional bakers were male. It is ironic, however, that females continued to be the bakers in the household economy where it remained a labour-intensive activity. Ale-making remained a lucrative household industry. The equipment required for making ale in the cottage industry phase–large pots, vats and ladle–were available in most households. Moreover, it was a labour-intensive activity. The final product spoiled rapidly and transported poorly. It required highly skilled people able to deal with these uncertainties–hence the preponderance of ale-wives. However, when hops were introduced from Europe and beer-making became a commercial activity, brewing became men's work and the ideology of woman's nature was used to exclude them. However, women continued to work in the liquor sector as bar maids, i.e. in the service sector rather than in the profitable production sector. This is but one example of such practices that occurred in the textile industry, lace making, garment manufacturing–a whole range of activities that had been considered as commensurate with women's nature and which continued to remain as women's work in the household sphere.

The relegation of women to low technologies was perpetuated through the denial of training to them. Young males were apprenticed and received formal training. Females learned their skills informally from their parents or through domestic service in artisan households. Orphaned children who received formal training in charity institutions learnt crafts that were labour-intensive such as spinning or sewing. Boys were taught to read and write–knowledge that was denied to girls–hence the large preponderance of illiterate working women in printing shops. Typesetting and pulling the press were male activities since women could not read enough to typeset (Davis 1986). In the textile factories women were not taught to repair the machines they worked on and their consequent dependence on men was used to justify their lower wages (Bradley 1986).

How was the relegation to lower skilled jobs institutionalized in society? Ideology was used to justify the exclusion of women from formal training. This related to the definition of femininity and prioritization of women's work in favour of household maintenance. A woman's participation in household production of crafts was periodic since her activity was determined by free time left after fulfilling the household tasks that included food preparation, child care and the like. Thus unwinding the cocoons and preparing the thread for bobbins was a female task since this could be accommodated with the many household tasks that women had to perform as mistresses, wives and mothers.

Are there any deviations from this? Is there any evidence in labour history of women's competence in male dominated sectors, i.e. in cases where women had penetrated into male preserves? Women's production during the craft industrial stage could be of three kinds: they worked as independent artisans and entrepreneurs; as unpaid helpers of male members of the household; and as wage-earning artisans. Only in the first case do we find that women had access to capital and technology. In the latter two cases–as household workers and wage labour-they worked at the low technology end of the industry. A brief discussion of women in male preserves can be very illuminating. In Lyon in the 16th century, for example, there were high-level female entrepreneurs such as printers, publishers, silk manufacturers and barber surgeons and cabinet makers (Davis 1986). Such independent entrepreneurs were either the daughters or widows of influential and respected crafts families and as such inherited the capital and technology. They were not perceived as threats since there were too few of them and they were maintaining family enterprises for their sons or sons-in-law. Even so, restrictive actions were taken so as to limit their capacity for growth and development during downturns in their industry. Davis mentions the limitations imposed on female barber surgeons and their journeyman helpers in Lyon during 1540, journeywomen in 1554, and the 1561 and 1583 rulings against female master silk makers.

The textile industry is used to illustrate these concepts in greater detail since textiles and kindred products are industries which have been overrepresented by women. The textile industry absorbed a large percentage of the female labour force in the U.K. when textiles were an important industry in that country. In developing countries today, where much of the textile and apparel industry has migrated, it continues to absorb the majority of women who are employed in the manufacturing. Moreover, the textile industry was one of the earliest industries to be affected by technological developments associated with the capitalist production systems.

The textile industry provides a clear example of the shifting sex composition of jobs in both weaving and spinning. Handloom weavers were men when textile production was a cottage industry. Weaving shifted to women during the putting out system associated with proto-industrialization. Handloom weaving once again became a male activity when weaving shifted to factory production. When factories became fully equipped with powerlooms women, once again, became weavers. Women were spinners in the spinning jenny and water frame stage and men became spinners when the more productive mule spinning was introduced (Hartmann 1979). The tasks of weaving and spinning moved in and out of female employment during different historical periods. This was primarily due to changes in technology.

The specific example of the hosiery industry in Leicester is used to illustrate, in further detail, the switching of tasks between men and women, with the progression of technology and the need to maximize returns to capital. Bradley (1986) and Osterud (1987) provide good documentation of the dynamics of job transformation between female and male workers and the association between feminization of specific tasks with technological development. The operation of knitting frames was considered to be a male task in the 18th century. However, from the beginning of the 19th century there are accounts of women being engaged in operating frames. This was in spite of the fact that the Charter of 1745 forbade women (except widows) to work frames. For example, the Royal Commission in 1845 found that 25 per cent of the frames in the town of Leicester, and as much as 50 per cent in the surrounding villages, were worked by women. Some individual employers had 66 per cent of their frames operated by women. What underlay the encroachment of women into a male preserve? The total profits that entrepreneurs could make depended partly on the rents they collected on machinery, such as frames. It was profitable for them to distribute their work over a large number of workers. The total work was divided in a way to maximize rental incomes from the frames–hence the importance of female labour. However, in operating these frames women were to be found in the economically unstable and less expensive wrought hose branch while men had begun to shift to knitting in the higher paid glove production.

There was increased feminization when hosiery production moved to the factory. Women in the early days of factory production worked on machines in the new factories. Bradley (1986) notes that by 1845, women were working in large numbers in the factories operating machines since men were not willing to accept the regular hours and discipline of the factory. For example, Thomas Collins in 1845 had installed 55 rotary machines and employed a predominant female workforce to operate these machines. However, the decline of cottage industry due to factory competition brought more males into factory production who became the rotary machine operators by displacing women. Women became relegated to subsidiary and supportive tasks while men became the weavers. By early 1890's the rotary machines, especially the Cotton's Patents, were almost all worked by men. While 31 per cent of hosiery workers in 1861 and 73.5 per cent by 1901 were females, the majority were now employed in specific female jobs such as seaming, folding and pressing. However the practices of a few firms such as Stretton's, that continued to use women on the Cotton's Patents in spite of union protests, proved that women were competent to use complex machines.

There was, once again, a redefinition of female tasks as labour shortages during the 1914-18 war allowed women to work on all types of knitting machines and enter into other higher paid male preserves such as countering and trimming. Women were the major workforce in the hosiery industry until the mid 20th century. However, men once again became the knitters as improvements in the knitting technology increased productivity and wages. In 1983, when one person was able to tend 18 machines instead of one, and wages increased in that sector, men again became the knitters in the sock industry in Leicester. In summary, knitting was a woman's task during the cottage industry phase when frames were rented by the household; in factories when the narrow frame had become obsolescent with the development of the more efficient wide frame which men began to operate; on wide frames during the world wars when there was a shortage of male labour. Women were used on new technology when men refused and were supplanted when its inevitability was demonstrated. They were displaced to old technology so that obsolescent technology could be retired at a rate which could still provide profits to entrepreneurs.

What is true of textiles is true of other industries as well. Abbott (1969) mentions that when cigar-making was a home industry in the USA before 1800, it was a woman's activity in the agricultural household. Early factories employed women who were displaced by male immigrants willing to work for similar low wages. By 1860 only 9 per cent of the workers were women in an industry that had been dominated by women. In 1869, when the wooden mould was introduced from Europe, women became the primary workers. Similar gender switchings, related to technology, have been documented for the printing industry (Baker 1964, Hartmann 1979). This theme of the association between technology, job switching and women's employment will be continued in the next section and documented for the service sector.

The well specified female and male areas of activity that characterize gender concentrations in occupations at any point in time are primarily related to the needs of capital. Technological development is a manifestation of this need. Sexual stereotyping and sex segregation in occupations are institutionally created and ideologically supported. Occupational sex segregation and ideology of the nature of women have been used to exclude women from new and productive technologies. Patriarchal values have been instrumental variables.

Role of Women in the Development of Technology in the Service Sectors

The steady growth in women's labour force participation in the contemporary period is related to sectoral shifts and the increasing importance of the service sector in the economy. Women moved into the service sector with the progressive mechanization of the female dominated goods producing sectors such as textiles and the decline of the family farm. For example, in the USA female non-agricultural employment in domestic and personal services declined from 67 per cent in 1870 to 32 per cent in 1930.

Employment in the service sector is also characterized by sex segregation and low wages. Feminization of a particular service is also directly related to technological developments in that particular service. The introduction of improved processes and related employment displacements are also associated with the progressive development of technology in the service sector. The clerical sector is used to illustrate the relationship between technology and women's employment in the service sector and the arguments made in the paper thus far are continued.

The 1910-20 decade was characterized by a significant occupational redistribution with massive incorporation of women into service occupations. In 1870 women accounted for .2 per cent of the labour force in the clerical occupations. By 1980, four out of five clerical workers were women (Maillier and Rosser 1987). In 1911 clerical work provided jobs to 3 per cent of the total female labour force; by 1981 more than 33 per cent of a much larger labour force were employed in that sector. As in manufacturing technology, the form of new machines went hand in hand with new ways of work organization. Feminization of the clerical sector was as intrinsically related to machines as it was to new patterns in the organization of work.

What is the relation between technical advances and the increased participation of women in clerical occupations? The feminization of clerical work force occurred in the late 19th and early 20th century when the character of clerical work and its organizational structure changed radically (Davies 1982). The premodern office was small with a low level of technology, characterized by close working relations between clerks and employers. In the USA in the pre-Civil War period the office was a male preserve and there were no women workers (Davies). The typical clerk, prior to this transformation, was an apprentice manager or businessman. He performed a wide variety of tasks in order to learn different facets of the business. Clerical work was viewed as temporary and a period of preparation for higher and more rewarding tasks. In the late 19th and early 20th centuries clerical work underwent dramatic changes in the type of technology used by workers and the organization of the workplace. Technologies such as the typewriter, telegraph, telephone, calculating and duplicating machines revolutionized the office. This resulted in the need for a larger workforce, standardization of tasks and greater specialization among workers. By the end of the transformation clerical work was primarily a dead end occupation; most clerical workers could hope to remain in their positions during their working lives. This transformation was accompanied by an enormous expansion of clerical work, changing sexual composition of the workforce and introduction of new technology that made clerical work into a series of routine, repetitive tasks and female clerical workers into office operatives. In the clerical sector the development of typewriters and telephones had much to do with the feminization of the workforce since the typewriter vastly increased the demand for correspondence and the keeping of records, i.e. filing. Feminization proceeded at different rates within the clerical field. It proceeded most rapidly amongst typists and stenographers–both of which were marked by new technological developments. In 1880 women constituted 40 per cent of all stenographers and typists. In 1900 and 1930 the proportion had increased to 75 per cent and 95 per cent respectively. Bookkeepers and accountants continued to be male and it is only in the last two decades that there has been a significant change in these clerical tasks.

Machines did not cause the routinization of work, though they certainly facilitated it. The successful invention and manufacture of the typewriter resulted from developments in the organization of work that made these machines necessary. Women facilitated their rapid diffusion because they adapted to the conditions of work and accepted the rigid hierarchal structure of authority. The rigid hierarchal structures within an office diminished opportunities for upward mobility. A typist who was involved in a restricted and highly specialized task lost the opportunity to gain knowledge that would allow him to take decisions over a range of tasks that management role implied. Feminization of the clerical work facilitated technological change.

Female employment is likely to be significantly influenced by new technological developments such as micro-electronics. New developments in information processing will cause the elimination of much of the clerical staff, particularly those involved in recording, storing, retrieval of information (Maillier and Rosser 1987).

The earlier round of technology increased job opportunities in a variety of new sectors, either through the replacement of males or in new tasks which technology opened up, i.e. typing, telephone switchboard operating. With the elimination of paper as a medium of information storage and storage of information on discs will cause a basic restructuring of the workforce and a severe cutback in typists and file clerks. Higher level of training in computers and word processors is likely to lead to a demand for a higher paid and more male workforce. While this is not a negative trend and a better sexual balance in all jobs is desirable, nevertheless most jobs that will be eliminated will belong to women typists and clerks.

Conclusion

Society has witnessed a deluge of technological developments since the dawn of the Industrial Revolution. On the aggregate these developments, relative to earlier societies, resulted in increased employment opportunities, increased productivity, increased prosperity and higher levels of material and non-material consumption for both men and women. The increasing paid labour force participation of women is a direct consequence of the increasing incorporation of improved technologies in production processes and the improved organization of work that this often entailed. However, two factors have been constant in this incorporation. First, due to the patriarchal form of societal structure, women have been assigned to the lower technology end of production processes. As new innovations were adopted women were reassigned to tasks which had relatively more obsolete technologies. Second, they have been paid lower wages than men for their effort. As aggregate increase in employment has been accompanied by sectoral declines, women have been concentrated in the declining sectors due to their assignment to the low technology end of production. This paper argues that women have facilitated the adoption of new technology through their positive adjustments to displacements and "acceptance" of lower levels of technology and lower wages.

There is nothing that is deterministic about the relation between women and technology. The various arguments that have been put forward in favour of women's assignment to low technology jobs, such as their weaker physical constitution, poorer mechanical skills, inability to handle complex tasks, loss of femininity and like sexist justifications do not stand the test of historical analysis. Even a cursory glance at the relation between women and technology from a historical perspective provides evidence that there has been no task that has been too complex for women or technology too onerous for them to use when appropriate training has been provided. Occupational segregation with its attendant discrimination in training opportunities, access to improved technologies, and lack of comparable wages has perpetuated itself through dominance and subdominance relations based on gender, race, region of origin and like variables. The key question is whether greater awareness of women's issues will make this period of rapid technological change significantly different from earlier periods of technological revolutions.

Past advances in technology have decreased labour demand in some areas and increased it in others. We can expect the similar dislocations in the new round of technological developments that are currently underway. For example, in the manufacturing sector computer-controlled technology will tend to eliminate repetitive jobs. The effect of this will be felt disproportionately by women since they tend to be concentrated in jobs that involve repetitive tasks and that have a high potential for automation. Maillier and Rosser note that the repetitive assembly of electronic goods is a female dominated industry that is likely to be affected by new technology. In the dawn of the new information age and the related microtechnologies there is an opportunity to change from this unequal and socially unjust use of women's labour discussed in this paper. The advent of these new technologies has the potential for raising the quality of life in the manufacturing and service sectors. However, there is also a great potential for increasing social inequalities both gender and class. It will depend on who will have access to the opportunities that will be opened up as a result of the new technological developments.

REFERENCES

1. Abbott, Edith, *Women in Industry*, Arno Press, New York, 1969.
2. Baker, Elizabeth, *Technology and Woman's Work*, Columbia University Press, New York, 1964.
3. Bennett, Judith M., "The Village Ale-Wife: Women and Brewing in Fourteenth-Century England" in B. Hanawalt (ed.), *Women and Work in Preindustrial Europe*, Indiana University Press, Bloomington, U.S.A.
4. Berg, Maxine, P. Hudson and M. Sorenschor, *Manufacture in Town and Country Before the Factory*, Chapter 1, New York, Cambridge University Press, 1983.
5. Berg, Maxine, *The Age of Manufactures 1700-1820*, Chapters 3, 6, and 8, Fontana Press, London, 1985.
6. Bergman, Barbara, *The Economic Emergence of Women*, Basic Books, New York, 1986.
7. Berk, Sarah, *Women and Household Labor*, Sage Pub., California, 1980.
8. Bradley, Harriet, "Technological Change, Management Strategies, and the Development of Gender-based Job Segregation in the Labor Process" in David Knights and Hugh Willmott Ced.), *Gender and the Labour Process*, Gower, UK, 1986.
9. Brown, Claire, "Home Production for Use in a Market Economy" in R. Thorne and M. Yalom (ed.), *Rethinking the Family: Some Feminist Questions*, Longmans, New York, 1982.
10. Chatterjee, Lata and T.R. Lakshmanan, *Facilitating Technical Change : The Role of Women*, 1987.
11. Davidoff, Leonore and Belinda Westover (ed.), *Our Work, Our Lives, Our Words*, Barnes and Noble, Totowa, New Jersey, 1986.
12. Davies, Margery, *Woman's Place is at the Typewriter: Office Work and Office Workers 1870 - 1930*, Temple University Press, Philadelphia, 1982.
13. Davis, Natalie Z. "Women in the Crafts in Sixteenth-Century Lyon" in B. Hanawalt (ed.), *Women and Work in Preindustrial Europe*, Indiana University Press, Bloomington, U.S.A.
14. Feldberg, Rosalyn, "Comparable Worth : Toward Theory and Practice in the U.S." in B. Gelpi, N. Hartsock, C. Novak and M. Strober (ed.), *Woman and Poverty*, University of Chicago Press, Michigan, 1983.
15. Gill, Colin, *Work, Unemployment and New Technology*, Basil Blackwell, 1981.
16. Glazer, Nona, "Everyone Needs Three Hands : Doing Unpaid and Paid Work" in Berk, S. (ed.), *Women and Household Labor*, Sage Pub., Califor-

17. Hartmann, Heidi, "Capitalism, Patriarchy and Job Segregation" in Z. Eisenstein (ed.), *Capitalist Patriarchy and the Case for Socialist Feminism*, Monthly Review Press, New York, 1979.
18. Humphrey, John, "Gender, Pay and Skill : Manual Workers in Brazilian Industry" in H. Afshar (ed.), *Women, Work and Ideology in the Third World*, Chapter 9, Tavistock, New York.
19. I.L.O. Office of Women, "Women, Technology and the Development Process" in R. Dauber and M. Cain (eds.), *Women and Technological Change in Developing Countries*, Westview Press Boulder, Colorado, 1981, pp. 33-47.
20. Joekes, Susan, "Working for Lipstick? Male and Female Labor in the Clothing Industry in
21. Morocco" in H. Afshar (ed.), *Women, Work and Ideology in the Third World*, Chapter 8, Tavistock, New York, 1985.
22. Joshi, H. and Joshi, V. *Surplus Labour and The City: A Study of Bombay*, Oxford University Press, Delhi, 1976.
23. Maillier, A.T. and M.J. Rosser, *Women and the Economy*, St. Martin's Press, New York, 1987.
24. Mann, Judy and Basia Hellwig, "The Truth About Salary Gap(s)" in *Working Women*, January, 1988, pp. 61-62.
25. Mather, Celia, "Rather Than Make Trouble, It's Better Just To Leave: The Lack of Industrial Strife in West Java" in Afshar (ed.), *Women, Work and Ideology in the Third World*, Chapter 7, Tavistock Publications, New York, 1985.
26. Matthaei, Julie, *An Economic History of Women in America: Women's Work, the Sexual Division of Labor and the Development of Capitalism*, Schocken Books, New York, 1982.
27. OECD, 1984 Employment Outlook.
28. Osterud, Nancy, "Gender Divisions and the Organization of Work in the Leicester Hosiery Industry" in Angela V. John (ed.), *Unequal Opportunities : Women's Employment in England 1800-1918*, Basil Blackwell, 1986.
29. Reskin, Barbara (ed.), *Sex Segregation in the Workplace*, National Academy Press, Washington D.C., 1986.
30. Reskin, Barbara and Heidi Hartmann (eds.), *Women's Work, Men's Work : Sex Segregation on the Job*, National Academy Press, Washington D.C., 1985.
31. Robinson, John. P., "Housework Technology and Household Work" in Berk, S. (ed.), *Women and Household Labor*, Sage Pub., California, 1980.
32. Roos, Patricia A., *Gender and Work : A Comparative Analysis of Industrial Societies*, State University of New York Press, Albany, 1985.
33. Roos, Patricia and Barbara Reskin, "Institutional Factors Contributing to Sex Segregation in the Workplace" in B. Reskin (ed.), *Sex Segregation in the Workplace*, Ch. 13, National Academy Press, Washington D.C., 1984.
34. Tilly, Louise A. and Joan Scott, *Women, Work and Family*, Holt, Reinhart and Winston, New York, 1978.
35. Treiman, Donald and Heidi Hartmann (eds.), *Women, Work and Wages : Equal Pay for Jobs of Equal Value*, National Academy Press, Washington D.C., 1981.
36. UNIDO, *Women in the Redeployment of Manufacturing Industry to Developing Countries*, Papers on Structural Change 18, 1980.
37. Urquhart, Michael, "The Employment Shift of Services: Where did it Come From?" *Monthly Labor Review*, April Vol., 1984, pp. 15-22.

10

LEGAL ETHICS IN A GANDHIAN PERSPECTIVE[1]

CLARK D. CUNNINGHAM

When my wifc and I came to India for the first time two years ago, our first stop after we left Bombay was at the Gandhi Vidyapeeth in Vedchhi, Gujarat. It is an educational institution on Gandhian lines. We spent four very meaningful days there. The second day we were there the Dean of the College of Education, Jyotibhai Desai (who has become a very food friend) gave us a copy of *Hind Swaraj* and told us that if we are going to read anything about Gandhi, we should start with *Hind Swaraj*, which is a very slender book. I read it while we were there. About half way through, I came across a very short chapter called, "The Condition of India, Lawyers". The chapter shocked me because Gandhi talked about having abhorrence for the legal profession, and towards the conclusion of the chapter he said, lawyers should "abandon their profession and consider it just as degrading as prostitution."[1] I found these statements distressing and also surprising because I knew Gandhi had more than 20 years of a successful and honourable practice as a

---

1. Gandhi Memorial Lecture delivered on 30th January, 1986, at Gandhi - in Action, 1, Arvind Nagar, Ghonda, New Delhi.

lawyer, primarily in South Africa. It was hard to believe that someone who had practised law for 20 years had come to this conclusion about his profession. (Though perhaps the same chapter has a sentence which should apply to Gandhi himself: "Whenever instances of lawyers having done good can be brought forward, it will be found that the good is due to them as men rather than as lawyers.")[2]

I was certainly interested in this issue. I read more of Gandhi while we were in India and when I returned to the United States I attempted to put some of the thoughts of Gandhi into practice in my own work as a legal aid lawyer. Later when I began teaching legal ethics, to challenge my students I included in the assigned readings that passage from *Hind Swaraj,* as well as other writings of Gandhi. The students appreciated this assignment, it sparked discussions, and I continued to wrestle with and think about that passage. So I welcomed (though it was a bit of work) the suggestion to give this talk. I spent several days still wrestling with and thinking through the issue. I am just going to share with you my continuing thoughts on the subject and look forward to your response.

I will begin by discussing the traditional view of the role of law and lawyers, both in the United States and India, a common heritage we have, going back to Great Britain. I will then briefly talk about some classic legal ethics issues and use them to illustrate the difference between the traditional view of the lawyer's role and Gandhi's view. Next I will try to look a little deeper into why Gandhi had given such an extraordinary rejection of law. Finally, I shall conclude with some thoughts as to what kind of new roles lawyers might have in a non-violent society such as Gandhi advocated.

II

The traditional justification for a lawyer's role starts with the whole concept of the rule of law, which is almost a sacred notion in British political and social thought. The rule of law is conceived as a civilizing force which replaces violence as a means of resolving conflicts. Not only is law non-violent, that is not forceful, but theoretically the rule of law is an equalizing power. All men and women are supposed to be equal before law and, therefore, the conflict is resolved without regard to the physical, economic and political power of one or the other. Many of us know that this ideal is not always realized, but theoretically that is the ideal of the rule of law.

Unfortunately, as law developed in the last 900 years in the British tradition, it has become ever and ever more complex, both in terms of substance and procedure. Thus for the last several hundred years, there has been an increasing role in society of a person who becomes specialized in knowing about the law to aid the average person in taking advantage of the rule of law. The traditional notion of a lawyer is that in a sense he *becomes* his or her client for the purpose of that representation. In fact, it is not too uncommon to hear law-yers in the courts speak in the first person when they are talking about their client. They say, "But your Honour, we cannot possibly do that," or "Your Honour, you have to understand our position." as if the lawyer is, in fact, the client. The way this role works out–where the lawyer in fact becomes the client within the rule of law – is that the client is expected to give the lawyer his utter trust. The client tells the lawyer his darkest secrets that are relevant to the case, things he would not tell anyone. In return for that extraordinary trust, the lawyer is supposed to return utter loyalty, zeal and confidence.

Now one of the major dilemmas of legal ethics is reconciling this special duty to the client with the duty to your own conscience as a lawyer or your duty to the court. It is generally accepted that the lawyer's duty to the client does not require the lawyer to do anything dishonest or deceptive or illegal. But there is a line drawn between those actions for which the lawyer is responsible versus the actions of the client. Balanced against the lawyer's conscience and public duty are the client's right to make his or her own decisions and the obligation to protect the confidences the client has reposed in the lawyer. I will illustrate from my own practice.

As a legal aid attorney, my speciality was welfare law, that is, the right under the American legal system for low-income people to receive certain benefits from the Government: free health care, free food, and a minimum cash payment. The welfare system in the United States is very complicated. I think anyone who studies it realizes that in many ways it is extremely unfair and does not work very well. One of my clients deliberately committed welfare fraud, which is a crime in the United States, because she was living with her daughter and son-in-law. The daughter was illegitimate, a fact, of course, my client did not want other people to know. However, under the law if you are living with someone who is a member of your family, whether or not illegitimate, you have to report that fact to the government when you apply for benefits, because the government will assume that if you are living with your daughter, the daughter should support you and that you are not entitled to benefits.[3] But my client could not dare to disclose that fact to the government, and yet she had no other way of living. So she simply did not tell the welfare officials that the family she was living with was related to her. She disclosed this to me. As is typical, I had told her, "Tell me everything. I will not tell it to anyone else."

We discussed the fact that her benefits had been cut off for reasons that had nothing to do with this welfare fraud–but, in fact, for reasons that were unjust. Initially I was going to represent her in talking to the welfare agency about giving her benefits back because the reason they denied her the benefits was wrong. But I then stopped and said, "I cannot do that because as soon as I begin talking to the welfare office about your case, I am going to be forced to lie to them because I am going to assert that you are legally entitled to these benefits. I may in fact even have to talk about why they should not look into the income of the people you are living with. I simply cannot lie to the welfare agency. But, of course, I cannot tell them what you have told me. Therefore, I simply cannot help you at all on this particular problem." I continued to help her on other issues. But I did not call up the welfare agency or the police and say, "This person is defrauding the government," because that would have been a violation of the client's confidence, that she had given me the secret with the assumption I would tell no one.

My behaviour would have been considered acceptable, at least under American legal ethics because the client's wrongful act was not my act; I had not assisted her in committing that wrongful act. I confronted this problem in another welfare case. I had a client who had had a part-time job and not told the welfare department about it. Now the case for which I was representing her did not involve the part-time job, it involved some other issue where she was legally in the right. The reason she did not report the part-time job was that every dollar earned by a person receiving welfare is subtracted from what she receives from the government.[4] It is, in fact, a 100% tax. For example, if my client was receiving $ 200 a month from the government and she went out and earned $180 a month, she would then receive only $20 a month instead of $200. So, she has actually worked for nothing. My client told me, "I cannot live and support my children on what I receive from the government. I am doing it for my family. I will take the risk of breaking the law; they have to eat, they have to be housed." I said, "There may come the time during the hearing when the judge will ask you, 'Do you have any other income?" What are you going to say to him?' She replied, "I am going to say that I do not have any other income." I said, "You know that is perjury." She said, "I know, but in fact I am going to do it." I told her that, while I cannot ask her that question because I would be, in fact, helping her to lie on the stand, the judge may ask her. And, in fact, that happened during the hearing. The judge asked her and she lied. I knew that she had committed a crime, but did not do anything about it. We went forward through the hearing, I did not tell the judge and we won the hearing.

Whether a lawyer's obligation not to allow perjury to occur outweighs the duty to protect confidential information of the client is a very controversial topic. A case is now pending in the United States Supreme Court involving this issue. On the eve of trial a criminal defendant told his lawyer he was going to testify to a different version of the facts than he had earlier told the lawyer. Convinced that his client was going to commit perjury, the lawyer told the client that if he told the new version on the stand, the lawyer would tell the judge that his client had perjured himself. As a result of this threat, the client did not tell the new version to the jury and was convicted. A federal court of appeals struck down the conviction on the grounds that the lawyer's conduct denied the defendant effective legal representation, thus holding that the lawyer's duty to honour the client's confidences outweighed his obligation to the court to prevent perjury.[5]

It is clear that Gandhi would not have acted as I acted in the second case. In his autobiography Gandhi said, "I built up such a reputation that no false case used to come to me. Indeed some of my clients would keep their clean cases for me and take the doubtful ones elsewhere."[6] "On one occasion, whilst I was conducting a case before a magistrate in Johannesburg, I discovered that my client had deceived me, I saw him completely break down in the witness box. So without any argument I asked the magistrate to dismiss the case. The opposing counsel was astonished and the magistrate was pleased. I rebuked my client for bringing a false case to me. He knew that I never accepted false cases and when I brought the thing home to him, he admitted his mistake and I have an impression that he was not angry with me for having asked the magistrate to decide against him."[7] Gandhi felt clearly his obligation to the truth, as he saw it, was supreme and could not in any way be outweighed by whatever duty he might have to the client.

Now this story by Gandhi raises two questions in my mind? What if Gandhi had been wrong when he decided in the middle of the trial that his client had deceived him? V.S. Hegde has hypothesized that Gandhi's answer to this dilemma would be that the miscarriage of justice arising out of the lawyers' wrongly distrusting his client is less likely to happen than the miscarriage that would arise when lawyers allow their clients to give false testimony.[8] I am not sure that would have been Gandhi's answer. I think his answer would relate much more deeply to his own personal commitment to the truth. Yet what Gandhi did in that case seems inconsistent with his own principles. My limited understanding of Gandhi is that he always acted according to what he believed was true; such action he called "soul force".

But as Gandhi pointed out, if soul force "is used in a cause that is unjust, only the person using it suffers. He does not make others suffer for his mistakes. Men have before now done many things which were subsequently found to have been wrong. No man can claim that he is absolutely in the right or that a particular thing is wrong because he thinks so, but it is wrong for him, so long as that is his deliberate judgement."[9] It would have been fine for Gandhi to have taken that action if he only affected himself,, but in so acting he affected his client. It seems to me instead that the better thing to do would have been to confront the client, and call on the client to do what is truthful.

In fact, that was more commonly Gandhi's practice. Gandhi in his autobiography also talked about a case of a co-worker and frequent client, Rustomji, a Parsi, who was a very successful trader in South Africa. Gandhi had known him for many years. One day Rustomji came to him and said, "Bhai, I have deceived you. My guilt has been discovered today. I have smuggled and I am doomed...I have kept nothing else from you, but I thought I ought not to bother you with such tricks of the trade and so I never told you about the smuggling. But now, how much I repent it!"[10] What the police had caught him for was a very minute amount of smuggling. But Gandhi persuaded the client to come forward and confess all of the smuggling, far beyond the present case and offer to pay a fine which was double the profit from the smuggling. The Attorney General accepted the arrangement. There was no criminal sentence and Rustomji framed in his office the confession as a reminder.

The story of Rustomji, however, shows the other problem of Gandhi's practice from the traditional lawyer's prospective. Recall that the smuggling had been going on for years, and his client never told him about it. Why had his client never told him? I think Gandhi told us himself: "My clients used to only bring me their clean cases. False cases they took to other lawyers."[11] So what happened was, because Gandhi acted as a judge to his client, his client had not confided everything in him. Thus his client had lost the benefit of Gandhi's advice and engaged in smuggling for years without "bothering" his lawyer with his "tricks of the trade." The story of Rustomji thus illustrates why as lawyers we should honour our client's confidences, and even when we know the client is committing a crime not be obliged to disclose it. Because otherwise, the clients would not tell us. It would have been better for all concerned if, years before, Rustomji had confided fully in Gandhi and Gandhi could have advised him much earlier.

In my own practice I have discovered that my clients sometimes think that they are guiltier than they really are. To give another welfare fraud illustration: I had a client who, in the process of discussing a case involving foreclosure of her house, told me that she had lied to the welfare department. She had told the officials that she was renting a house from her mother when in fact she owned the house herself. She had done so because she thought she could not get welfare if she had owned her own house. That belief was mistaken because under most welfare programmes a person is allowed to own a home. When I told her this, she said, "Oh my God! Here I have gone years committing fraud when I didn't even have to." Now in this case, because she had come to me without being caught or charged, I was able to do something rather like what Gandhi did. I negotiated with the prosecutor an arrangement where she would not be prosecuted, she could reimburse whatever extra money she had and set the record straight. Experiences like this show that the lawyer's ability to advise his client requires that total protection should be given to the client's confidences.

III

Gandhi's insistence on serving the truth over the duty to the client is really a sign of a much deeper issue. In his autobiography, after explaining how he honoured truth as a practising attorney, he concluded with this sentence: "Let the reader, however, remember that even truthfulness in the practice of the profession cannot cure it of the fundamental defects that vitiate it."[12] Now what fundamental defect in law did Gandhi see, after 20 years of practice? Why did he say it was as degrading as prostitution? To answer this we must return to the fundamental concept of the rule of law, which Gandhi rejected. Legal ethics as traditionally observed in the United States and India are based on the adversary concept. Although the rule of law transforms physical violence into litigation, law still retains the model of a battle or a game–although litigation is stylized and acted out in a courtroom rather than on a field of combat. In litigation there is still a winner and still a loser. The ethical lawyer is simply a lawyer who fights fair, who fights the battle on behalf of his client according to the rules. The attorney is, in a sense, a champion.

But Gandhi radically rejected the whole adversary concept of the rule of law. In a startling passage in *Hind Swaraj* he says: "Men were less unmanly when they settled their disputes either by fighting or by asking their relatives to decide for them. They become more unmanly and cowardly when they resorted to the courts of law. It was certainly a sign of savagery when they settled their disputes by fighting. Is it any less so if I ask the third party to decide between you and me? Surely, the decision of the third party is not always right....We in our simplicity and ignorance imagine that a stranger by taking our money gives us justice."[13]

It seems to me that this passage is perhaps the real key to the whole book. As I understand it, *Hind Swaraj* says that true home rule is really self-rule; thus political liberation is meaningless without spiritual liberation. So the word "Swaraj" is the pivot on which the whole concept revolves. This is perhaps Gandhi's most fundamental insight, to link the political liberation of India with the concept of Swaraj. The rule of law is still not self-rule because it is imposed from outside of a person. It is perhaps imposed by a legally constituted government rather than by a more forceful and powerful individual, but it is still not self-rule. That is why Gandhi could say that law is still a form of brute force. Against brute force, Gandhi puts "soul force." Soul force resolves conflicts by changing the character of the opponent. Thus there are neither winners nor losers when soul force resolves a conflict. Rather there are changed people. In contrast, at the end of litigation, typically there is no growth or change in the litigants, no reconciliation. Adversaries remain adversaries. What simply happens is that someone has won and someone has lost. This concept Gandhi has fundamentally rejected in *Hind Swaraj*.

Soul force is an appealing approach if the two adversaries reconcile. But what if the more powerful refuses to change? Is that not why we have the rule of law: if the adversary is more powerful and will not be reconciled? Gandhi replied, it is better for the innocent to suffer than to resort to law. That is a very difficult concept. But as I thought about it, it seems to me that it contained some-practical truth. Even a court victory does not really shift power.

I thought of my own practice as a legal aid attorney. The poor remain poor, no matter how good a lawyer I am. One of the kinds of cases legal aid attorneys frequently handle are landlord-tenant cases; low income tenants in bad housing. Frequently the tenant withholds rent to try to force the landlord to make repairs or provide heat. I would go to court and often win such cases for the tenants. The tenant would not have to pay rent or the court would order the landlord to fix the toilet or restore heat. But often the tenant would then move because even though the court had ordered the toilet to be fixed, the landlord was still the landlord and he would make the life for that tenant so miserable that he had to move out. Likewise, I often resolved one welfare problem, only to have the same client calling me back two weeks later with another problem. The basic inequity in the distribution of power and wealth remains.

In the United States we may suffer from a kind of myth about courts and the justice that they can do. One of the classic of justice being done in the courts is *Brown* v. *The Board of Education*. That is the famous desegregation decision of the Warren Court in the early 1950s in which the Supreme Court said, "Separate is not equal; schools must be racially integrated under the U.S. Constitution." The struggle to have the civil rights for the Black people of the United States has been one of the great events in the United States since World War II; and many say, it is because of the Supreme Court's great decision, *Brown* v. *The Board of Education,* that this all happened. I do not think so. The 1950s after the decision was a difficult time when very few schools were integrated and there was great racial strife. True liberation of the Blacks in the USA really began with Martin Luther King and the civil rights struggle that he brought–of course, deeply inspired by Gandhi. It is those events of the early 1960s we really should look to as having fundamentally transformed racial injustice in American society, though the struggle is still going on.

A wonderful example of transformation accomplished by the civil rights movement is George Wallace. He was the Governor of Alabama in the 1950s who made himself a folk hero of the racist people in Alabama by personally standing in front of the schoolhouse doors to prevent integration, deliberately breaking the law. The irony is that George Wallace, who re-entered politics years later was once again elected Governor of Alabama - only this time he deliberately sought out the support of Black people; indeed the only reason he was elected Governor was because Black people voted for him. At that stage he had a whole new image and a whole new campaign which appealed to Blacks for support. I am not sure I would totally trust him, but Wallace may have been transformed in the way Gandhi hoped.

In Gandhi's vision of a non-violent society, what role is there for a lawyer? It seems to me, looking to Gandhi as an example, there are still two roles for lawyers, roles which he exemplified. One is the lawyer as a friend of the client. A good example is what in a way was one of the most important lawsuits of the 20th century: the lawsuit that brought Gandhi from India to South Africa, Abdulla Sheth's case. Abdulla Sheth was a very prosperous Muslim merchant who had immigrated from Gujarat to South Africa and was involved in a lawsuit with his relatives over trade accounts worth hundreds of thousands of dollars. It was to work on that major lawsuit that Gandhi went to South Africa. After a several-month stay in Natal, Gandhi was sent by his client to Pretoria, where the lawsuit was being litigated and the defendant also stayed. As Gandhi was getting on the train Abdulla Sheth cautioned him to be very wary when he arrived. Gandhi said, "I do intend cultivating the acquaintance of the other party. I shall like to be friends with them, I will try, if possible, to settle the case out of court. After all, Tayeb Sheth is a relative of yours." Abdulla Sheth was taken aback and he said, "There would be nothing better than a settlement out of court. But we are all relatives and know each other very well indeed. Tayeb Sheth is not a man to consent to a settlement easily. With the slightest unwariness on our part, he would screw all sorts of things out of us and do us down in the end. So please think twice before you do anything."[14]

Gandhi went to Pretoria, spent months studying the case and became certain that it was in the interest of both parties to end the case quickly. So he approached Tayeb Sheth and after great efforts persuaded him to come to mutual arbitration. He said, "I felt my duty was to befriend both parties and bring them together. I strained every nerve to bring about a compromise."[15] And after straining every nerve Tayeb Sheth agreed to arbitration. The arbitration resulted in an award to Gandhi's client, but the award money would have bankrupted Tayeb Sheth. Thus Gandhi had to turn the tables, and he strained every nerve to persuade his own client to accept a long-term, no interest payment plan so that Tayeb Sheth would not become bankrupt. Gandhi said, "Both were actually happy over the result, and both rose in the public estimation. My joy was boundless. I had learnt the true practice of law. I learnt to find the better side of human nature and to enter men's hearts. I realized the true function of a lawyer was to unite parties riven asunder. The lesson was so indelibly burnt into me that a large part of my practice as a lawyer was occupied in bringing about private compromises of hundreds of cases. I lost nothing, thereby, not even money and certainly not my soul."[16]

This concept of the attorney as a friend throws a different light on the classic ethical dilemmas I described earlier. Certainly, if you intervened in a problem as a friend of somebody, you would be still personally responsible for what you have said and especially for any untruthfulness you spoke. No matter how good your friendship was, you would never allow yourself to be involved in any kind of falsehood when advocating for your friend. Because Gandhi saw himself as the friend of the client, he could not in any way compromise himself, even if he violated what might be considered as a duty to the client.

The second role of the lawyer that I see in Gandhi's non-violent society is the lawyer as a voice. For soul force to work, the opponent still must hear you and must understand you. In fact, much of Gandhi's role was to become a voice. After Gandhi came back to India, he turned to journalism as a more effective way of giving voice to the oppressed of India. If we think of the lawyer as the voice of the client, a lawsuit is changed from a conflict to a conversation and the court from an arena where a stylized battle is changed into a forum. "Forum" is a frequent synonym for "court." The world "forum" originally referred to the central square of a city as the marketplace, like the place in Athens where everyone used to meet and chat, and especially where Socrates used to sit and hold forum. A forum is, thus, a place where people gather to talk and exchange ideas.

Therefore, if we think of the court as forum and the lawsuit as conversation, the lawyer is not really speaking to the judge at all. Under the Gandhian approach you are not appealing to the judge to exercise the power of the State to make you a winner; what you are really doing is speaking to your opponent. The courtroom provides an opportunity to do that with the hope of changing your opponent, of resolving your conflict with him. An example is what in Gandhi's life was called "The Great Trial," the trial in Gujarat in 1922, after which he was sentenced to six years' imprisonment for treason. Why was it called "The Great Trial?" The whole trial lasted only 100 minutes and it was not really a trial at all because Gandhi pleaded guilty. The 100 minutes consisted primarily of his statement of why he had acted as he did. It is considered a great trial because in so speaking Gandhi gave voice to what perhaps millions of Indians were feeling. He was not in any way trying to move the judge not to sentence him, indeed he welcomed the maximum sentence of six years. Nonetheless even the judge was deeply moved, saying as he passed the sentence required by law, "I hope the Viceroy feels moved to set aside the sentence, if so, I would be the happiest man in India." It was a great trial because, in a sense, it was a great conversation and people across India heard him.

IV

I will conclude by taking these two concepts of the lawyer's role and applying them to a case arising out of a protest against nuclear arms in the United States. Near my hometown of Detroit is a plant that manufactures engines for the Cruise Missile, which is one of the most frightening weapons in the nuclear arsenal. It can be delivered by a very small airplane and yet carries a nuclear warhead. Most of us in Detroit did not even know the plant was there until people concerned about peace started a series of non-violent protests at the plant, largely consisting of either entering the premises or blocking the gate. What happened, of course, was that they were arrested. In fact, the company got so tired of the protests that it went to the court and obtained an injunction to prevent people from stepping on the property.

Two different kinds of cases came out of these protests. In one case a group of people who were arrested were represented by lawyers and presented a legal defence to the charge of criminal trespass. The legal defence they raised was the defence of duress. The basis of this defence is that you committed the crime because you were in fear of some greater harm occurring. For example, if you trespass on someone's land to save your child from certain death this would be a defence to the trespass. This defence was used to argue that the protesters were so afraid of nuclear holocaust that, in fact, they felt compelled to do this act of trespass.

One of the judges who heard the case was himself sympathetic to the nuclear arm protest movement and was a member of an organization advocating for nuclear disarmament. He accepted the duress defence and acquitted the defendants. Most of my friends said, "What a great legal victory! What a great precedence!" I became very unpopular by saying, "I am not so sure." First of all, from a purely legal stand point the judge was probably wrong in applying that defence. Besides that, he appeared to reach that legal conclusion because he was sympathetic to the cause of the people in front of him. The result was that the prosecutor went to the next higher court and obtained an order disqualifying that judge from hearing any more cases involving the protests at the plant. There was a great deal of adverse publicity which I think detracted from the protest movement. Moreover, I think the legal argument was inconsistent with the very act of civil disobedience. These people were not moved by fear; their act should have been viewed as an act of courage. In traditional civil disobedience you act willingly to accept the punishment of the law. Therefore, the legal defence raised was really inconsistent with the principles of the protest. In my opinion what happened was that lawyers acted according to their roles and won, theoretically. But I think it was a hollow victory. They got a figure of authority to give them victory but nothing really changed. In fact, more people were arrested, other judges heard the cases, there was neither a shift in power nor any change in justice.

Contrast this first case with a different case. A friend of ours, our neighbour and our minister, was also arrested. He and three other people arrested with him initially said, "We do not want lawyers. We are going to plead guilty and do our 30 days in jail." And that is what they did. But the judge that heard the case was not satisfied with putting them in jail for 30 days. He wanted them to promise, under oath, never to go back again to the plant and commit civil disobedience in defiance of the injunction. My friend and the other three people could not do that because, as my friend told the judge, "To swear that I will obey this court order is to say that I will place what I believe God is telling me to do second to the order of this court. I cannot do that. I simply cannot do that." The judge replied, "You will sit in jail until you say you are going to obey the court's orders," and sent him back to jail. That is when our friend asked to talk to me and said, "Perhaps I need a lawyer." I went in and talked to him. He said, "I do not want to be out of jail before 30 days, but I want to say that I have the right to protect my conscience."

So that was the argument I made to the Court of Appeals and that was not the only place we made the argument. We went to his bishop and to a bishop of the Roman Catholic Church about what had happened. The two of them wrote an open letter to the judge saying that this was an issue of religious freedom and conscience. The letter was published on the second front page of a major Detroit newspaper. There were editorials, great discussions and debates in the public eye, thus really raising the issue, I think, in the right context.

The Court of Appeals freed my friend and the other three without reaching the issues of religious freedom and the right of civil disobedience. They ruled on a legal technicality, which as a lawyer, I should have been happy about. But in fact, there was not a great victory because later other people were arrested and went back in front of the same judge who wanted the same promise to be made. When they appealed our Court of Appeals upheld the judge saying that the right to civil disobedience had to yield to the court's order. Some people sat in jail for two or three months, one among them was in his eighties. But they did not stay in jail forever because (and I think this is something which would have pleased Gandhi) the armament plant went before the judge and asked him to release them. True, the adverse publicity may have been too much for them to be let out of jail. Thus the second case shows how the courtroom can be a forum, as a place for the issues to be raised for other people to hear about it.

As a postscript, what is happening?[17] Whether or not there will be more protests at the plant I do not know; the plant is still making Cruise missiles. There are other strategies being taken by the peace movement in addition to civil disobedience. They are now going to churches in the surrounding communities and talking to the people who work at the plant asking them to think about perhaps not working there any more because of the moral issues that are raised.

Hundreds and hundreds of lives were touched by these events. My own life was touched. As I had to defend our neighbour, my client, I myself had to think about the sacrifice he was making. I have talked about it to many people, including now you friends tonight, and I used the case as an example in my classroom. Several hundred of my students participated in a mock argument on this issue. Indeed one of my students, an older student, came to me and said, "I am a business executive for Williams International (the plant) and I really appreciate the way the class has made me think about what it is we are doing."

So in all sorts of unexpected and mysterious ways the courts were used as a way of voicing in a non-violent way profound concerns. Most people, most of my friends, state that the whole non-violent approach to the nuclear arms race is silly, that no matter how many people sit in jail and outside the gate, there are going to be Cruise missiles. Indeed, if I step back, the whole Gandhian approach to lawyering may seem hopelessly naive. What possible impact could this approach have on the arms race or on issues of social injustice?

I am still thinking through whether or not these new roles for lawyering are ones that I should perhaps adopt. But as I question, and perhaps as we talk, there is at least one answer that I think is a powerful one: and that is, simply, the life, the miraculous life, that ended 38 years ago (on January 30, 1948). That perhaps is a sufficient answer.

REFERENCES

1. *Hind Swaraj* p. 57 (Navajivan Publishing House. Ahmedabad, 1938).
2. *Hind Swaraj* p. 55.
3. The requirement that the income of one's adult children sharing the home be considered in calculating welfare benefits does not apply to all welfare programmes in the United States.
4. There are certain exceptions which allow, under some programmes, a portion of earned income to be retained without a corresponding reduction in welfare benefits.
5. On February 26, 1986, the U.S. Supreme Court reversed the Court of Appeals and held that the lawyer's actions did not deny the defendant effective representation, noting that the only "right" denied the defendant was the right to lie on the witness stand. *Nix* v. *Whiteside*, ___U.S.___ 106 S.Ct. 988 (1980).
6. *An Autobiography* p. 302 (Navajivan Publishing, Ahmedabad, 1927).
7. *Ibid.* p. 305.
8. "The Practice of Law and Gandhi." 4 *Gandhi Marg* 722.727 (Gandhi Peace Foundation, November, 1982).
9. *Hind Swaraj* p. 79.
10. *An Autobiography* p. 307.
11. *Ibid.* p. 302.
12. *Ibid.* p. 305.

13. *Hind Swaraj* p. 56.57.
14. *An Autobiography* p. 92-93.
15. *Ibid.* p. 111.
16. *Ibid.* p. 112.
17. Several months after the talk was given the Michigan Supreme Court decided to review the decision of the Court of Appeals upholding the judge's order that the protesters promise not to commit future civil disobedience at the plant. *In re Contempt of Peter Dougherty et. al,* Michigan Supreme Court Nos. 77337, 77338. On behalf of Michigan bishops of the Methodist, Episcopal (Anglican) and Roman Catholic churches I filed an amicus (friend of the court) brief with the Michigan Supreme Court raising the same issues of religious freedom and freedom on conscience I raised on behalf of my earlier client. A copy of this brief has been given to A.B. Bhardwaj, coordinator of Gandhi-In-Action, 3 Lajpat Bhawan, New Delhi-110024.

11

RELEVANCE OF MAHATMA GANDHI'S APPROACH TO COMMUNAL HARMONY

M. L. SHARMA

In a vast country like India inhabited by people following a variety of religions, speaking various languages and observing different cultures, customs and traditions, communal harmony is absolutely necessary for national integration, peace and prosperity. Besides, the issue of communal harmony is quite relevant and significant under the present circumstances in which communal frenzy and religious intolerance have been posing a serious threat and danger to our national unity. Before independence, we used to curse the British for communal divide and violence. But foreign rulers are no more here to sow the seeds of communal disruption, division and hatred. An observer's comments, in this connection, are quite relevant and eye-opener:

> "It is unfortunate that even after almost four decades of independence we need more conciliation committees and more tightening of the official machinery of administration, like our erstwhile alien rulers, than tracing the root of the problem and finding solution to it."[1]

Similar views have been expressed, by an eminent journalist who says that as India approaches the 40th anniversary of its freedom, the evil of communalism clouds its horizon as menacingly as it did in that fateful summer in 1947.[2]

Mahatma Gandhi preached non-violence throughout his life and lived and died for communal harmony and unity. He was such a great man who never felt, thought and acted in terms of communalism or narrow sectarianism. He fought for the safeguard of the rights and interests of the minorities. He had no malice, ill-will and animosity towards any community. His soul was an ancient violin wonderfully tuned and radiating focus of goodwill and love. Undoubtedly, centuries together would not dim the image and the splendour of his idealism since his mission in his life was the service of mankind and humanity through love-truth and non-violence (Ahimsa).

Restless Until the End

Accordingly, when we talk about communal harmony, we cannot forget the contribution of this great man of India. Remember, he was the most unhappy man, upset and very much hurt with the violence and communal hatred all around him. It is a fact that his soul was restless until the last moment of his life and he wished that rather than he be a helpless witness to communal (Hindu-Muslim) atrocities, he should be removed from this earth. For instance, he openly threw himself into the flames of communal frenzy and communal rivalry in Bengal, Bihar and Delhi. He went on foot from place to place, village to village spreading the message of non-violence, love and friendship, brotherhood and mankind, instilling a sense of courage and a ray of hope in the hearts of those cowed down by violence and communal fanaticism. He fully believed and was convinced that communal fanaticism could be eliminated from the ignorant people only through love and compassion, non-violence and service of men irrespective of their caste, colour and creed. Moreover, he had already experienced and realized this essential truth at an early stage when he was in South Africa and held fast to it till his death. Similarly, during the days of the "Khilafat Movement" and the agitation against the "Punjab Wrongs", he laid utmost emphasis on Hindu-Muslim Unity by which expression he meant communal harmony and Unity in its widest sense. His writings and speeches delivered on different occasions in those days are full of passionate appeal for strengthening communal harmony and amity which were then manifesting themselves and for making them a permanent feature of our national life. It was on account of his strong desire to establish harmony between the Hindus and the Muslims that he went for an all-out effort to help the "Khilafat Movement" which he regarded as a movement for the redrerss of a very genuine grievance of the Muslims and he hoped that by rendering them assistance during that period of their trial the Hindus would be winning their lasting goodwill. His policy as well as intention always was to ask the Hindus to leave it to the Muslims not to do anything which could hurt their religious feelings and to ask the Hindus to see to it that nothing was done by them which could hurt the Muslims. For instance, one major cause of conflict between the Hindus and the Muslims, particularly in Northern India, used to be the slaughter of cows especially on the day of Bak-rid. Gandhi in the days of "Khilafat Movement" used to say that it was for the Muslims to protect the cow and it so happened that in 1921, when the Non-cooperation Movement was at its height, cow sacrifice on the day of Bakr-id was almost negligible in the country as a whole. Speaking on the vow of Hindu-Muslim Unity, Gandhi advised that meetings should be seriously considered. He expressed that before the unity became a reality, both the communities would have to give up a good deal and would have to make radical changes in their ideas. He pointed out:

> "Members of one community when talking about those of the other at times indulge in terms so vulgar that they accentuate the relations between the two. In Hindu society we do not hesitate to indulge in unbecoming language when talking of the Mahomedans and vice versa."[3]

Similarly, he pointed out that the standing complaint of Hindus against Muslims was that the latter were beef-eaters and that they purposely sacrificed cows on the Bakr-id day. Now it was impossible to unite Hindus and Muslims so long as Hindus did not hesitate to kill their Muslim brothers in order to protect the cow. He explained:

> "For I think it is futile to expect that our violence will ever com-

pel Mohamedans to refrain from cow-slaughter. I do not believe the efforts of our cow protection societies have availed in the least to lessen the number of cows killed every day. I have had no reason to believe so. I believe myself to be an orthodox Hindu and it is my conviction that no one who scrupulously practises the Hindu religion may kill a cow-killer to protect a cow. There is one and only one means open to a Hindu to protect a cow and that is that he should offer himself as a sacrifice if he cannot stand its slaughter. Even if a very few enlightened Hindus thus sacrificed themselves I have no doubt that our Mushalman brothers would abandon cow-slaughter. But this is Satyagraha, this is equity; even as, if I want my brother to redress a grievance I must do so by taking upon my head a certain amount of sacrifice and not by inflicting injury on him. I may not demand it as of right. My only right against my brother is that I can offer myself as a sacrifice."[4]

Again to him it was only when Hindus were inspired with a feeling of pure love of this type that Hindu-Muslim Unity could be expected and as with the Hindus, so with the Muslims. He said that the leaders among the latter should meet together and consider their duty towards the Hindus. When both were inspired by a spirit of sacrifice, when both try to do their duty towards one another instead of pressing their rights, then and only then would the long-standing differences between the two communities could cease. Each must respect the other's religion, must restrain from even secretly thinking ill of the other. We must politely dissuade members of both the communities from indulging in bad language against one another. To him, only a serious endeavour in this direction could remove the estrangement between the two. "Our vow would have value only when masses of Hindus and Mussalmans join in the endeavour."[5] This naturally led to people to hope that the Hindu-Muslim tangle could be solved. Similarly, another cause which used to stir up feelings and led to trouble between the two communities was the question of music accompanying processions in front of mosques. Gandhi appealed to Hindus not to insist upon playing music near mosques which disturbed Muslims in their prayers and became a cause of provocation.

Unfortunately the communal concord achieved during the period of non-cooperation proved shortlived and there were riots again between Hindus and Muslims in different parts of the country. However, Gandhi did not lose faith in the absolute necessity of unity and harmony between the Hindus and Muslims or in the method which he had been pursuing to establish it. There were Hindus also who never accepted his principle or his method at any time and they feared that his effort in connection with the "Khilafat Movement" would only result in strengthening the fanatical elements amongst Muslims without ultimately bringing about communal unity on which Gandhi was so keen, and when these riots occurred they were able to point out that they had foreseen and foretold the consequences of the movement which Gandhi had led. It was not, however, till several years later that what appeared to be a complete break between the Hindus and the Muslims on the political front actually took place. As the movement for Swarajya gained in momentum, and it seemed that power would pass into Indian hands, the political elements among the Muslims conceived the idea of securing for their community their share, if not a dominant position, in the Indian polity. This movement was started long before but it gained momentum particularly after the advent of the Simon Commission. Late Dr. Rajendra Prasad observed:

> "The British Government was also interested in encouraging a fissiparous tendency. It ultimately led to the formulation by the Muslim League of its separate demands which would put the Muslim community in a position of parity as against all the rest of the people although they were less than 25 per cent of the population. The theory that Hindus and Muslims constituted two separate nations was sedulously propagated and when it was accepted by the Muslim League, it led to the demand for a partition of the country and the establishment of Pakistan".[6]

However, it must be mentioned here that though there were some Muslims who were opposed to this yet it cannot be denied that the majority of the Muslims supported this movement wholeheartedly and the country had to yield at last. Even during all this period of more than 20 years Gandhi held fast to his views about Hindu-Muslim unity and his opposition to the theory of two Nations.

Unwavering Faith

In spite of this misunderstanding of his actions and motives, he never wavered in his faith. Moreover, like some Muslims, some groups of Hindus also considered his activities as against and prejudicial to the Hindus blaming him for showing undue favour and yielding too much to the Muslims. It was due to the fact that such Hindus never felt that the policy of appeasement which the Mahatma had been following would ever bear fruit. Some of them even did not hesitate to accuse him of treachery to the Hindus. Even after that Gandhi did not bother about his life and felt the agony and rushed to Bengal to stem the tide of communal hatred that had manifested itself in such an ugly shape after the ruthless killings in Calcutta and the atrocities that were committed in Noakhali and other places in East Bengal followed by the terrible happenings in Bihar in 1946. His heart was broken when the disaster followed the partition of the country. History is witness to his tireless efforts made to bring about communal harmony and stem the waves and to heal the wounds. Moreover, it is due to tireless efforts and secular attitude of the Mahatma that the exodus of many Muslims from India was stopped and today India has a Muslim population in millions spread all over the country. However, the happenings and incidents of that period had so soured his heart that he had almost ceased to have any interest in life. He expressed it publicly time and again that he had no desire to live and be a helpless witness to what had been going on in the country. At the same time he had never lost faith and he was working and hoping for the day when relations of concord and harmony could again be established between the Hindus and Muslims and when those who had migrated to the other side would not only find it possible to return to their old homes but would actually be welcomed by the members of the other community. He was, therefore, opposed to anything being done which could make the return of those who had migrated impossible. It shows that his whole policy had been based on an unalterable faith in human nature and a firm belief in non-violence.

Religious Tolerance and Gandhi's View on Hinduism

Gandhi believed that irrespective of one's religion and faith, one had to feel his identity with everyone of the millions of the inhabitants of our motherland. He said:

> "In order to realise this every Congressman or (anybody else) would have to cultivate personal friendship with persons representing faiths other than his own. He should have the same regard for the other faiths as he has for his own."[7]

Similarly, he was not happy while listening to the disgraceful cry at the railway stations such as "Hindu Water" and "Muslim Tea", and separate rooms or pots for Hindus and non-Hindus in schools and colleges, communal schools, colleges and hospitals.[8] In 1938, Gandhi elaborated:

> "My Hinduism is not sectarian. It includes all that I know to be best in Islam, Christianity, Buddhism and Zoroastrianism. I approach politics as everything else in a religious spirit. Truth is my religion and ahimsa is the only way of its realization. I have rejected once and for all the doctrine of the sword. The secret stabbings of innocent persons, and the speeches I read in the papers are hardly the thing leading to peace or an honourable settlement. "...I go as a life-long worker in the cause of Hindu-Muslim unity. It has been my passion from early youth. I count some of the noblest of Muslims as my friends. I have a devout daughter of Islam as more than a daughter to me. She lives for that unity and would cheerfully die for it. I had the son of the late Muazzin of the Juma Masjid of Bombay as a staunch inmate of the Ashram. I have not met a nobler man. His morning Azan in the Ashram rings in my ears as I write these lines during midnight."[9]

Similarly, Gandhi emphasized that the Gita, the Koran, the Bible, the Granth Sahib and the Zend Avasta contained gems of wisdom. Now it is up to the followers whether they follow or belie their teachings.[10] In this respect, Gandhi's comments on the subject are quite relevant when a deputation of the Hindus and the Sikhs from Rawalpindi and Dera Gazi Khan met him and explained their grievances to him. Gandhi's reply was that the Hindus and the Sikhs had made Rawalpindi what it was. They were all well off there but became refugees without shelter later on. It hurt him deeply. Why should innocent persons–Hindus or Sikhs or Muslims–be killed in the name of religion? Religious intolerence is one of the major reasons for this problem. Gandhi had admitted that religion was the personal affair of each individual but it must not be mixed up with politics for that matter.[11] And the Hindus, the Muslims, the Sikhs, the Christians, the Parsees, the Jews should be Indians first and Indians last.[12] While elaborating this issue Gandhi remarked:

> "If some misdirected individual took it into his head to desecrate a temple or break idols, should a Hindu in return desecrate a mosque on that account? Did it anyway help to protect the temple or to save the cause of Hinduism?"[13]

Gandhi pointed out that he was as much an idol-worshipper as an idol-breaker, and he believed that all Hindus and Muslims upheld the same view whether they admitted it or not. He said that mankind thirsted for symbolism. He questioned: were not Masjids or Churches or for that matter Gurdwaras in reality the same as Mandirs (temples)? He answered that God resided everywhere no less in stock or stone than in a single hair on the body of man. But men associated sacredness with particular places and things more than with others. Such a sentiment was working of respect when it did not mean restrictions on similar freedom for others. To every Hindu and Muslim, Gandhi's advice was that if there was compulsion anywhere, they should gently but firmly refuse to submit to it. Personally, he himself would hug an idol and lay down his life to protect it rather than brook any restriction upon his freedom of worship. That required courage of a higher order than was needed in violent resistance.[14]6 Thus it is on that ground that Gandhi declared time and again that he would not give up repeating the names of Rama and Rahim which meant to him the same God.[15]

Furthermore, in the eventuality of a communal conflict Gandhi's advice is that we should forget the past and should learn the duty of having friendly feelings towards all and being inimical to none.[16] He reminded, for example, that the crores of Muslims were not all angels nor were all the Hindus and the Sikhs. There were good and bad specimens among all communities. Would they be less than friendly towards the so-called criminal tribes amongst them?[17] In such circumstances both men and women of one community should go to the men and women of other communities and establish friendship with them. Besides, they should invite them on ceremonial occasions and be invited. The girls and boys of various communities should be attracted to common schools rather than communal schools. They should mix in sports. He pointed out:

> "The condition of keeping me in your midst is that all the communities in India live at peace with one another, not by force of arms but that of love... there is no better cement to be found in the world."[18]

That is why once Gandhi advised the people of India as a whole not to be violent and take the law into their own hands and commit inhuman acts. To him that would mean the end of society.[19]1 Therefore, Gandhi realized the importance of self-purification which could purge out the dross from the hearts of the conflicting communities. Accordingly, all should turn the searchlight inward and to cast out all hidden impurity. In April 1946, Gandhi stayed in the quarters of an untouchable (Harijan Colony) in Kingsway, Delhi, and as usual started conducting a public prayer meeting there every evening. The first evening he asked those present whether they would object to the recitation of some verses from the Koran. Many of them objected to it. They told him that he had no authority to intone or use an Islamic holy book at Hindu service. On that point Gandhi broke off the meeting. He raised the same question the next evening. Again there was opposition to it. Likewise, Gandhi also refused to pray with the congregation. The same thing happened the third evening. Gandhi repeated the same thing fourth evening. As a result and to everyone's surprise, no one objected as the objectors had withdrawn. In the end, non-violence prevailed and Gandhi proved to be victorious.

Conclusion

When we come to Gandhi's approach to communal harmony, we find that Gandhi opposed communal virus of return blow for blow which is nothing but perpetuating our mental slavery and tearing up our motherland into bits, namely, Hindustan, Pakistan, Brahministan and Achhutistan[20] (land of Untouchables) and now one more such a place–Khalistan. Everybody knows how dear to his heart was the dream of a united India–a peaceful and a prosperous India–an India in which all Indians, irrespective of their religion, language or political affiliation, could live together as one big family in an atmosphere free from communal frenzy, mutual rivalries and prejudices. He sacrificed himself so that a united India might live together. Dr. Rajendra Prasad has rightly said that it was the tragedy of the first magnitude that the unscrupulous people who could not reconcile themselves to his approach to communal harmony, conceived the idea of removing his body from the scene of his activity and achieved success in their design. Similarly, Muslims as a body also did not "fully appreciate the value of his good services till his tragic death, hut he bore witness to the truth that was in him by smilingly laying down his life for it. No man can do more".[21]

Thus, here lies the importance of Gandhian approach to communal harmony. Today, movements are launched with communal violence and quelled with more violence. Bloodshed continues unabated, communal riots erupt on the flimsiest of provocations. This is more important in the sense that we have been unable to overcome or stop violence by violence or forcible methods. Gandhi had opposed and rejected the theory of return-a-blow-for-a-blow or bullet-for-a-bullet, which was not the solution of any of our problems. It is the height of communal virus when we have a general rather wrong impression that while a person is being killed in violent incidents in Delhi, we say he would be a Sikh and if another killed in Punjab, he would be a Hindu. Whereas, the truth is that violence does not see a Hindu or a Muslim or a Sikh or anybody else. Such a thinking creates undesirable and unethical values such as anger, hatred, suspicion and spirit of revenge. Therefore, there is confusion. Such confusion cannot be removed until and unless we all, irrespective of our caste, colour and creed cultivate in us higher values and virtues such as liberal attitude, truthfulness, humility, compassion, tolerance and loving kindness which Gandhi preached throughout this life.[22]

Thus, Gandhi's approach to communal harmony has a meaning, a worth and is meaningful step in the proper direction but this single step should not be considered as a panacea or a single pill or tablet course for the eradication of a serious disease of communalism. However, this one step of humility, tolerance, liberal attitude, self-restraint, self-purification, love, compassion and loving kindness can show us the proper way to go ahead for the second step to reach our destination–communal harmony, peace and amity. Therefore, the first step is most important, fundamental, and decisive also.

REFERENCES

1. B.S. Gupta. "Education and Integration" in *The Tribune* (Chandigarh), 2.11.1987, p. 4, col, 5.
2. Ibid., 1.6.1987, p. 4, Col. 3.
3. *Young India* (Bombay), 7.5.1919, Vol. I, No.1, p. 9.
4. Ibid.
5. Ibid.
6. Rajendra Prasad, "Foreword" in M.K. Gandhi, *Communal Unity* (Ahmedabad, Navajivan Publishing House, 1949), p. v.
7. M.K. Gandhi, *Constructive Programme : Its meaning and place* (Ahmedabad, Navajivan Publishing House, 1983), Reprint edition, p. 8.
8. Ibid.
9. *Harijan* (a journal of applied Gandhism: 1933-55), 30.4.1938 (New York, Garland Publishing, Inc., 1973), Vol. VI, p. 99.
10. Ibid., 5.10.1947, Vol. XI, No. 36, p. 354.
11. Ibid., 7.12.1947, Vol. XI, No. 45, P. 459.
12. Ibid.
13. Ibid., 30.3.1947, Vol. XI, No. 9, p. 86.
14. Ibid.
15. Ibid. 20.4.1947, Vol. XI, No. 12, P. 118.
16. Ibid., 25.1.1948, Vol. XI, No. 52, P. 531.
17. Ibid.
18. Ibid. p. 536.
19. Ibid., 1.2.1948, Vol. XII, No. 1, p. 10.
20. *Harijan,* 30.3.1947, Vol. XI, No. 9, p. 86.
21. Rajendra Prasad, "Foreword" in M.K. Gandhi, *Communal Unity,* op.cit., p. VII.
22. *Harijan*, 2.4.1938, Vol. VI, p. 65.

12

SEARCH FOR UNITY IN DIVERSITY: GANDHIAN MODEL

S. VARADARAJAN

In the past 40 years since the attainment of Independence, the country has no doubt taken long strides in economic development–in greater industrialization, increased food production, more energy supply and advancement in science and technology–all reflected in what the economists call GNP. Politically also the democratic practice is satisfactorily progressing, the country remaining the largest democracy in the world. But the human relationship which is far more important than others has greatly suffered. Peace and happiness which was the dream of Gandhiji have receded farther and farther. The sword of disintegration seems to be hanging over the country by a very slender thread. And a Herculian effort is being made to preserve national integration.

Before looking for a remedy in keeping with Gandhiji's ideals, for such an alarming situation let us try to lay our finger on the factors which have contributed to the deterioration of human relations in the country and threatened national integration. These are several. I prefer to call them disharmonies. First and the foremost is the communal disharmony–disharmony between some of the religious groups in our country such as Hindus, Muslims and Sikhs. The disharmony between these groups has sharpened so much that it is causing frequent violence, arson, loot and loss of life and property, assuming the most ghastly form–terrorism–with no solution in view so far. Then come the disharmony between various castes, as also between Harijans and caste Hindus; the cultural and linguistic disharmony, particularly after the formation of cultural and linguistic States; disharmony between the haves and have-nots, between various political parties in the country and between factions in the same party struggling for power–all causing tension and unrest in the country. It is not that these factors were not there earlier. They were very much there. But during the past four decades these disharmonies have much sharpened and pushed them to the point of confrontation and conflict. As a result violence has become the order of the day and every situation is becoming a law and order problem. How long the country can continue like this?

What is the reason for such rapid deterioration of human relationship in the country? It is due mainly to greater and greater importance being given to narrow loyalties of caste, creed, group and religion, overlooking the larger national interest. It is due to continuous increase in selfishness and individual and group egos. These are all aberrations of our own creation. We have the wrong type of training and the wrong type of environment. Feeling of separateness leading to the point of hatred and enemity. Our present-day education and upbringing does not develop in us feeling of love and brotherhood between individuals and among various sections of our community/people. The very mentality and outlook are vitiated.

The situation has become so serious and assumed such a dimension that one wonders whether there is any remedy for it and whether it can be set right at all. But one thing is clear–that no non-Gandhian method can ever bring about any improvement in the situation, it can only worsen it. It should be realized that the method of love and non-violence alone can remedy the situation and bring about harmony, resulting in peace in the country.

Again the unrest in India or outside is the reflection of disharmony within man. There is a fatal imbalance between what man is and what he wants to be. Peace and happiness emanate from inner contentment for which one has to lead a life based on human values. Gandhiji sought to set right this malady in human personality. He worked for a major change in human nature. He worked incessantly to bring about a change in the human heart so that it is ruled by love and nonviolence and not by selfishness, jealousy and hatred. He wanted men to control their unbridled sensual pleasures which generate selfishness and consequent evils. It is for this reason that Dr. Radhakrishnan called Gandhiji "A revolutionary thinker who belongs to ages, to history."

Gandhiji wanted a social order which would ensure the greatest good of all, *Sarvodaya* and not merely the greatest good of the greatest number. He wanted a society in which all had equal status, mutual respect, and freedom and equal opportunity to develop to his or her best. He wanted a society in which economic progress and social justice would go together.

To understand the basis of all this, one should understand Gandhiji's personality properly, and his beliefs and faiths. If one goes through the life, thoughts and actions of Gandhiji, one would get a glimpse of these. For him there was inseparable relationship between Truth and Non-violence. For him Truth was Reality or God. His firm faith was that Truth, in the immanent form, manifested in the world, in animate and inanimate entities. When once he realized this Truth he identified himself with the entire humanity and acted accordingly. Thereby he became Mahatma. His firm faith was that "There is only one religion, the religion of Love; there is only one caste, the caste of Humanity; there is only one language, the language of the Heart; and there is only one God and He is Omnipresent". So upliftment and integration of humanity was the mission of his life whether it was related to labourers in South Africa or peasants in Kaira or Harijans in India or to equal status for women and the downtrodden–it was all the same for him.

Attainment of Truth was the main purpose of Gandhiji's life, which he experimented throughout his life. The best a man in search of Truth can and ought to do is to abstain from any form of injury to others in thought, speech and action *(manasa, vacha, karmana)*. This is the beginning of Ahimsa or Non-violence. "But the utmost step and form of non-violence or love would be not only selfless service but also sacrifice of oneself, if need be". Therefore, the realization of Truth for Gandhiji was only through non-violence, through *Satyagraha.*

For the integration of humanity belonging to different groups, parties, castes, creeds and religions, it is necessary to have a feeling of oneness over and above all the apparent differences and to have a sense of unity for making a common cause to achieve peace and happiness. Such a feeling could be there among men only when it is realized that there is the same divine principle in the core of the personality of every individual. This is the unifying principle in all the diversity of men. This is the basic truth which Gandhiji wanted all men to realize. His main aim was to spiritualize people. The various struggles and Satyagrahas he lead such as Champaran, Jalianwala Bagh, Kaira Satyagraha, Salt Satyagraha, Individual Civil Disobedience Movement and Quit India Movement and also his Constructive Work Programme were all meant to awaken the soul-force in the masses of India and to spiritualize them. This would lead to a life of love, brotherhood and selfless service. This would dispel gradually all disharmony among individuals and groups and pave the way for peace and happiness. This is the way to bring about integration of people not only in India but also in the world. Gandhiji believed that this was not only the best way but the only way for human development and world peace. "Gandhiji is the immortal symbol of love and understanding in a world wild with hatred and torn by misunderstanding", says Radhakrishnan.

How to achieve this? Education is the only means by which it is possible to build a democratic human community with a sense of human values, universal outlook and tolerance. It is only through education that it is possible to inculcate selfless love, brotherhood and unselfish service to the needy. Materialistic education of today, it has become abundantly clear, generates selfishness and greed, narrow loyalties and individual goals which have been responsible for the strife-ridden world of today, threatening to destroy not only all the cultural, scientific and technological achievements of man but also humanity itself. Therefore the urgent need is the introduction of an education with value orientation, incorporating the teachings of Mahatma Gandhi as a part and parcel of its curriculum and thereby start the process of re-integration. This is the only way to save ourselves, our country and humanity.

13

GANDHIAN MODEL OF COMMUNAL UNITY : AN AXIOM FOR NATIONAL INTEGRATION

M. SUBRAHMANYAM

Immediately after achieving political independence from the British, India, under the leadership of Jawaharlal Nehru, was successful in bringing territorial integration of the nation. But the territorial integration did not bring the desired unity among different communities. The partition of India, as demanded by the Muslim League, reluctantly accepted by the Indian National Congress and conceded by the British, did not put an end to the mistrust, and the riots that followed between the two numerically large communities, i.e. Hindus and Muslims, only increased it. Time is a great healer, and within four decades of independence, the mistrust has been reduced to the minimum, but recurrence of communal riots all over India in general, and in northern and western parts in particular, still poses a major threat to the democratic life of Indians. The problem of communal riots, sometimes appears to be the instigation of a foreign hand. This, in fact, poses a major problem before the Indians, i.e. the National Sovereignty.

Strictly speaking, Indians can put an end to the communal disharmony which raises its ugly and inhuman face from time to time. It requires no new model to be formulated and put into execution by the government. In fact it hardly requires government interference. Only principled assistance. All that is required is that the government keep its position impartial, and keep away from the electoral politics. The age-old and tested model is found in the voluminous pages written by Mahatma Gandhi. The only effort Indians need is to turn to Gandhiji, and to follow his message. To Gandhiji, communal unity is not merely a political expediency, but an article of faith and an ethical and spiritual maxim of conviction.

Gandhiji, in 1908, yet to emerge as a leader of the Indian national movement, through his most important and controversial writing, *Hind Swaraj*, expressed his views lucidly regarding the entire communities of India as one nation. He wrote: "India cannot cease to be one nation because people belonging to different religions live in it. The introduction of foreigners does not necessarily destroy the nation, they merge in it. A country is a nation only when such a condition obtains in it. That country must have a faculty of assimilation. India has ever been such a country. In reality, there are many religions as there are individuals; but those who are conscious of the spirit of nationality do not interfere with one another's religion. If the Hindus believe that India should be peopled only by Hindus, they are living in a dreamland. The Hindus, the Mohamedans, the Parsis and the Christians who have made India their country are fellow countrymen, they will have to live in Unity, if only for their own interest. *In no part of the world are one nationality and one religion synonymous terms, nor has it ever been so in India.*[1]

"Of all the leaders of Indian National Movement, M.K. Gandhi (1869-1948)", says Mackenzie Brown, "is least susceptible of analysis in point of either the theory or action alone. He did not consider himself a philosopher, yet his ideas have permeated in political and social life of India."[2] Gandhiji's predecessors, who indulged in much intellectual and political gymnastics on Swaraj, considered Swaraj mainly from the political angle.[3] They felt once political independence was achieved, the rest of the problems affecting India would be resolved, hence, they did not attempt to focus much on the social and economic problems. But, Gandhi, ever since he took part in the freedom struggle, gave a serious thought to the meaning and scope of Swaraj. "It has been said that Indian Swaraj will be the rule of the majority community, i.e. Hindus" Gandhiji said, "there cannot be a grosser mistake than that. If it were to be true, I for one would refuse to call it Swaraj and would fight it with all the strength at my command, for me Hind Swaraj is the rule of all people, is the rule of Justice."[4]

Gandhiji was an embodiment of Hinduism. His religion was not that of a narrow perspective. It was elastic, humane and universal both in theory and practice. It was not a religion of ritual practice nor a dictum of a particular sect. It was a religion which propagated the ever cherishable maxims of *Sarva Dharma Samabhava* and *Vasudhaiva Kutumbakam*. He believed in the greatness of all religions. He professed, "all religions were equally true, though being received and interpreted through human instruments equally imperfect". His vision was, "the different religions were beautiful flowers from the same garden or branches of the same majestic tree". That is why he was always against any kind of religious conversions. According to him "one must stick to one's own religion, as everyone's religion was best for himself."[5]

Gandhi was a "remarkably integrated personality and continues to be of enormous interest as regards his ideological and political legacy, his role in the history of India, and his links with the country's past and future".[6] Even since Gandhiji was drawn into politics, he understood that communal harmony among all communities in general, and Hindus and Muslims in particular, was the prime need for realizing Swaraj, and thereafter to sustain them as a democratic nation. In 1919, the Muslim leadership of India expressed its anguish against the British approach towards Turkey and the Caliph, and to express it they organized the All India Khilafat Conference. Gandhiji did not undermine the Muslim sentiment. He fully shared their concern and influenced the Congress to support and join them. He presided over the meeting of the Khilafat Conference held on November 24, 1919, at Amritsar. Addressing them in Urdu he said: It ought not to appear strange for the Hindus to be on the same platform as the Muslims in a matter that specially and solely affects the Muslims. After all, the test of friendship is true assistance in adversity and whatever we are, Hindus, Parsis, Christians, or Jews, if we wish to live as one nation, the interest of any of us must be the interest of all. The only consideration can be the justice of a particular cause. We talk of Hindu-Muslim Unity. It would be an empty phrase if the Hindus hold aloof from the Muslims when their vital interests were at stake. Some have suggested that we Hindus can assist our Muslim countrymen only on certain conditions. Conditional assistance is like adultrated cement which does not bind.

In 1920 there was a new turn in Indian politics. The Khilafat question was agitating the Muslim mind and the Hindus could not forget the Jalianwalla Bagh tragedy. At this time a special session of the Congress was held at Calcutta from September 4 to 9. Lala Lajpat Rai presided. The Khilafat question and the Punjab wrongs were mentioned at the session and it was suggested that the attainment of Swaraj was of the utmost importance to restore justice. This could be done by following a progressive non-violent, non-cooperation movement. This resolution was passed by an overwhelming majority. It was supported, among others, by Motilal Nehru, Maulana Shaukat Ali and Mohammad Ali. But, C.R. Das, Lala Lajpat Rai and few leaders from Bengal and Maharashtra opposed the resolution.

On March 19, 1920, moving the historical resolution at a Khilafat meeting held in Bombay, Gandhiji said, "So far the resolution is a joint transaction between the Hindus and Muslims and others to whom this great land is their mother country or their adopted home", and observed further, "And it commits the joint movement to a policy of non-violence in the course of struggle. But the Muslims have special Koranic obligations in which Hindus may or may not join. They, therefore, reserve themselves the right, in the event of the failure of non-cooperation-cum-non-violence, in order to enforce justice to resort to all such methods as may be enjoined by the Islamic scriptures. I venture heartily to associate myself with this resolution."[8] One cannot miss the spirit of Gandhiji, accepting and respecting the code of conduct of other religions. "We know this that there will be neither peace nor rest for the Government and people, until the wrong is righted and the feelings of eight crore of Muslims are duly respected." Gandhiji prevailed over the Indians in support of the Muslim sentiment and concern. He made the entire nation march along the Muslim community in pursuit of their desire. He maintained, "I hope it is unnecessary to show why it is obligatory on Hindus to march side by side with their countrymen. So long as the means and the end are honourable, I can imagine no better cement for perpetually binding us both...."[9] For Gandhiji the unity of Hindus and Muslims was not a passing phase of freedom struggle. It was because they share the same destiny, the unity consists in our having a common purpose, a common goal and common sorrows', and it is" best promoted by cooperating to reach the common goal by sharing of one another's sorrows and by mutual toleration".[10]

No Compartments in His Heart

Some sceptical among both Hindus and Muslims had mistaken Gandhi as partial towards the other community, and expressed their apprehensions. Taking note of that, he clarified, "I have same love for the Mussalman as for the Hindu. My heart feels for the Mussalman as much for the Hindu. If I could tear it open, you would discover there are no compartments in it, one reserved for the Hindu, another for the Mussalman and so on."[11] Communal unity was his passion from his early youth. For that, he lived, continuously pleaded for, fasted and purified himself, and ultimately breathed his last. Such was his spirit. How did that passion develop? That develops out of love, Gandhiji explained, "Love is the basis of our friendship as it is our religion. I seek to gain Mussalman friendship by right of love and if love persists even on the part of one community, unity will become a settled fact in our national life."[12]

During the national movement and, thereafter, "Cow" was a major problem for forging communal amity among Indians. Gandhiji, like many Hindus, believed in the protection of cow, as it is useful for agriculture, and that being the main occupation of millions of Indians. He desired the Indians to adhere to cow protection. But when some Hindus complained against the food habits of Muslims, he questioned them, why they were not complaining against the food habits of their rulers, the English. He blamed the protagonists of cow protection for the ill treatment of the so-called sacred animal by Hindus. His contention was to convince the Muslims by peaceful means to stop consuming beaf, but not through confrontation and adopting coercive methods. Gandhiji observed: "But, just as I respect the cow, so do I respect my fellow men. A man is as useful as a cow, no matter whether he be a Mohamedan or a Hindu. Am I, then, to fight with or kill a Mohamedan in order to save a cow? In doing so, I would become an enemy of the Mohamedan as well as the cow.

Therefore, the only method I know of protecting the cow is that I should approach my Mohamedan brother and urge him for the sake of the country to join me in protecting her. If he would not listen to me I should let the cow go for the simple reason that the matter is beyond my ability. If I were overful of pity for the cow, I should sacrifice my life to save her but not to take my brother's. This, I hold, is the law of our religion.[13]

Gandhiji was a pantheist. His God is *Truth.* It is the *jijnasa* of the Upanishads. It is an irrevokable faith in *Yekopasana*. His *Iswar* is none other than *Allah.* He saw no difference between true Hinduism and Islam. He highlighted "the contribution of Islam to Indian culture." He observed, "Islam's distinctive contribution to India's national culture is its unadulterated belief in the oneness of God and a practical application of the truth of brotherhood of man for those who are nominally within its fold. I cast these two distinctive contributions. For in Hinduism the spirit of brotherhood has become too much philosophised. Similarly, though philosophical Hinduism has no other God but God, it cannot be denied that practical Hinduism is not so emphatically uncompromising as Islam."[14]

Writing about the 21-day fast undertaken by Gandhiji on September 18, 1924, to arrest the communal riots that had gripped Bombay, his biographer, Louis Fischer, describes the impact of the fast: In the seven hundred thousand villages of India, Hindus and Muslims had always lived together in peace. The Hindu-Muslim tension of the twentieth century was a man-made, middle class, urban disease. Indians are often ambitious and dynamic. A city like Bombay throbs with vitality. The inhumanly crowded towns, with their herring barrel tenements and frustration which comes from animal-like poverty and very limited opportunities to earn, learn and advance, make urban Indians easily excitable."[15]

Gandhiji never conceded the theory that Hindus and Muslims are two different nations as advocated by the communal organizations such as the Muslim League and Hindu Mahasabha. For him, as mentioned before, religion was never a determinant of nationality. "Religion", Gandhiji said, "is no test of nationality, but a personal matter between man and his God. In the sense of nationality they are Indians first and Indians last, no matter what religion they profess."[16] This concept he always maintained. His appeal to his countrymen was "to examine religion from the point of religionists themselves". He was opposed to the concept of one nation and one religion. His message was, tolerance for all religions and their existence side by side with one another. In a nation that was powerless, Gandhiji became a symbol of strength. In a nation of slaves he behaved like a free man, he was a man of God.[17] His countrymen also responded to his feelings. His impact upon them was that of a Messiah. The Muslims in Calcutta or Agra, the Hindus in Amritsar or Allahabad would not be compelled to change their conduct because Gandhiji was dying for Hindu-Muslim amity. They would change, writes Fischer, if at all, because the Mahatma's great sacrifice established a spiritual bond between him and them, a kind of common wavelength, a means of communication over which he conveyed to them the importance, the necessity, the urgency, the sacredness of the cause for which he was fasting. It was his way of going out to them, of entering their hearts, of uniting himself with them.

Law of Majority has no Place

Gandhiji envisaged India to follow a written constitution. That should provide utmost priority to democracy from grass-root level. It should guarantee equal civil and political rights to all its citizens. Democracy he never agreed as "rule of the majority over minority". Advocating the need to honour the minority opinion and wishes, Gandhiji pointed out that "the rule of majority has a narrow application, i.e. one should yield to the majority in matters of detail. But it is slavery to be amenable to the majority, no matter what its decisions are. Democracy is not a State in which people act like sheep. Under democracy individual liberty of opinion and action is jealously guarded". "I, therefore, believe that the minority has a perfect right to act differently from the majority as long as it does not act in the name of the Congress."[18] In matters of conscience the law of majority has no place.[19]

Immediately, with partition and independence, India was in the grip of communal strife and riots. The entire country was in a pool of blood. Punjab, U.P., Bihar and Bengal were the worst hit. India, in her history, had never witnessed such an inhuman and cruel incidents where man slaughtered man in the name of religion. No authority with its physical force of maintaining law and order succeeded in putting the strife down. And whether it was Bengal or Delhi or any other place in India, it was only Gandhiji's moral influence, which could put a stop to the communal massacre. But for the Mahatma, no leader could even go near the human butchers to pacify them. His moral and personal influence, his commitment to love for the entire humanity, the trust the different communities had in him, and his instrument of Satyagraha which he exercised for right purposes alone could bring the situation under control and save India.

The British imperialism never left any stone unturned to damage the integration of the people of India, in the hope that they could perpetuate their rule over India. But for Gandhiji, and his commitment to preserving the harmony and unity among the various religious groups and intra-religious sections, and his supreme sacrifice for that cause, the imperial authority may have succeeded in fragmenting the Indians as they wished. And if, the fabric of Indian unity remained intact, whether in 1924, 1931 or 1947, it was again Gandhiji with his "Passive Resistance" that averted the colossal split among the Indian community.

No body in his heart was interested in the partition of India. It was an outcome of the dialectical process of the British imperialism and its confrontation with the liberation struggle of the Indian masses. The responsibility cannot be attributed solely to any person or organization that had taken part in the historical process. And Gandhiji, till the last, had exerted to avert that. But, man makes his own history, not always as he wishes. History failed the Mahatma. The Hindu communal elements blamed him for the partition and all the aftermath that followed. When a young couple from Maharashtra arrived in Delhi and undertook fasting, threatening they would not end it until Pakistan was abandoned, the Mahatma addressed them at two successive prayer meetings. "Are you fasting against Pakistan", he asked them, "because you hate Moslems or love Moslems? If you hate Moslems you may not fast. If you love Moslems, you should go and teach other Hindus to love them." The young couple abandoned the fast and returned.[20]

History records the sincere effort of Gandhiji to bring back the waring crowds of Hindus and Muslims to their senses, immediately after independence. In 1947, during his fast until death, until the communal riots stopped, Gandhiji in the midst of the people of Calcutta said firmly: I will not rest till every Moslem in the Indian Union who wishes to be a loyal citizen of the Union is back in his home living in peace and security and until the Hindus and Sikhs have returned to their homes.[21] In his address to the RSS volunteers at Delhi, during the riots that spread following independence, he advised them, "there is no gain in returning evil for evil. Both sides appear to have gone crazy. The result can be nothing but destruction and misery for both sides. The RSS was a well-organized, well-desciplined body. Its strength could be used in the interest of India or against it. Allegations had been made against the RSS. Gandhi told them, "it had been accused of fomenting riots and planning assassinations. It is for you to show by your uniform behaviour that the allegations are baseless".[22] The preceptor and practitioner of Truth and Non-violence, at the end of his life, emphasized the need, when it is relevant, truth has to be uttered, however unpleasant it may be .... Misdeeds of Hindus in the Indian Union have to be proclaimed by the Hindus from the housetops if those of the Moslems in Pakistan are to be arrested or stopped. As a Hindu he was sternest with Hindus.[23] While answering to the question, does Hinduism permit killing an evil doer? his reply was, one evil doer cannot punish another; to punish is the function of the government, not of the public.[24]

Gandhiji was both politician and saint, a combination of roles not unusual in earlier epochs, but almost unique in the 20th century. He alone of the front-rank political figures of our times claimed constantly and in public to be doing God's bidding, to be acting at the prompting of "the inner Voice", he alone had sought to cast out devils and to win over opponents by prayer and fasting; and he alone made prayer-meetings a main avenue of approach to the public.[25] Over the years the universality of Gandhiji's philosophy has come to acquire greater and greater significance for the tortured soul of the entire humanity, and thinkers all over the world have turned their attention to a study of Gandhiji's life and philosophy with a view to seeking an effective and abiding solution for the world's complicated and multiplying ills.[25]

India a Mini Universe

We live in an age of science and we cannot be called upon to accept incredible dogmas or exclusive revelations. It is again an age of humanism. Religions which are insensitive to human ills and social crimes do not appeal to the modern man. Religions which make for divisions, discord and disintegration and do not foster unity, understanding and coherence, play into the hands of opponents of religion.[26] India is a mini universe, it is the only place since civilization and culture emerged on its soil, which has projected herself as a model of positive secularism. Peoples of different races, languages and cultures met on the soil of India, and, though we notice occasional conflicts and clashes, they have settled down as members of a common civilization whose primary characteristics are faith in unseen reality, of which all life is a manifestation, primacy of spiritual experience, a rigid adherence to intellectual norms, and an anxiety for harmonizing apparent opposites.[27] But unfortunately, the 40 years' history of India after independence reveals a distortion of that common culture, if not withering away of it as a whole. The indices for distortion of that image are due to multiplicity of reasons. To enumerate some of them, lack of equal opportunities to all sections of people; projecting a negative dimension in a democratic polity; capitalizing the grievances of some sections of society for immediate political gains; and attempts in disguize by those who are opposed to a just world.

In fact, what Gandhiji, throughout his political life, strived for was communal harmony and national integration but did not develop any new model of his own. It was the same age-old practice and experience of Indians since time immemorial. But this practice was thrown into the background. Karl Marx has rightly noted that "the British were the first conquerors, superior, and, therefore, inaccessible to Hindu civilization. They destroyed it by breaking up the native communities, by uprooting the native industry, and by levelling all that was great and elevated in the native society. The historic pages of their rule in India report hardly anything beyond these destructions.[28] Gandhiji wanted to purge modern Indian society of its evils and help it to gain back its former glory.[29] But the crux of the national problem in India is, "we want integration and unity and what not, and at the same time we want to perpetuate the very thing that has kept us apart +– all exclusive religion. We want to identify our people not as Indians, but as Hindus, and Muslims, and Christians, and Sikhs, Parsis and Jews".[30] If we want abiding unity in this country we are not going to achieve it merely by having a common language, a common script and a common this and that. Such patchwork integration will lead us nowhere. If there is one thing that we need very much in common, it is common culture, a common Indianness, a common set of *samskaras*.[31] Here, the teaching of the Mahatma and his lifelong effort and sacrifice become relevant. He understood that the unity of this esteemed land lay not in its uniformity but in its picturesque diversity. His appeal to his fellow compatriots was and is to preserve that inheritance of unity in diversity, through mutual respect, tolerance, cooperation, trust and love.

Any Indian worth his name, interested to see his nation live in peace and achieve economic development without much tension, needs to adhere to what Gandhiji stood for his entire life. Any Indian who has the genuine desire for his country and its people to attain glory and progress and to scale the higher heights of socio-economic growth, the need of the present is to restore communal harmony and unity in the country with a sense of live-and-let-live. The revival of the age-old model which has been retouched by Gandhiji is the right choice of the people of India to adhere to. The past, present and future civilization of this ancient country safely rests on that model. The only thing required at present is a strong will and commitment by the people to carry forward that axiom.

REFERENCES

1. M.K. Gandhi, *Hind Swaraj, Collected Works of Mahatma Gandhi*, Vol. 10. Publications. Division, New Delhi, p. 29.
2. D. Mackenzie Brown, *Indian Political Thought from Ranade to Bhave*, University of California Press, Berkeley, 1961, p. 108.
3. B. Pradhan, Swaraj the Gandhian Vision, in B.C. Das and G.P. Misra (ed.), *Gandhi in Today's India*, Ashis Publishing House, New Delhi, 1979, p. 39
4. Gandhi, *Young India*, July 12, 1924, p. 78.
5. T.K.N. Unnithan, *Gandhi and Free India, A Socio-Economic Study*, p. 56.
6. Rosteslav Ulyanovsky, *Present Problems in Asia and Africa: Theory, Politics, Personalities*, Progressive Publishers, Moscow, 1978, p. 163.
7. D.G. Tendulkar, *Mahatma, Life of M.K. Gandhi*, Vol. I, p. 330.
8. Ibid., p. 346.
9. Ibid., p. 3347.
10. *Young India*, Feb. 25, 1920, p. 3.

11. *Young India,* Aug. 13, 1921, p. 215.
12. *Young India,* Oct. 20, 1921, p. 333.
13. *Hind Swaraj, Collected Works,* Vol. 10, p. 30.
14. *Young India,* March 3, 1929, p. 95.
15. Louis Fischer, *The Life of Mahatma Gandhi,* Vol. I, Bharatiya Vidya Bhavan, Bombay, p. 240.
16. Ibid., p. 281.
17. Ibid., p. 281.
18. *Young India,* March 23, 1922, p. 129.
19. *Young India,* Aug. 4, 1920, p. 318.
20. Op. cit., Louis Fischer, Vol. 2, p. 288.
21. Ibid., p. 297.
22. Ibid., p. 297.
23. Ibid., p. 302.
24. Ibid., p. 298.
25. Penderel Moon, *Gandhi and Modern India,* The English University Press, London, 1968, p. 1.
26. Kaka Kalelkar, Foreward, in K. Ahluwalia and Shashi Ahluwalia (ed.), *Facets of Gandhi*, Indian Academic Publishers, New Delhi, p. V.
27. S. Radhakrishnan, *Religion and Culture,* Hind Pocket Books, Delhi, 1968, p. 89.
28. Ibid., P. 110.
29. Karl Marx and F. Engels, The Future Results of British Rule in India, in *The First Indian War of Independence,* Foreign Language Publishing House, Moscow, p. 34.
30. Op. cit., T.K.N. Unnithan, p. 98.
31. T.K. Mahadevan, *Gandhi My Refrain,* Popular Prakashan, Bombay, 1973, p. 62.
32. Ibid., p. 63.

14

DEVELOPMENT PLANNING AND SPATIAL INEQUALITY: THE RELEVANCE OF THE GANDHIAN APPROACH

LATA CHATTERJEE

Introduction

More than three decades ago Myrdal (1957), in analysing problems of recurring poverty in developing countries, had argued that one of the primary goals of State policies should be to increase the spread effects of development. He emphasized the need for a conscious effort by decision makers to distribute the benefits of development in an equitable way, since a structural characteristic of efficiency-oriented planning practice would be the generation of a variety of negative backwash effects that would increase economic injustice and socio-economic polarity among different groups of society. It is a pity that his theory has been incorporated into standard, even elementary, texts in development theory but has yet to be successfully adopted in development planning practice. This is not because development planners are not cognizant of the backwash effects; an almost forty year record of development planning provides numerous empirical illustrations of the validity of Myrdal's argument. This is also not because there is a lack of goodwill among development planners. Development planning has drawn more than an average number of people concerned with issues of ethics and social justice.

This disparity between acceptance of the concept of core periphery in theory and it's lack in practice largely results from two factors. First, we have a limited understanding of the logic of spatial processes in development. Second, while economic growth is a necessary component of development, we have been inadequately concerned with the choice of instruments that promote economic growth. Instruments of economic growth greatly vary in their propensity for generating negative backwash effects. Many conventional efficiency oriented instruments, such as subsidised credit and tax write offs, that are used to attract investments to depressed regions have intensified instead of reduced equity problems. We need to focus more analytical attention on the choice of appropriate instruments for equitable spatial development.

Conventional instruments for increasing efficiency and equity are derived from the concepts of welfare and spatial economics that emphasize the benefits of agglomeration and scale economies in production and consumption. Such instruments favour regional concentration of investment and planning. Concerns with social justice and equity are addressed through redistribution policies at the secondary income stage. However, this approach ignores two fundamental realities, that is, the minimal resources available in developing countries for social security types of redistribution, and the distortion of these limited resources for transfer payments in favour of the socially, economically and politically powerful groups in society.

Accumulating evidence of these distortions has led to a fresh interest in the search for alternative models of development that can build in social justice at the choice of instrument stage. Gandhian economics has much to offer in this regard. Gandhi asserted that equity should be a paramount concern in the development of ex-colonial, low income countries. Thus he argued for strategies that would permit balanced rural and urban development and favoured the use of appropriate technology for this end. He claimed that indiscriminate modernisation, while growth producing, would increase unemployment and cause further immiserisation of the weaker economic elements of society. Since economic and industrial modernisation involves spatial concentration of investment in countries with limited resources, Gandhian economic thought also has relevance for the design of spatial strategies for development. While Gandhi did not directly address the issue of spatial equity, his emphasis on local area development, maximization of employment through choice of appropriate technologies and like emphases have relevance for the design of spatially equitable planning strategies. In this paper tentative ideas on the relevance of Gandhian economic thought to spatial justice and equitable regional development are presented for the purpose of encouraging discourse and dialogue.

The paper is divided into three sections. In the first section the spatial organisation of production in Ghana is discussed. Colonial policy in Ghana produced an unequal spatial system with identifiable variations in regional wealth and welfare. This unfortunate legacy has been accentuated by planning strategies in the post-independence era and this paper describes spatial elements in the development strategies of Ghana. In the second section the regional impacts are traced, particularly the human consequences of spatial inequality expressed in terms of well being and deprivation. In the third section Gandhian ideas are explored as an alternative for using the spatial system as an instrument for a more equitable and socially just development. Through reviewing planning practice in Ghana, the paper will make a case for an alternative approach to regional development that has the potential for increasing social welfare and economic justice.

Spatial Organization of Production and Services in Ghana

In 1957, at the time of it's independence, Ghana was among the most developed countries of Africa. With a per capita income of $500, in 1960, it could qualify as a middle income country according to the World Bank criteria for the classification of third world countries (Roemer 1984). In the thirty years since it's independence, the GDP per capita declined at an average annual rate of 0.7%. During the seventies, however, per capita GDP declined by 2.5% annually and by 1980 Ghana's share of capital investment to GDP had declined to 5% in comparison to 20% in the 1950's. These are among several available indicators that document the failure of

Ghana's development planning. Since Ghana provides an unambiguous example of a country that made serious attempts to plan for economic development and where the development strategies failed to meet their efficiency and equity objectives it's experience is used to illustrate some of the points regarding the alternative of Gandhian ideas for socially just and economically effective spatial planning in developing countries.

Ghana has an unbalanced spatial economy with an overconcentration of basic infrastructure and production possibilities in the South, especially within the golden triangle encompassing the cities of Accra-Tema, Sekondi-Takoradi and Kumasi. These three agglomerations accounted for 41% of the total urban urban population in 1984 (Economic Intelligence Unit, 1985). The uneven urban distribution is shown in Fig. 1. In 1970 only 11 out of 135 centers with populations over 5000, were located in the backward Upper and Northern regions. Moreover, these towns also poorly integrated with the national urban system. For example, Ghana's 700 mile railroad does not serve these northern regions. Even a cursory glance at the spatial distribution of urban, infrastructural, industrial and service levels demonstrates the presence of structural dislocations within the Ghanaian space economy.

The source of this uneven spatial development lies both in colonial practices as well as in the growth oriented strategies adopted by the development planners. The colonial policy geared to resource extraction and development of the country for the interests of the imperialists laid the foundation for the current uneven regional pattern. The economic prosperity of Southern Ghana was brought about by the development of the cocoa industry. The higher rate of urbanization, the more balanced size distribution of urban centers and the better integration of the urban areas in the cocoa producing areas, such as the Ashanti region, reflects the higher levels of economic development achieved in the southern area. In like vein there is a concentration of urban centers in areas where mineral extraction was developed for the export market such as in the Western and Ashanti regions. The development along the coast and in the colonial capital of Accra - now the Greater Accra region - also has its roots in colonial policy.

Figure 1 The Urban Pattern in Ghana: 1970

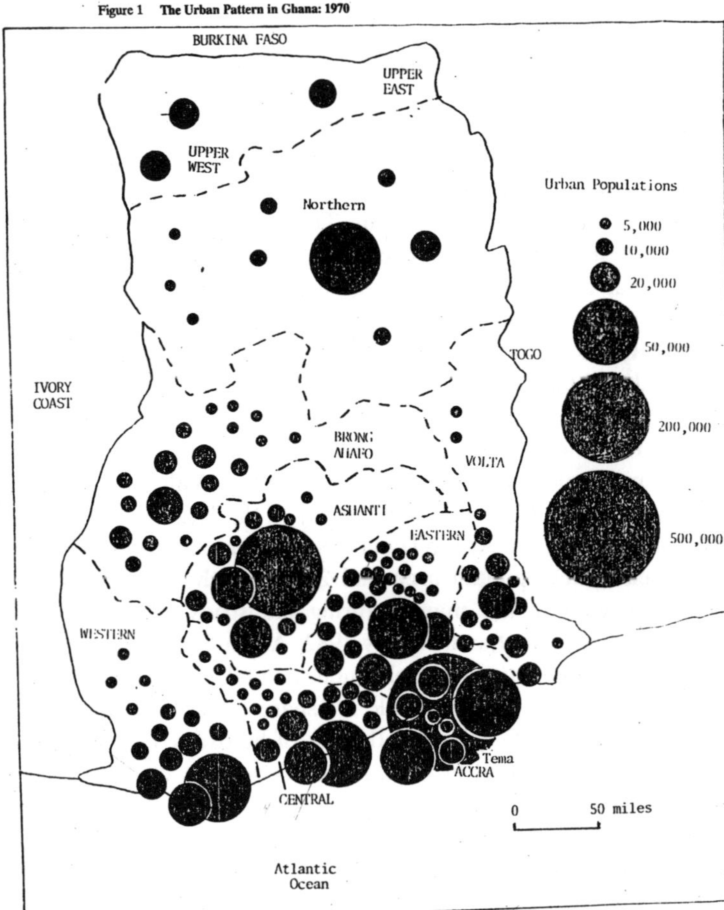

Source: Computed from Census Data. Central Bureau of Statistics.

This uneven pattern was accentuated, however, by development planners. Ghana adopted the principles of the then prevalent growth oriented development theory and this choice accentuated regional inequalities. Nkrumah pursued a policy of rapid economic growth consistent with the ideas of the " big push" theory. The big push advocated an unbalanced growth strategy, wherein modern, import substituting industries were considered as lead sectors. Industrialization was expected to absorb the surplus labour from the agricultural sector, improve the agricultural worker/land ratio and generate the demand for the agricultural output. The big push, based on massive capital investments, was expected to break the vicious cycle of poverty that described developing countries. As is clearly evident, these strategies, accepted as common wisdom in the development community, violated almost all of Gandhi's prescriptions for a post colonial development.

One result of these policies has been the increase of Accra-Tema's importance as a manufacturing centre. With the opening of the modern port of Tema in 1962, many of the larger processing industries moved to the Accra-Tema district. For example, in 1962, the Accra-Tema metropolitan area had 26.2% of the total number of people engaged in the manufacturing industries and 31% of the value added by manufacturing. By 1982, Accra-Tema accounted for 55% of the manufacturing employment and 60% of the value added in the manufacturing sector while it's share of the national population was around 8.5% (Central Bureau of Statistics 1984). In terms of manufacturing output in 1982, Accra-Tema, the Western and the Ashanti regions accounted for 40.2%, 39.7% and 13.9% respectively of the national output. The Northern and Upper regions, on the other hand, had only 2% of the manufacturing establishments, 1.5% of the manufacturing employment and 9% of the value added. Thus, they not only had a disproportionate share of establishments, the establishments were less productive and more obsolete. Their value added was lower than their share of establishments would warrant.

Such a spatial distortion in the manufacturing sector can be attributed to the fact that many of the plants were geared to the use of imported industrial inputs. Moreover, Ghana tried to encourage foreign investors through fiscal incentives. It was therefore logical for the industrialists to have located their establishments within the

Accra-Tema metropolitan area. However, a dominating structural feature of such capital intensive industrialization is the relative unimportance of flows inside the industrial system. Since such an industrial strategy generates few backward linkages, there has been little benefit to the economy of this strategy. Indeed the import demands put an onerous strain on external payments and despite the imposition of taxes and controls fueled deficits. Roemer (1984) notes that the cumulative government deficit from 1960-65 was 50% higher than recorded deficit of an annual 15% due to the use of short term borrowing from equipment manufacturers and others to finance long term debt.

TABLE 1: **Agricultural Employment in Ghana 1970-1985**

Region	Share of National Income	Share of National Population	Agricultural Labour Force as Percentage of Total	
	(in percentage.)		1970	1985
Greater Accra	35.8	9.9	9.6	6.6
Western	17.2	8.9	48.0	68.5
Ashanti	15.2	17.3	54.7	54.0
Eastern	12.7	14.7	56.1	53.8
Central	7.9	10.4	54.4	57.8
Volta	3.6	11.0	54.6	57.5
Northern	3.0	8.5	80.2	71.7
Brong Ahafo	2.6	8.9	73.2	71.6
Upper	2.0	10.1	70.9	65.3

Source: World Bank, Ghana Agricultural Sector Review, Vol. III, 12, 1978. Washington, D.C.
Economic Intelligence Unit 1985.

In addition, the emphasis on capital intensive industrialization caused economic growth to decline through the negative impacts generated on the agricultural sector. Neglect of the agricultural sector and capital intensive industrialization increased regional inequalities since the Northern, Upper and Brong Ahafo - the poorest states – are primarily agricultural. In these states more than 70% of the population were engaged in agriculture (Table 1). Policies aimed at the expansion of capital intensive, large scale, modern industries, can be expected to have the greatest negative impact on regions where agriculture is the economic mainstay. These three states had 27% of the population and only 7.6% of the national income.

With the bulk of economic activity concentrated in the South, Ghana's rail and road network revolves around these activities. As noted earlier, the entire rail network serves only the South-connecting Accra-Tema-Sekondi-Takoradi and Kumasi with branch lines to the Prestea and Awaso mines and Kade. The road network spans 20,000 miles of which feeder roads account for 68% of the total network in the country. Since these feeder roads, even though unsurfaced and of poor quality, connect the small towns and villages they are of great importance to the rural economy. Unfortunately, government expenditure on feeder roads has been relatively minimal. The Economic Recovery Programme (1984-86) intended to rehabilitate only 2,900 km. or 13% of these roads. Trunk and secondary roads, which account for 32% of the total network and which serve the urban centers of Southern Ghana, have received a disproportionately larger share of government road allocations. The World Bank has approved $ 22 million for the rehabilitation of three major roads in Accra and major highways linking Accra-Tema and Kumasi (Economic Intelligence Unit 1985). Another $ 60 million has been earmarked for the rehabilitation of the Tema and the Takoradi harbors. The World Bank and the African Development have committed $ 40 million for renovation of the rail network in the Western region. Accra has a $ 26 million urban development project.

With budgetary allocations for infrastructure in the more developed South it should not be surprising if regional inequalities increase and the peripheral areas of the northern and upper regions continue to be isolated. Even in the urbanised South there is uneven development; the urban and industrial areas are receiving the budgetary allocations so there are marked inequalities even within the more prosperous regions.

Attempts to maximize national economic growth not only failed in its objectives, but also generated unfortunate side effects such as increase in spatial inequalities within and between regions, aggravation of poverty in the neglected regions and a transfer of poverty to the economically favoured core areas through population migration.

The Human Dimension

Ghana's development planning has intensified regional disparities. While regional disparities, in and of themselves, do not necessarily imply injustice (for they may reflect real differences in natural resource endowments), they do raise questions about social justice when inequalities result in geographical differences in life chances. If life chances of individuals are determined by the geographical region they live in, then the concept of territorial justice becomes an important geographical issue.

Life chances are a function of real incomes and the level of services that are to be found in a region. Absolute poverty has the most serious negative impact on human wellbeing and poverty elimination is a recognised development objective in all planning circles. It is important to note that reduced inequality and elimination of poverty are not synonmous. As Streeten and Stewart (1981) point out that poverty elimination is concerned with absolute income levels of certain groups of society while reduced inequality is concerned with relative and not absolute income levels. Policies which raise the average income of a poor region cannot be assumed to reduce the absolute poverty of the poorest groups within that region. Increasing incomes in the upper levels of the income distribution, for example through relocation incentives, may be an efficient strategy for reducing regional inequalities but is not relevant to poverty elimination. This will be confusing place prosperity with people prosperity.

It is necessary to use indicators in order to assess absolute poverty levels in different regions. The Physical Quality of Life Index (PQLI) is used in this paper to portray spatial variations in the life chances in Ghana. The PQLI index has been derived by using three indicators and the method suggested by the Overseas Development Council (Morris 1979). The three indicators - infant mortality, life expectancy and literacy - are combined into a weighted composite index in the PQLI.

The PQLI is not without shortcomings and these have been dis cussed by Larson and Wilford (1979) and summarised briefly in Areetey Attoh and Chatterjee (1988). For example, the PQLI index does not take into account additional variables that are relevant to the quality of life of an individual. It assumes that human beings value life expectancy, improved health, survival of their children, enhanced potentials for earning and the ability to read more than all else. In spite of criticisms about the universality of such assumptions, the PQLI is a useful indicator for it pays attention to basic needs which have been identified as being important development objectives by analysts. Perhaps it's greatest strength is that the three variables measure "results" or "outputs" of development rather than inputs such as monetary flows or level of subsidies.

The results of the PQLI ratings of the nine States of Ghana are presented in Table 2. The results indicate, not surprisingly, a higher level of well being in the southern states, particularly in the Greater Accra region. The lowest levels are in the Northern and Upper regions - the states with the lowest per capita income. Infant mortality in these two States is more than three times that of Greater Accra. Literacy rates are less than one sixth of that of Greater Accra and average life expectancy of 38-39 years can be contrasted to the 68 years of expected life in the Greater Accra region. Thus regional inequalities are severe enough to affect life chances and southern Ghana has a higher level of well being relative to the northern states.

TABLE 2: **The PQLI: Infant Mortality, Literacy, Life Expectancy at Age One**

Region	Infant Mortality		Literacy		Life Expectancy		PQLI
	Rate	Index	Rate	Index	Rate	Index	Index
Greater Accra	56	78	50.9	60	64	68	69
Western	111	53	37.9	38	45	18	36
Central	140	40	33.3	33	44	16	30
Eastern	124	47	42.8	43	48	26	39
Volta	130	45	37.5	38	54	42	42
Ashanti	124	47	27.9	28	52	37	37
Brong-Ahafo	142	39	38.0	38	47	24	34
Northern	168	27	7.7	8	39	3	13
Upper	192	17	7.4	7	38	1	8

Source: 1. Republic of Ghana, *Education Statistics: 1972-1973*, Central Bureau of Statistics, Accra, 1976.
2. S.K. Gaisie, Determinants of Population Growth in Ghana, Ph.D. Thesis, Australian National University, Canberra, 1973.

An Alternative Model for Regional Development

Regional inequalities, decline in standards of living and increasing poverty in Ghana results from choices made by local and national elites attempting to maximise their own welfare. The reasons for and the characteristics associated with such choices have been analysed very clearly by core - periphery and dependency theorists. The manner in which international elites form alliances with national elites, use instruments such as capital intensive technology, subsidised credit, international trade, exchange rates and like to further their class interests has received considerable analytical attention in the last three decades. The literature is dominated by the discussion of causes and effects, there is much less focus on what can be done to stop and redress this. Reformers who have tried to go against these dominant trends associated with neocolonialism have been foiled by their national and international elites. In this section there is a discussion of Gandhi's ideas about development strategy that has the potential to address this.

Gandhi's ideas about strategies that oppressed groups can adopt to gain their political freedom and civil liberties are well known. Gandhi also had very firm ideas about desirable development strategies for ex-colonial countries after their achievement of political freedom. However, his ideas about development strategies are less well known since India, after her independence, chose to ignore Gandhi's ideas for economic reconstruction in favour of alternative development strategies that emanated from Western universities. Given the failure of development planning to increase the welfare of the economically oppressed and to provide basic needs to all citizens of a country, it appears an opportune time to explore the attributes of the Gandhian model for development particularly with respect to the achievement of economic freedom and economic justice.

Gandhi wrote extensively on the characteristics of desirable development strategies, particularly with India's impending independence he became very concerned about protecting the welfare of the politically and economically weaker groups. Among the various ideas he expounded, three are discussed in this paper for reasons of feasibility. Firstly, the relevance of the collaborative principal is described. Secondly, the planning implications of his emphasis on small community development are explored. Thirdly, the issue of appropriate technology, physical and institutional, discussed. This section draws on Das's (1979) exposition of Gandhian economic thought.

The underlying basis of the Gandhian system is an emphasis on the collaborative principle. The concept of collaborative economic behaviour differs from it's two primary alternatives - the competitive, individualistic behaviour underlying the market system and the collectivist, bureaucratic behaviour underlying centralised planning systems. In the former the welfare of each individual is maximised through the self seeking, autonomous behaviour of each, in the latter the welfare of each individual is maximised through the collective. In the collaborative system, the unit whose welfare is being maximised is a social microgroup that is larger than a household but smaller than a collective. Gandhi believed that human welfare, particularly of disadvantaged and poverty groups, would be maximised not through the anarchy of the market place where economically powerful individuals could express their preferences at the cost of the economically weaker groups in society, nor through the centralised system where the politically powerful groups could express their preferences through political controls but through small groups that could be unified around their common interest. These groups would cooperate within to maximise their welfare. Das (1979, p. 120) notes that there is an increasing recognition of the importance of collaborative economic behaviour of microgroups in market and centralised systems. For example, in market societies, manufacturing firms have incorporated microgroup production systems in labour management practice. In collectivist, centralised systems the importance of the micro brigade is recognised, for example in Cuba and China. Thus Gandhi's emphasis on the microgroup as the unit was farsighted.

If the collaborative principle were to be adopted, then this would imply that the economically weaker groups of a geographical area would work with local elites to improve the welfare of the locality or the group and combine against the interests of external, exploitative elites. This would be contrary to the increasingly dominant model in developing countries wherein local elites combine with external elites to maximise their narrow self interest. Gandhi was no stranger to the presence of selfishness and greed. However, he believed that the weaker members of a society could use non-violent struggle to ensure the downfall of exploitative elites and the rise of decision makers that would respect the collaborative principle and group welfare. His political success shows that active, non-violent, mass-resistance can bring about the emergence of good decision makers. Unfortunately his principles have not been tested in the economic sphere except in some spectacularly successful isolated cases.

The tribal system in Ghana with the election of responsible Chiefs who maximised group welfare provides an example of the successful operation of the collaborative principle. Unfortunately, these cultural systems are being destroyed and replaced by either the anarchy of the market place or the retention of the Chiefdom system wherein power is used by titulary rulers to maximise their own, instead of group, welfare. The corruption associated with the atomistic definition of welfare has emerged as a major reason for inefficiencies and inequities - regional or interhousehold.

Gandhi repeatedly pointed out the dangers of attempting to modernise production technology at a rate faster than the economy could support, particularly where capital intensity depended on foreign capital and international trade. He predicted that the short term gains would lead to structural unemployment and lowering of the living conditions of the weaker members of society. Such a strategy would lead to all of the characteristics that have been highlighted by dependency theorists - the emergence of local elites allied to international elites in the core countries, corruption, distortion of policies in favour of capital intensive development and like. These characteristics of dependency are descriptive of Ghana as well as most developing countries. Gandhi had foreseen these events as being the logical consequences of a capital intensive, manufacturing based development strategy.

Gandhi had emphasised the importance of investment in agriculture and the use of appropriate technology for the production of basic necessities such as clothes. Emphasis on these sectors would increase the consumption of all and provide the necessary basis for industrialization. Current emphasis on basic goods production to meet the basic needs of all are recent statements that rarely acknowledge Gandhi's half a century earlier similar concerns about the meaning of development. Ghana's neglect of the agricultural sector has caused rampant inflation of food prices, shortages of commodities and the high import content. A Gandhian strategy would have benefited the northern states that are primarily agricultural. Regional inequalities and the low PQLI index of the northern States would thus have been avoided. Clearly Ghana's record, certainly not unique among developing countries, provides evidence of Gandhi's foresight and intuition.

Gandhi emphasised the revival of rural economies, village development and the control of disfunctional urbanization. These were perceived by his more modern contemporaries as being archaic since, in the western world, increased urbanization had gone hand in hand with economic growth. Given the realities of the expansion of megacities in the developing world and the difficulties faced by third world countries in providing basic services to the poor, Gandhi's ideas hardly seem unrealistic and utopian. The successful record of countries such as Japan, Taiwan and Korea in market societies and of China in a socialist context, that had emphasised agricultural development as a precondition of industrial development, show the wisdom of Gandhi's policy for economic reconstruction of ex-colonial countries.

A central component of rural development was his emphasis on the recognition of local economic planning which would use local resources optimally, to produce locally the items needed to meet the basic needs of the community. While local area planning is emphasised in many developing countries, this is not consistent with Gandhi's ideas since his concept can be interpreted as small area or microgroup participatory planning. Local area planning in the context of the collaborative economic principle is different from local area planning based on bureaucratic endeavours and leadership. Moreover, Gandhi's ideas of local self government and local self determination is applicable to other microgroups such as the tenants of a government housing project, a factory division, a marketing cooperative to name a few. These are all areally based microgroups and extension of Gandhi's ideas are as relevant as his statements about the village economy.

Only a few of his ideas are discussed here because attention to these concerns has the potential for changing Ghana's downward slide, improving the regional distribution of resources and increasing the welfare of the masses. Ghana has experimented with the international trade based market system, rapid capital intensive industrialization for a pan-African market, with socialism and emphasis of Soviet type of development. None of these strategies appear to have worked. At this conjuncture Gandhi's ideas has considerable potential.

Concluding Comments

It is common knowledge that regional conflict in developing countries is a catalyst for super power confrontations. Problems of poverty, malnutrition, poor life chances of large numbers of domestic groups, and competing ideologies about mitigating these problems become the basis of violent civil strifes. These rapidly escalate and become internationally cast in terms of super power rivalry. As long as ideas about development strategies are drawn from either the political ideology of the socialist left or the conservative right such internationalising of domestic problems will continue. Since the world is divided along these political ideologies into the first and second world, the countries of the third world will exacerbate their problems as long as they are drawn into super power rivalries and provide a remote controlled theatre for violent struggle.

The root cause of these violent rivalries lies in regional and intergroup inequalities. Exploitation of peoples between the various regions of a country is dangerous for the third world countries. Therefore the desirable solution lies in the minimisation of these inequalities. Since attempts to reduce inequalities after the fact have not succeeded, the alternative model that would minimise inequalities at source and through the use of appropriate institutions is certainly worth consideration.

Development planning has focussed on such questions as what share of national income should be allocated to peripheral and backward regions. How much of this allocation should be given to infrastructure, agriculture, industry, housing and health. What incentives should be given to investors, domestic and foreign, in order to induce them to invest capital and locate in these regions. There is little discussion of what type of infrastructure is most beneficial to the masses that cause these regions to be defined as backward. There is little discussion of what forms of technology are most appropriate for agricultural or industrial development. Or for that matter in what form should the capital in its money form be translated into its physical and technological form. How can these be linked to social welfare, democratic expression of the preference of the masses and political stability. As long as we continue to view the problems of poorer regions and groups of people only in terms of their monetary expression, the problems of the poor will not be appropriately addressed. We need to focus on the identification of appropriate institutions and forms of technology instead of only on expenditures, capital investment and like. Gandhi's ideas on economic and spatial justice have much to contribute in this regard.

REFERENCES

1. Aryeetey Attoh, S. and L. Chatterjee, 1988, "Regional Inequalities in Ghana: Assessment and Policy Issues, Tijdshrift voor Economische en Sociale Geografie 79, 1: 31-38.
2. Central Bureau of Statistics, Government of Ghana.
3. Economic Intelligence Unit, 1985, Quarterly Economic Review of Ghana, Sirra Leone, Liberia Annual Supplement, The Economist, U.K.
4. Bose, N.K., ed. 1948, Selections from Gandhi, Navajivan Publishing House, Ahmedabad, India.
5. Das, A., 1979, Foundations of Gandhian Economics, St. Martin's Press, New York.
6. Desai, V.C.A Gandhi Anthology, Vol. 1 & 2, Navajivan Publishing House, Ahmedabad, India.
7. Gandhi, M.K., Towards Non-Violent Socialism, Navajivan Publishing House, Ahmedabad, India.
8. Gandhi, M.K., Young India, 1919-28, Ganesan, India.
9. Gupta, S., The Economic Philosophy of Mahatma Gandhi, Ashok Publishing House, Delhi, India.
10. Larson D. and W. Wilford, 1979, The PQLI: A Useful Social Indicator? World Development, 7, pp. 581-584.
11. Morris, M.D., ed., 1979, Measuring the Conditions of the World's Poor: The Physical Quality of Life Index, Pergamon Press, New York.
12. Roemer, Michael, 1984, "Ghana, 1950 - 1980: Missed Opportunities" In A. Harberger ed., World Economic Growth, ICS Press, SanFrancisco.
13. Streeten P. and F. Stewart, 1981, New Strategies for Development: Poverty, Income Distribution and Growth in P. Streeten ed., Development Perspectives, pp. 148-174, Oxford University Press, Oxford.

15

TOWARDS A GANDHIAN APPROACH TO PLANNING

B.P. PANDEY

"Real Planning", wrote Gandhiji,[1] "consists in the best utilization of entire manpower of India." This is in complete consonance with the ideal of "Full Employment" as economists call it. As everyone had to be ensured an opportunity to earn his bread, the need for full employment arose. "We should be ashamed of resting or having a square meal", Gandhiji told his countrymen, "So long as there is one able bodied man or woman without work or food."[2] Thus work and food went together in the Gandhian scheme of things and in the Indian situation these two had to be made the basic goals of planning.

The social structure that Gandhiji envisaged for free India was defined by him as follows:

"In this structure composed of innumerable villages, there will be ever widening, never ascending circles. Life will not be a pyramid with the apex sustained by the bottom. But it will be an oceanic circle whose centre will be the individual already ready to perish for the village, the latter ready to perish for the circle of villages, till at last the whole becomes one life composed of individuals, never aggressive in their arrogance, but ever humble, sharing the majesty of the oceanic circle of which they are an integrated unit. Therefore, the outermost circumference will not wield power to crush the inner circle but will give strength to all within and derive its own strength from it."[3]

In such a structure of society a decentralized State power is needed. The people's power will be the core of State power in such a society. He expressed his strong disapproval of centralization of authority and power in a small coterie or oligarchy in a democratic State. That would be a negation of democracy. "True democracy", he pointed out, cannot be worked by 20 men sitting at the centre. It has to be worked from below by the people of every village."

In the Gandhian way of thinking, planning must touch the life of each and every citizen and the commonest among the common men must understand the goal and meaning of planning. There must be participation by the masses in the process of development and the State should have a minimum role to play in such a process. There should be little scope for the members of the State to exploit their position, and they should be paid an allowance based not on the fabulous profits of merchants but on the average earnings of the citizens of villages.

Such a planned development would be labour-intensive and not capital-intensive; the production for exports would receive the least priority; the goal of forest policy would be to protect and preserve the forests so that they meet the needs of people and keep up the level of their economic activity rather than to maximize revenue; there would not be any greedy exploitation of mineral resources; the transport and communication policy would serve the interests of the villagers' economic activity and it would not be used for impoverishing and draining the village economy; and there would not be any centralization of production of consumption goods. The top priorities of such a planning would be (i) agricultural development, (ii) development of village industries, (iii) promotion of housing, health and cleanliness, (iv) spread of education in villages, (v) promotion of village organization and (vi) encouragement to cultural development of villages.

Jawahar Lal Nehru who became the first Prime Minister of India wanted to see India as modern scientifically advanced industrial nation at the earliest. He had been highly impressed by the industrial advance that the Soviet Union had made within a short period through socialism and planning. He wanted to replicate the Soviet experience in India without going communist. He thought that he would build a "socialist pattern of society" in this country through a strong vibrant "public sector" that occupies "commanding heights" of the economy and by preventing the capitalist private sector from concentrating economic power in its hands and acquiring monopoly power. The latter objcctive was to be achieved through use of State power for democratizing the industrial subsector in which the private sector would be allowed to operate and imposition of an elaborate system of controls and licensing that would circumscribe its entire operation.

When the First Five Year Plan was prepared, a series of discussions on the objectives and strategy of planning took place between Vinoba Bhave and the members of the Indian Planning Commission sometime in the middle of 1951. They differed completely on the fundamental issues. Vinoba pointed out that the planners had not suggested adequate measures for the upliftment of the poor and the backward in the draft outline of the First Five Year Plan. He disapproved of the pattern of economic reconstruction visualized by the Planning Commission. He wanted that in keeping with the provisions of the Constitution, the basic objective and foundation of planning should be to provide food, work and wages to every citizen within a definite period of time and that India should achieve self-sufficiency in food by a definite date. He reiterated that in order to provide work for all, our villages will have to be made self-sufficient and the village and cottage industries will have to be accorded the topmost priority not as a transitory step but as a permanent policy. He questioned the planners' emphasis on the growth of large-scale industry and their policy of encouragement to cach crops in place of food crops for earning foreign exchange. He also objected to the Government's programme of artificial means of family planning.[4] But the Planning Commission did not accept Vinoba's views.

The Basis for Gandhian Planning

Gandhi in his writings did not develop any planning model but he expressed some economic ideas on which an analyst can base the formulation of a model for planning. The economic ideas and principles enunciated by Gandhiji have been quoted and analysed in the following paragraphs.

Gandhi rightly pointed out, "According to me the economic constitution of India and for that matter of the world should be such that no one under it should suffer from want of food and clothing. In other words, every body should be able to get sufficient work to enable him to make two ends meet. And this ideal can be universally realised only if means of production of the elementary necessities of life remain in the control of the masses. They should be freely available to all as God's air and water are or ought to be...their monopolisation by any country, nation or group of persons would be unjust... the neglect of this simple principle is the cause of the destitution that we witness today not only in this unhappy land but in other parts of the world too."[5]

Undoubtedly Gandhi wanted a Planning Model for India which could solve the unemployment problem in the country. This idea of Gandhiji is relevant not only in connection with India but all the underdeveloped and overpopulated countries which can adopt such a model. Gandhiji's philosophy of *swadeshi* led to self-reliance as a major objective of Indian planning. For providing full employment to the people of India Gandhiji wanted a widespread network of khadi and village industries in the countryside for poverty alleviation and for solving the problem of unemployment. He said, "if the government can provide full employment to our people without the help of khadi and village industries, I shall be prepared to wind up my constructive programme in this sphere." Regarding minimum standards for the people Gandhiji said to Shriman Narayan, "Whatever minimum standards you prescribe should be made available to all citizens without any distinction more especially to the poorest sections." During the course of his discussion with Gandhiji, Shriman Narayan said that Gandhiji was very keen to bring about maximum regional self-sufficiency in regard to food, clothing and shelter in the rural areas.

Gandhiji wanted modernization and reconstruction but he was of the opinion that side by side with economic development and progress proper emphasis should be laid on promoting ethical and spiritual values in life. To Gandhiji, the essence of *sarvodaya* was *antyodaya* or concern for the lowliest. Unless the priorities in planning are reoriented to the felt needs of the poorest of the poor, more planning on a comprehensive scale becomes more or less a luxury that an underdeveloped country like India can hardly afford.

The Mahatma believed in micro planning by creating models of economic development which could inspire the neighbouring areas and ultimately the whole nation. Talking to workers at Sevagram, Gandhiji said, "Shaping Sevagram into an ideal village of my dreams is as difficult as to make India an ideal country. But if one can produce one ideal village he will have provided a pattern not only for the whole country but perhaps for the whole world."

Mahatma highlighted the role of decentralized production in the countryside for the simple reason that in a densely populated country like India, the problems of higher production and full employment could be solved not by mass production but by "production by the masses".

Regarding the decentralized planning certain critics raised the objection that the basis of Gandhian programme is decentralization but the core of planning is centralization, so how could Gandhism and planning go together. Gandhiji answered this question as below:

"Your objection to the word 'plan' is technically valid. But I am inclined to say there is no substance in the objection. I must dissent from the view that the core of planning is centralization. Why should not decentralization tend itself to planning as well as centralization."[6]

Fundamentals of Gandhian Planning

In this connection we should like to discuss three basic principles of Dr. Sun Yat Sen – nationalism, democracy and livelihood. Our planning should be based on the indigenous culture and civilization of the nation and should be in the nature of an organic growth, it should also promote welfare and happiness of the whole nation and not merely of a small selected class or group. This should be the first principle of any plan of economic development. Secondly, our planning should not result in regimentation of the masses. We must plan for democracy and not for totalitarian control. Economic planning should necessitate the least amount of State control and coercion. We should remember that political democracy is impossible without economic equality. The third principle of planning should be that every citizen of a nation is entitled to earn his or her livelihood by just and honourable means. Each citizen has an inalienable right to work and to reap a decent harvest of his honest labour.

Mahatma Gandhi has emphasized the above three principles of planning as enunciated by Dr. Sun Yat Sen but in different words. Gandhiji did not want the development of India on industrial lines. "My views on national planning differ from the prevailing ones. I do not want it along industrial lines. I want to prevent our villages from catching the infection of industrialism."

Gandhiji wanted purity of means and ends in the system of planning. Gandhiji will have nothing to do with violence because in a planned society planning is only a means and not an end in itself. Even if it were the end he does not subscribe to the theory that the end justifies the means. In order to conserve the purity of the end, the means employed for its attainment must be equally pure. That is why Gandhiji maintains that even a socialist society should be established through non-violence and not through a bloody revolution.

The planning model based on Gandhian ideology should be based upon the following economic principles expressed by Gandhiji:

1. *Simplicity and Limited Wants*: Voluntary limitations on wants correspond to truth.[7] Gandhiji was of the opinion that multiplicity of wants is the great vice of the modern materialistic civilization. The Western concept of modernization does not suit the idea of simplicity and minimum wants. In our planning process the economic and social policies should be made in consonance with the needs of millions who fall below the line of poverty.

2. *Non-violent Ownership–Trusteeship*: The limitations of wants can pave a way to change of heart of those who own the means of production. The trusteeship allows the right to private property in the means of production as long as it is responsible to the needs of

the community. The trusteeship is sarvodaya extended to "firms".

3. *Non-violent Production-Appropriate Technology*: "Appropriateness" is used to designate the production function that maximizes human need satisfaction. No technology should be used which economizes on manual labour while there are unemployed workers in the community.

4. *In an Agrarian Economy Like Ours*: we need a decentralized system of economy, polity, planning, production and decision making. It also fits into a democratic structure. If "appropriate technology" is the means, "decentralization" is the end. Without following a decentralized structure of our economy, we cannot develop our villages as desired.

We can use machines whenever they are badly needed but there should not be a craze for machinery.

5. *Non-violent Consumption–Non-possession*: This concept is related to the minimization of wants. Non-possession follows strictly from "ahimsa". After all every body has got a right to get the basic necessities of life, so one should follow the golden rule to refuse to have what millions cannot. This will prohibit the infinite multiplicity of human wants. The idea of non-possession can be propagated and practised through a social movement. Without this the anti-poverty programme run by the government will not bring the desired results.

6. *Non-violent Work–Bread Labour*: Gandhiji was of the opinion that everybody should do labour to earn his bread. He was convinced that just one hour of daily manual work would induce doctors and lawyers to moderate the fees that they charge for their talents. The poets and philosophers will be induced for better creativity in their arts through manual labour.

7. *Non-violent Allocation–Cooperation*: Gandhiji was not a believer in competition which generates fear and insecurity which in turn breed greed and violence. Cooperation on the other hand appeals to the human element of need to serve each other.

8. *Non-violent Distribution–Equality*: Equality meant to Gandhi

primarily two things: (i) Every body has a basic right to live, meaning thereby his essential needs should be fulfilled, (ii) equality means absence of exploitation.

9. *Self-reliant Village Economy*: If we are interested to make village republics and if our motto is to see an oceanic circle, it is very essential to make the village "self-reliant". It fits with the concepts of *decentralization* and *swadeshi*.

10. *Non-violence in Reforming Economic System*: Gandhiji never wanted capitalism but he wanted its destruction by non-violent means. He wanted to transform capitalism into communitarian socialism through the trusteeship model. He wanted a peaceful communitarian socialism rather than the Marxian path of class war and violent revolution. He was of the view that a communitarian society can be achieved by peaceful means.

In this way we find that by fitting the economic ideas of Gandhiji into the axioms of truth and non-violence we can make an attempt to develop a Gandhian model for planning.

Investment Criteria in Gandhian Economics

By integrating various economic ideas of Gandhiji, it is possible to construct a model of Gandhian economy.[8] A non-violent, non-exploitative and egalitarian social order is conceptualized by such a model. Such a model is guided by the fundamental principle of *sarvodaya*–welfare of a whole society like any other model. Gandhian model also may generate a number of economic activities or functions+ such as savings, investment, production, distribution, consumption and growth. Each of these functions is based on Gandhian moral, ethical and philosophical principles. The doctrines of swadeshi, non-possession, trusteeship, non-violence, economic equality and bread labour are some of the essential elements that constitute the philosophical infrastructure of the Gandhian economic system.

Undoubtedly an economic system needs an organizational structure. Several Gandhian economists have tried to develop such an infrastructure. The work of Suresh Desai[9] is a notable example in such an area. In such a model the investment decision maker at all levels–private and public–is a trustee, guided by the principles of economic equality, non-possession, non-stealing, non-exploitation, *swadeshi* and *sarvodaya*. For a trustee who is acting as a decision-maker, it has to be constantly reminded that any investment has an economic purpose as well as a moral purpose, the conventional set of investment criteria are sensitive to the economic purpose but not to the moral purpose of society. The fundamental principles of Gandhian economics as enunciated in the preceding paragraphs enable us to define such moral purpose and design accordingly a set of investment criteria, suiting to Gandhian economy. This is where Gandhian welfare economics can meaningfully integrate economics and ethics.

It is generally said that the Gandhian model conceptualized in such a manner is slow moving. But we have an example of communist China bearing the testimony of Gandhian model with its village orientation, local technology and small units of production. Gandhian values have got some positive contributions to make to economic growth as enumerated below:[10]

1. Capital formation has always been considered as a prerequisite of growth. In this context, Gandhi's emphasis on prudent, frugal and unostentatious life is highly relevant.

2. Similarly his emphasis on *swadeshi* helps to check the demonstration effect which is another important constraint on development.

3. Gandhiji's emphasis on village and cottage industries is of utmost importance. Prof. D.H. Cole says, "Gandhian campaign for the development of the home made cloth industry–khaddar–is a practical attempt to relieve the poverty and uplift the standard of the Indian villages."[11] Prof. G. Myrdal, in his *Asian Drama*, has advocated decentralized industry as best suited for India and has fully supported Gandhi's programmes for the protection and promotion of cottage industries in the villages. Gandhiji was an advocate of "appropriate technology" that is, technology with human face.

4. That unbridled growth leads to stagnation and decay is now

fully brought out by those like *Limits to Growth*. Thus what is needed is optimization of resources. The Gandhian concept of economy of permanence is suited in this context.

5. People's participation in development programmes is desired by Gandhiji.

6. It was "self-reliance" from personal and territorial points of view which Gandhi advocated for poor countries.

7. Most of the growth models have got distributional defects. Gandhian model establishes an organic relationship between production and distribution. Such a relationship does not give rise to distributional defects. Production by masses means distribution to the masses.

8. Gandhiji has democratized the whole process of development having an emphasis on decentralization.

9. Gandhi wanted to build up a new India in terms of *Gram Swaraj*.

Lastly, Gandhi always stressed the human factor in economic development. He wanted a balanced regional growth. He emphasized the activities such as sanitation, health, agriculture and basic education as priority sectors. He wanted redistribution of wealth for greater equality. Gandhiji wanted an "integrated planning" for the country but not in the way as it is being implemented today.

Conclusion

Under the framework of Gandhian alternative, we want a decentralized economic order. We want participation of people in formulation and implementation of programmes. The decentralized system in production, in planning, in decision-making and in administration is required at all levels. Village and cottage industries in our rural economy can solve the problem of production, distribution, consumption and exchange. The concepts of "truth", "non-violence" and "swadeshi" will fit in our decentralized economic order.

REFERENCES

1. *Harijan*, March 23, 1947, p. 79.
2. *Young India*, October 6, 1921, p. 314.
3. *Harijan*, July 28, 1946.
4. See, Nargalkar, Vasant, *The Greed of Saint Vinoba*, Bhartiya Vidya Bhavan, Bombay, 1963, pp. 188-193 and Nfarayan, Shriman, *Towards the Gandhian Plan*, p.7.
5. *The Hindu*, June 28, 1946.
6. *Harijan*. 29.9.1940
7. Gandhi M.K., *Voluntary Poverty* compiled by G. Ravindra Karkar, Navajeevan, 1961.
8. A.M. Huq, Investment Criteria in Gandhian Economics, *Gandhi Marg*, May 1986.
9. Suresh A. Desai, The Role of Price System in Gandhian Economics, Gandhi Marg, March 1981.
10. Thanu, L.C., "Relevance of Gandhian Thought to Economic Growth", *Gandhi Marg*, No. 83, Feb. 1986.
11. Narayan, Shriman, *Gandhi the Man and His Thought* (1969), p. 43.

16

GANDHIAN CONCEPT OF INDIAN VILLAGE

SURESH MISRA

Gandhi's philosophy offers a practical way to a peaceful social revolution to improve the quality of life. What he preached was not only for the Indian masses but for the entire deprived people of the world. His message was not for a particular time but for the future of the mankind, especially his theory of non-violence and peaceful co-existence.

But his immediate concern was the Indian masses, especially in the countryside. Gandhiji was of the view that the Indian problem was not merely political or economic but manysided. In fact people needed courage and sense of self-respect to enable themselves to come out of the slavish mentality developed over centuries of bondage. In his view if these conditions were to be changed, politics, education, social reform, economy, and technology had to suit the genius of the society.

Gandhi, therefore, devoted himself completely to the cause of village reconstruction. He tried to uplift the standard and quality of rural life through the active participation of people themselves. It was easy for the masses to understand him better because he spoke in their language and lived like them–a life of utter simplicity and succeeded in enlisting their participation in the struggle for freedom.

According to Gandhi, the individual was of supreme importance. He believed in the inner development of man. He said man must pursue truth and non-violence in life if he wants inner contentment. Purity of means was more important than the desirability of the end. He believed that if the means were pure, one was bound to reach the goal. As far as possible any imposition or curtailment of individual freedom should be avoided. Equality which is the basis of economic independence must be achieved through peaceful and non-violent methods. Perhaps Gandhi's attitude to violence makes his message of special significance to the modern age. For him personal liberty was of the great value.

Gandhi's love for the Indian masses was great. It is difficult to deny the fact that he knew India the best. He knew it with his ears and his eyes. He was intensely concerned about poverty. He wanted to utilize the energies of the vast army of rural unemployed to produce more goods for the nation and some wealth for themselves. He measured progress in terms of human happiness and wanted a social order that would secure the greatest good of all. He wanted a society in which every man would have equal opportunity and freedom to develop. He knew that the villages were the nerve-centres of India and if India were to develop and prosper it should not copy the European model of development. Rather it should evolve a model that would suit its millions of starved children.

As early as 1936, Mahatma Gandhi remarked, "I would say that if the village perishes India will perish too." He added, "I have believed and repeated times without number that India is to be found not in the few cities but in its 7,00,000 villages. Perhaps it was only Gandhi who understood the real India best. His role was crucial in awakening the most dormant and stagnant sector of Indian society, viz. the Indian village. By drawing the village into the mainstream of national awakening, Gandhi played a unique role in Indian history. Without the awakening of rural India under his leadership the economic growth and social development which followed India's achievement of freedom would have been inconceivable.[1]

It is, therefore, not surprising that constructive programmes for rebuilding the life of the countryside became an integral part of the total programme of Mahatma Gandhi. In fact to build the Indian village was in a way his main mission. The prevailing situation could be changed with the active participation and cooperation of the villagers themselves. The blueprint that he has given is unique provided the real essence of his programme is understood in the Indian context. The basic principles that formed his idea of rural reconstruction were: communal unity, removal of untouchability, prohibition, use of Khadi, promotion of village industries, upliftment of underprivileged classes and women, full employment, promotion of economic equality and self-sufficient village economy. Above all he preached a simple life and for the development of moral values in society he conceptualised an integrated rural development programme that would serve the Indian needs best.

Man of Great Practical Wisdom

Gandhi was not only a man of ideas but also a person of great practical wisdom. He worked out meticulously the details of a wide variety of practical things which are vital to building a graceful village life. His conception of an ideal village was a comprehensive one encompassing the economic, political, social and educational dimensions. Gandhi's conception of village was not anchored on the "Modern (urban industrial) notion of development" but on the post-modern perspective of quality of life."[2] His main emphasis was on the quality of life. He said, "My ideal village will contain intelligent human beings. They will not live in dirt and drunkenness as animals.... There will be neither plague nor cholera, nor small-pox. No one will wallow in luxury. Everyone will have to contribute his quota of manual labour.[3]

Gandhi's Gram Swaraj was not the resurrection of the old village but the formation of fresh independent units of villages having a self-sufficient economy. He clearly spelt out the political and economic relations that ought to exist in the village. For him Man was supreme. The end to be sought is human happiness combined with full mental and moral growth. Self-sufficiency in basic needs was one of the fundamental conditions of Gandhian Village reconstruction. Food, clothing and other basic necessities should be produced at the village level itself, this will lead to full employment and the employment of almost each able-bodied person and this will prevent the rural-to-urban migration in search of employment and better opportunities.

His main mission in life was to make villages a "thing of beauty". He said, "An ideal village will be so constructed as to lend itself to perfect sanitation. It will have cottages with sufficient light and ventilation, but of a material obtainable within a radius of five miles of it. The cottages will have courtyards enabling the householders to plant vegetables for domestic use and to house their cattle. The village lanes and streets will be free of all avoidable dust. It will have wells according to its needs and accessible to all. It will have houses of worship for all, also a common meeting place, common pastures for grazing its cattle, a co-operative dairy, primary and secondary schools in which industrial education will be the central factor and it will have village panchayats for settling disputes. It will produce its own grains, vegetables, and fruits and its own Khadi."[4] What is of importance is that Gandhi not only visualized the development of the village but the community as a whole. A theory of interdependence and co-existence which would lead to overall growth and development.

Traditionally, there has been a controversy about Gandhi's view regarding modern technology and heavy machinery and industry. I feel it would be a misunderstanding of Gandhian philosophy and ideology as well. In fact Gandhi was not against modern technology and industry. He never objected to industrialization. He maintained that what we need is not mass production but production by the masses. Given in the Indian context and in the light of the European exploitation of Indian craftsmen perhaps Gandhi did say the correct thing. He said "our people are poor, the solution to large-scale poverty does not lie in large - scale production which under a system based on private enterprise accumulates wealth in the hands of few but in spreading production in as many units as possible each of which will produce wealth for itself."[5]

Against Exploitation of Villagers

As early as 1936 he observed "there would be no objection to villagers using even the most modern machines and tools and they can make and can afford to use."[6] He was against the exploitation of villagers by the cities. He always had the common man in his mind. He asserted, "I do visualize electricity, ship-building, iron works, machine making and the like existing side by side with village handicrafts. Hitherto industrialization has been planned so as to destroy the village and village crafts. Under my scheme, nothing will be allowed to be produced by the cities which can be produced by villagers. The proper function of cities is to serve as clearing houses for village products."[7] However, Gandhiji preferred to replace large-scale manufacture by cottage production. To serve and to avoid starvation he believed that only cottage and village industries could bring prosperity back to India. He was not aiming at eradication of all machinery but only at its limitation. The political and economic compulsions of the time forced him to take a rigid stand against heavy industries. The British had totally ruined Indian village economy and Gandhi felt that in case India went in for heavy industrialization the poorer sections of society could never recover. His concern for the rural masses moulded his ideology.

Gandhi attached great importance to education. In fact he insisted on a sound good education and advocated free and compulsory education up to the final basic course. He attached special importance to women's education specially in health and hygiene. He believed that if every activity was conducted on a cooperative basis, there would be no caste as we have today. He attached great importance to village panchayats which would act as major popular agencies involving only the village people. In his structure composed of innumerable villages there will be ever-widening, never ascending circles. Life will not be a pyramid with the apex sustained by the bottom. But it will be a oceanic circle whose centre will be an individual always ready to perish for the circles of villages till at last the whole becomes one life composed of individuals never aggressive in their arrogance but ever humble sharing the majority of the oceanic circles of which they are integral units. Therefore, the outermost circumference will not weild power to crush the inner circle but will give strength to all within and derive its own strength from it. None will be the first and none the last.[8] In the final analysis, "the unit of society should be a village or call it a manageable small group of people who would in the ideal be self-sufficient as a unit and bound together in bonds of mutual cooperation and independence."[9]

To be self-sufficient is not be altogether self-contained. In no circumstances would we be able to produce all the things we need so, though our aim is complete self-sufficiency, we shall have to get from outside the village what we cannot produce in the village. We shall have to produce more of what we can to obtain in exchange what we are unable to produce. Thus, Gandhi spoke of collective inter-dependence and in a way asked for barter if it helped the community as such.

Trusteeship

Land was one of the main concerns of Gandhi. He argued for collective ownership and to be operated collectively. He advocated trusteeship of land. He said "the rich man will be left in possession of his wealth, of which he will use what he reasonably requires for his personal needs and will act as a trustee for the remainder to be used for society. He did not advocate the overthrow of the landed class but instead advised the zamindars that they "should give their tenants fixity of tenure, take a lively interest in their welfare, provide well-managed schools for their children, look after the sanitation and in a number of other ways make them feel that the zamindars are their true friends taking only a fixed commission for their manifold services. Thus Gandhiji wanted the zamindars to change their hearts and own only so much as they really needed and they should become trustees and trusted friends of the entire village community. This, he firmly believed, would pave the way for a non-violent society. It is here that the economists have greatly disagreed with Gandhi's concept of Trusteeship. By nature man is property conscious and it would be difficult to agree in practical terms that without State intervention the upper class would relinquish major part of its property and more so in a capitalist society where property relations and exploitation are best evident.

A feeling emerges that Gandhi did not give a major role to the peasants and saw them as passive people and advised them to wait for a change in the zamindar's heart. In fact, to an extent, Gandhi diluted the effects of Marxism through his theory of peaceful co-existence, non-violence and Trusteeship.

Keeping aside his theory of Non-violence and Trusteeship even his close associates and friends failed to understand the meaning and significance of the Village Society that he had advocated. Most of his close associates were people influenced by the European thought and way of life. In a letter to Pandit Nehru in 1945 he wrote, "I am convinced that if India is to attain true freedom and through India the world also sooner or later, the fact has to be recognized that the people have to live in the village, not in towns, in huts not in palaces. Crores of people will never be able to live in peace with each other in cities and palaces. They will have no recourse but to resort to both violence and untruth. I hold that without truth and non-violence there can be nothing but destruction of humanity. We can realize truth and non-violence only in the simplicity of the village life and the simplicity can best be found in the Charkha and all that the Charkha connotes. I must not fear if the world today is going the wrong way. It may be that India too will go that way and like the proverbial moth burn itself eventually in the flame around which it dances more and more fiercely. But it is my bounden duty up to my last breath to try and protect India and, through India, the entire world from such a doom. The essence of what I have said is that man should rest content with what are his real needs and become self-sufficient, if he does not have this control he cannot save himself."[10]

Probably Gandhi rightly predicted the destruction of mankind, the breakdown of moral values. He never asked men for more than they could give but only asked for all that they could afford to give. Few men in history have played the role that Mahatma Gandhi played and only with the weapon of non-violence. He touched the emotions and hearts of millions the world over. Today, when the entire world is reeling under the threat of nuclear holocaust Gandhiji's teaching of love, non-violence and truth has achieved greater significance. His life has itself become a message for the mankind. He did not leave any set theory or doctrine of Gandhism but his life, his simplicity reflecting his ideology and his philosophy has a great appeal for every human heart. May be, we are forgetting Gandhi in this materialistic world but Gandhi as a man will continue to inspire the mankind through generations to come.

What, therefore, is needed today is not so much the seminars and conferences to remember Gandhi as to work with true dedication for the principles that he cherished and always valued. It is a pity that just within 40 years of Independence, the Father of the Nation has become a mere ceremonial figure. The Great has become a dwarf among his own followers. Today the country needs to develop and propagate the ideals of this Great Man more than even before.

REFERENCES

1. P.C. Joshi, *Gandhi and Nehru: The Challenge of a New Society*.
2. T.K. Oommen, *Gandhi and Village. Towards a Critical Appraisal*, pp. 4-5.
3. M.K. Gandhi, *A Bunch of Old Letters*, 5.10.1945.
4. The Collected Works of Mahatma Gandhi.
5. *Harijan*.
6. *Harijan*, 29.8.1936.
7. *Ibid.*, 28.1.39.
8. T.K. Oommen, *Op. cit.*
9. N.K. Bose, *Studies in Gandhism*.
10. Jawaharlal Nehru, *Glimpses of World History*.

17

A JOURNEY TO SARVODAYA[1]

R.R. DIWAKAR

Gandhi was no doubt gifted with an adamantine will. He has equally the tenderest of hearts. It would not stop at mere sympathy for the sufferers of misery and degradation but move further to empathy – identification with the sufferer. He had seen and felt life at all levels.

Indian labourers, to save themselves from hunger, had fled to South Africa. Gandhi had seen and felt their degraded condition and their utter loss of the sense of human dignity. He spent the best part of his life to restore it through self-suffering Satyagraha.

Religions have been preaching pity, upgrading it by the word compassion for the poor and the downtrodden. They had tried to explain away the plight of the poor by saying that it was due to past

---

1. This article is based on the Presidential Address delivered by the author at the Twenty-sixth Sarvodaya Sammelan held at Jayaprakash Nagar from 13 to 15 April 1985. and first published in *Gandhi Marg* No. 76, July 1985, pp. 197-208.

karma or sin. Philosophers and philanthropists laid unction to their own sympathetic souls by gifts and charity for the poor. Socialists provoked class-war – there was a change of masters, no doubt; but the poverty of their spirit and love of power did not raise the spirit of the poor to new heights.

None of the redeemers of the poor and removers of their poverty, with all their alleviative and ameliorative measures, could root out the basic cause of poverty. Because they failed to ask a question!

Gandhi dared to ask the question and endeavoured to find a reply: Why are the poor poor at all?

Is poverty God-ordained? Can God who is All and Totally Good be so cruel as to create the poor? He cannot create what He Himself is not! Is Karma or Fate or Original Sin the cause of poverty and of the millions of the poor struggling to rise above the so-called poverty-line? No Creation could have been started like that.

Today's man cannot and ought not plead an alibi for the poor condition of his brothers and sisters with whom he claims close relationship as Homo Sapiens.

Yes, today and now, Gandhi would say: We and everyone of us have to own responsibility for the whole 'human condition' and begin remedying it.

The new knowledge that science has brought to us, says: All that exists and moves is but the play of Energy in Flux. We are one in essence and in fact. The old knowledge too has been saying the same thing in a different language: that it is Self-conscious Infinite Energy (GOD) manifesting itself as all creation. Conversion of these perceptions – new and old – into wisdom is today's self-conscious man's duty and responsibility here and now.

Gandhi spelt this wisdom in the form of Sarvodaya and the good and the progress of all sentient beings. That has to be our end and aim. It has to be based on the idea of total Trusteeship principle sans egocentrism and homocentrism, both of which are running riot now to the ruin of all.

It is the man-made socio-economic and political structures which are, singly as well as collectively, responsible for the present plight of man all over. Gandhi began a new journey for a legitimate, just and noble destiny with his new and only weapon. Truth through Ahimsa – Nonviolence.

The Origin

Like many other great concepts, the evolving and expanding concept of Sarvodaya had a small and humble beginning. By chance Gandhi's friend Polak gave him a small book *Unto This Last* by Ruskin while the former was on a railway journey in South Africa. Gandhi's hungry mind full of the milk of human kindness, groping for solutions to man's problems of poverty, suffering and misery on account of exploitation by his own kind, devoured the contents. He was so impressed by the book that he translated the book into Gujarati and called it *Sarvodaya: The Rise and Progress of All.* A fresh outlook, as of a crimson sunrise on a foggy day seemed to dawn on his consciousness as a sovereign ideal and a remedy to overcome all kinds of disparities and tensions in the relationship of human beings. The deplorable condition of the deprived of mankind revolting to every aspect of human dignity on account of man's injustice to man was ever present in the highly sensitive mind of Gandhi. He was seeking a way, worthy of man made in the image of God, to elevate him to his divine destiny.

In view of the extra emphasis often given to Western sources almost to the exclusion of indigenous sources, in the formation of the ideology and the build-up of Gandhi's personality, I would submit that the roots from which he drew the basic strength of his character and the fundamentals of his beliefs and ideas were in the nurture he had in the Indian spiritual culture of Oneness of Existence from his childhood, and the subsequent conscious absorption of the the essential teachings of the Gita and other holy books. But the natural catholicity of his mind made no such distinction of East or West. Light from whatever source it came was always welcome and Gandhi made it his own. And, then, it was 'Gandhian', and no longer Western or Eastern or even Indian. The originality of approach to all human problems was his own. His conscious awareness was like an extraordinary prism. When any flash of light entered the same, it came out in the form of brilliant rainbow colours which expressed themselves in the form of Adhyatma, Abhaya, Satya, Ahimsa, Prem, Sarvodaya, and Satyagraha.

Incidentally the word 'Sarvodaya' was a new contribution made by Gandhi to the already vast vocabulary of the ancient Sanskrit language. Like Gandhi's earlier addition of the word Satyagraha to Sanskrit, this word too went on gathering a rich connotation. Between them, these two words spell the whole teaching of Gandhi: the rise and all-round progress of all beings through Satyagraha, Ahimsa-oriented adherence to one's Truth unto Death.

I have deliberately used the expression 'all beings' because the Indian mind has never excluded sentient beings other than human beings, from the scope of its philosophy and its ethics. Gandhi himself in one of his intuitionist outbursts said, "all life is one". His love for the cow was, as he once put it, symbolic of his love for the whole dumb but sentient creation.

The Purpose of Life

India's history and her culture span over three millennia at least, if not more. There have been philosophies of life current in India since those remote times. They have not been merely systems of thought-structure spun out by the intellectuals, but they have been disciplines as well for living and rising to higher and noble levels of consciousness. Except the utterly atheistic and materialistic philosophy of the Charvaka School, other systems had as their aim the attainment of a twofold goal in life, and that was Abhyudaya – prosperity in worldly life, and Nishreyasa – the highest joy – abounding – of spiritual life, the Ananda of the Upanishads. Though this twofold aim and purpose of human life has been India's tradition, there has always been an overwhelming emphasis on spiritual attainment even to the detriment of worldly success sometimes and to a certain extent.

In common parlance, Dharma – religiously ordained human duties; Artha – acquisition of Wealth and its proper use, Kama –

natural human desires and urges as well as their fulfilment, and lastly but most importantly Moksha – the liberation of human consciousness from every kind of attachment, in order to attain Ananda – bliss, which is the natural condition and status of the human psyche, have been designated as the four Purusharthas or attainments in one's life. But it may be noted that Artha and Kama are sandwiched between Dharma and Moksha which are valued more than the other two!

It may be stated without any serious contradiction that almost all religions and philosophies of human life have the same twofold aim in life, namely well-being and success in the physical worldly life and the attainment of inner peace and unmixed happiness during one's own lifetime, and thereafter eternally for the soul. It is so because, a living human being is an unbreakable blend of the physical body with its senses and the subtle psyche which is spiritual in essence. So, a human being naturally seeks salvation for both of these two components of his being and existence while here on earth.

One more important aspect of the traditional beliefs, religions, philosophies, as well as spiritual thoughts is that the body-life-mind complex is temporary, perishable and of course expendable, while the psyche, the soul or the spirit inhabiting the complex is the eternal component of a human being which survives and is imperishable. Hence the greater or rather the greatest importance given to the life of the psyche, the spirit, the soul, the Atman or one may call it by any other name. I need not enter here further into other aspects of these beliefs. What I have stated already however was necessary from the point of view of understanding the concept of Sarvodaya and its implications.

The Beginnings

At the earliest stage, 'Sarvodaya' for Gandhi means three things: (i) the good of each individual in society consists in his effort to achieve the good of all; (ii) each function, be it physical, vital, mental, moral, aesthetic or spiritual necessary for a human society to progress is equal in value and there should not be any disparity in the remuneration due for it; and (iii) the life lived by performing duties involving labour is the best for all individuals.

For Gandhi, 'action' was the test of every theory and proposition. His two experiments; namely the Phoenix Settlement and Tolstoy Farm in South Africa, were both meant to implement the conclusions arrived at by him for bringing into existence an 'ideal human society' of his conception. Of course, all these experiments of his were subject to the greatest experiment of his life at that time, namely Satyagraha for the establishment of the rights of Indians in South Africa as equal citizens of the British Empire, without any distinction or discrimination on account of race or country or occupation.

I need not trace here the whole history as to how this Gangotri-like conception of Sarvodaya went on gathering speed and volume to become the Ganga of today at the hands of the originator and innovator Gandhi, and then how the stream swelled by the efforts of the saintly personality of Vinoba and strengthened by the dynamic revolutionary fervour of Jayaprakash. In fact, JP was the well-nigh for two decades or more known in India and abroad as the Sarvodaya leader. That is how Sarvodaya went on gathering more strength and richer connotation. Today it claims a place in the socio-economic philosophies of mankind. It would be an alternative to other existing ideologies for attaining and establishing a human society which can alleviate all disparities and distortions, which have crept into all the socio-economic-political structures and are stemming the tide of human progress as a whole. There are now vested interests which exploit society to the advantage of a comparatively small minority.

The 'Sarva' in Sarvodaya

The most important significance in the concept of Sarvodaya is to be attached to the prefix 'Sarva', that is, 'all' without exception. Further, Sarvodaya would very much begin by giving priority to the welfare and emancipation of the lowest of the low and the poorest of the poor. It is sometimes averred that Antyodaya is the very soul of Sarvodaya. Just as in a human family, the youngest and the most helpless child commands prior attention; so too, Sarvodaya social philosophy would well emphasise earliest attention to the most deprived among us.

Since Sarvodaya is a social philosophy meant for the whole of humanity and not restricted to any portion or section of it, a brief survey of the 'human condition' is necessary before I try to interpret at some length the concept of Sarvodaya.

The Human Condition

Even a cursory glance at a few tragic situations that are prevailing at present and are well known all over the world reveal the critical nature of the present-day human condition brought about by present socio-economic structures.

Let us look at the 'war and peace' situation and the proliferating arms race, not only between the Super Powers, but also between all other nations including India and Pakistan. No doubt, some negotiations have started recently between the Super Powers. But it is a safe bet to say that at the most there would be very marginal success as a result of their talks. Nuclear freeze would be a far cry and a cut here and a pruning there would be hardly a response to the demand of the whole of humanity for abandonment of nuclear weapons altogether. Today the impending disaster of a nuclear holocaust is the real cause of the 'angst' or the anxiety of every thinking human being. About $ 800 billions is the total military budget of the nations. What they manufacture and pile up is useful *only* for destructive purposes. Similarly, twenty million people of different nations, the very best and youngest are under arms and they are taught to kill and destroy their human brethren and all their handiwork. This is dehumanisation with a vengeance and a shame for the human race, which is called the crown of creation. We may just think out how we human beings have arrived at such a situation with all our vaunted civilization and our vanity for the advance in modern science and technology.

Is not enthroning nonviolence in the place of violence, as the United Nations Organisation demands, the *only* remedy and the Sarvodaya philosophy, the only philosophy which would bring humanity to its senses and ensure a sense of security for all?

Let me refer to another situation, in West Germany. That country has announced that it is going to slaughter 2,60,000 cows in order to keep up the price of milk at the present level. It is on account of the 'profit motive' and commercialisation of the life of the bovine population that West Germany has arrived at that equation. There is but a thin line between the situation and some exuberant scientist prescribing an innocent vaccine to be injected to prevent human sperms and ovums from breeding, since human population is proliferating. The gas-chamber is a case in point and the psychiatric treatment being meted out to political dissidents is a similar abuse of so-called modern science and its wonders. Are not all governments, whatever their nomenclature, using the latest discoveries of science to keep down dissidents by hook or by crook, by every advanced method of torture and brain-washing?

The Indian Situation

To refer to similar situation at home in India, we may have a close look at the situation regarding the pernicious evil of drinks, alchohol and drugs which deprive human beings, however temporarily, the use of the divine faculty of thinking and self-control, the only inbuilt safeguard against the misuse-abuse of energies with which they are endowed by nature. The National Congress organisation in its earlier days declared with a fanfare its policy for complete prohibition to ensure the health of body and mind of all Indians. But a few years after Swaraj the Congress governments installed by the votes of the people completely forgot all about it, perhaps on account of the pernicious lust for power and the lure of the excise revenue. Now there is a free flow of intoxicating drinks into the throats of the people and as free flow of money from the pockets, especially of the poor and the hungry, into the chests of governments. The ostensible policy of the government is the welfare of the poor of the land! And all this in contravention of the Directive Principles of State Policy laid down solemnly in our Constitution.

To draw the attention of the people of the world to another situation in India, I may refer to the slaughter of cows and their progeny and the export of beef to the tune of 80,000 tons during recent years. This is again in contravention of the provisions in the Directives of State Policy which would like to protect the cow and its progeny since it is the life-companion of the poverty-ridden peasant of India who forms 70 per cent of her teeming millions. No less a personality than the great Acharya Vinoba Bhave took up the cause, fasted against the attack on the cow, and pleaded for its protection in the whole of India. He found himself helpless against the policies of the government and sanctioned nonviolent Satyagraha which is going on for the last three years at Deonar Slaughter House in Bombay and other places. This was in spite of the fact that those in power paid court and extended reverential courtesies to the modern Rishi of Paunar and the originator of the Bhoodan, Gramdan, and Gram Swaraj movements in India. He attracted world attention and universal homage on account of his saintliness, his identification in action with the poorest and his compassion for the whole animal kingdom. Here again it is the profit-motive and commercialization without any consideration for human values. Ecologically cow and her progeny are a renewable source of energy.

Since the dawn of history man has reconciled himself with the absence of morality in the field of politics. Now there is no scope left for the exercise either of spirituality or religion or morality or even common concern for the good of all in any walk of life; so debased is the mind of human beings as regards the common good, and so narrow are the ego-centric drives, that people do not know much beyond selfish, individual material gain in order to satisfy sense-hungers. Ego-centrism is today the curse of the individual, homo-centrism is the curse of the whole human race, so much so that sans any control and any higher idea, man armed with modern science and technology looks like a wild primitive beast roaming over the globe without any regard for ecology and even for his own orderly development. He seems to be drunk with one passion of consumerism and sense-satisfaction, leaving the conscience, the inner soul or psyche to take care of itself.

Sensate Civilization

It is not without sound reason and deep study that Pitirim Sorokin, the greatest modern sociologist, named the modern Western civilization as Sensate Civilization, that is, a civilization which has its dominant thrust at selfish sense-hunger and its satisfaction. It was after the study of several civilizations of the past and the present that he came to the conclusion that man would have no future and would be completely lost if he does not abandon his utterly ego-centric and homo-centric stance. To save himself, man must become more altruistic, other-regarding, ecologically conscious, and adopt early enough a new stance based on them. He has elaborated this theme in his book *Reconstruction of Humanity* which he has dedicated to the Immortal Mohandas Karamchand Gandhi.

Gandhi, in his *Hind Swaraj* written as long ago as 1909, condemned Western civilization for similar, if not the same reasons. He foresaw where it would lead man, and his foresight has been justified. Man is today the slave of the machine-civilization sans moral content and even without an attempt to restore lost human values. The result is exploitation galore of the weak by the strong, of the poor by the rich, of the ignorant and illiterate by the intellectual and the literate. Governments today, whatever their designation on colour, enthroned by popular vote or otherwise, with the help of modern science and technology and with a disciplined violent force as the final sanction, are in a position to rule over vast masses in their name and with their resources but not necessarily in their interest and for elevating them to higher levels of real human existence. The very nature of governments has changed and all power is concentrated in their hands. Concentration of power, centralisation of authority and bureaucratisation of administration are the common features more or less of all governments.

Gandhi and Sorokin are not alone in the diagnosis of the present human condition. There are several others, like Schumacher who pleaded for what he called 'appropriate technology' and made popular the maxim, Small is Beautiful. Then there is Rifkin, the author of *Entropy*, who stands for a simpler lifestyle and pleads for it in the name of the Second Law of Thermodynamics and use of renewable sources of energy. There are several others who are not only disillusioned but disgusted with the restless and mad race after consumerism and the use of all science and technology for its fulfilment. Instead of peace and satisfaction we have bargained for total alienation and in the place of the art and science of living together as cultured human beings in a society based on love, mutual cooperation, friendliness and harmony, we are living in fear, in distrust of each other and in an atmosphere of insecurity and perpetual anxiety. Our governments are busy arming themselves against neighbours and trying to perpetuate their rule over their own citizens, however obnoxious it might have become in course of time on account of sheer exploitation of resources and inability to deliver the goods with an equitable hand and with justice.

Sarvodaya: The Alternative

It is always easy to find fault with what exists but difficult to find remedies to right the wrongs and think of a new social order. Gandhi, Vinoba, and Jayaprakash tried to find an alternative to the present predicament and the current predominantly materialistic ideas of human development. Gandhi and Vinoba were both spiritually oriented, that is, they believed in the eternal existence of an all-pervading Spiritual Energy and the oneness of all being and existence. Hence their early humanism and latterly Ecological Humanism was based on their realisation of their belief in an all-round Oneness of Existence and their capacity for achieving identity with that Reality of the Oneness of all Existence. Jayaprakash never laid any claim to any such realisation but he accepted the conclusions arrived at on that basis.

Along with these preliminary observations, I would love to point out that most recent experiments in physics, in Quantum Mechanics and Particles explorations it has been found that the subtlest of particles, the proton has been decaying. Therefore, there is no building-block for 'matter' as such. What exists is Energy 'dancing as it listeth' in the style of Nataraja! Fritjof Capra in his *Tao of Physics* has made a clear statement that the whole universe of Energy units is an organic whole in which each unit is interacting, interpenetrating and interdependent on every other unit all the time, and at every moment of its existence! Capra further asks scientists to be true to this reality of the situation and try to rearrange socio-economic and other structures on the basis of this Truth of the Oneness of all Existence.

When such is the conclusion regarding the so-called solid matter arrived at by scientists, how much more true it is about living sentient beings and still more true of human beings with active consciousness which is the cognitive apparatus. It has the ability to perceive, think, feel, and will to act with organic tools provided by Nature. So, Gandhi and Vinoba were not only truthful to their own spiritual realisations of Oneness of Being but they have been on the right track even according to the Truth of Physical Sciences!

Sarvodaya is a concept founded on the spiritual perception of oneness of all beings and all sentient creatures. Though they seem to be physically separate to our eyes and other senses, they are organically one like the bees in a bee-hive or the variety of cells in the human or any other living organism. Once this is realized, and it becomes an important experience in our consciousness, one need not argue out the importance and naturalness of the concept of Sarvodaya, that is, 'the rise and progress of all' in all matters and in all details. Just as there is never any necessity to argue out the oneness of interest of the members of a family, so too the oneness and identity of interest of the members of the Family of Man as well as of all sentient beings is an evident truth of existence. Sarvodaya means and includes not only the rise and worldly success and progress of all but also the attainment of spiritual elevation and illumination by all. This means that every individual in a Sarvodaya society is entitled to have equitable opportunities for the healthy development of the physical, vital, mental, aesthetic, moral and spiritual energies he or she is equipped with, consistent with similar opportunities to others. The obligation to develop one's energies is of course coupled with the responsibility to utilise the developed energies in the interest of others more than for one's own benefit. This ought to lead ultimately to a global human society in which love and identity of mutual interest rules the roost with the result of converting a human society into a divine society.

I would hasten to point out here one important difference between religious ideals which aim at the emancipation of human individuals and the Sarvodaya ideal which aims at the utmost good of the human community as a whole. Most religions believe in individual souls and the emphasis is on other-worldly interest, on the basis that the body is perishable and the soul is eternal. Sarvodaya always keeps in view not the individual or his other-worldly interest predominantly. It has the 'individual-in-society' in view and the worldly as well as otherwordly interest of all always. Similarly Sarvodaya differs from other spiritually-oriented philosophies which emphasise spiritual gains even at some sacrifice of mundane interests. Sarvodaya would not sacrifice either of the interests at the cost of the other. Sarvodaya would give equal importance to the first two verses of Ishopanishad, thus ensuring a healthy vigorous mundane existence to be used as a foot-stool for as vigorous a spiritual life of action as in the case of Gandhi himself. From this point of view simple and healthy socio-economic-political structures may have to be devised in the intermediate stages. The Sarvodaya approach is a holistic approach but showing no quarter to negative forces and energies which are or seem to be repugnant to the achievement of the ideal.

It is but natural that other social philosophies would look upon Sarvodaya with different eyes. Some may say that it is not a realisable ideal. Others may say that it is only a dream or that it is a utopia. But one need not be deterred from one's chosen path nor depressed by adverse criticism. Vast and immense is the world and endless is time! One has only to see if the direction is correct and then proceed without hesitation, saying, "One step enough for me".

As things stand, Sarvodaya Samaj is a kind of brotherhood without any organisation as such. Nor are there any rules or regulations to bind the members together. Those who believe in Truth and Ahimsa or Nonviolence as promulgated and practised by Gandhi in his own lifetime, and those who observe in their own lives the principle of the indivisibility of Ends and Means and that right and truthful means alone can yield good ends, are all members, whatever their race, nationality, religion, language or sex.

Here I would like to observe that Gandhi looks upon Truth itself as the highest ideal to be pursued and attained, and God is but the formal name of Truth. His other belief was that Truth can be attained only through the practice of Ahimsa. Thus truth through Ahimsa alone is the path to be tread along Gandhian lines. He gave the reason also as to why he said Truth alone is to be attained. God is denied by many as God has many meanings according to different religious traditions. But so far as Truth is concerned, no one who has arrived at his own Truth by the use of all the tools Nature has given him, dare deny the same, his own Truth.

Truth and nonviolence, or rather I would always prefer to use the word Ahimsa with its rich connotation, are in fact two social virtues which are absolutely necessary for any society even of two, and of course, all multiples of two to live together, to function together and be helpful in benefiting both. They have been tested by experience throughout the ages and sanctified by saints and seers and have found a place in sacred scriptures of many religions and in social philosophies.

For a believer in Sarvodaya philosophy and to be a member of the brotherhood called Sarvodaya Samaj the qualifications have already been mentioned. But I believe we cannot leave things at that. The observance of the sacrosanct vows – five of them, namely Satya, Ahimsa, Asteya, Brahmacharya, and Asangraha by all non-Indian members and the additional six vows of Shareer-shrama, Aswad, Swadeshi, Sarvadharma Samabhava, Abhaya, and Sparsh-bhavana, for Indian members – is essential. Just as in Yoga, Yama-Niyama are essential ingredients, so too for members of the Samaj, the vows are an essential discipline.

Sarvodaya is not meant only for India or Indians. Neither Gandhi nor Vinoba ever thought only in terms of India and Indians. In fact, Vinoba adopted a global slogan 'Jai Jagat'. So, what is already being done on a small scale, has to become a part of our activities, namely setting up a propagative unit under the auspices of the Samaj so that contacts could be established with cognate bodies and or individuals, literature could be published in different languages and the great ideal of Sarvodaya Samaj be communicated by all possible media all over the world. That in fact is the least that has to be done at the earliest. As we all know, Gandhi gave the greatest importance to communication. Ultimately, Gandhi became communication-incarnate. So, this great ideal, Sarvodaya which embraces within its loveful fold all human beings and all sentient creatures as well, deserves this service of setting up a Unit for Communication and for popularising the concept in all its manifold bearings.

18

EMPOWERING CITIES AND CITIZENS: COMMUNITY-BASED POWER

ROBERT T. NORMAN

American cities increasingly are involved in the global community, yet that social and economic involvement has not been matched politically. The empowerment of cities and citizens is needed to cope with what is happening in the global economy. This paper attempts to show how a community-based conception of power would help strengthen cities and improve the chances of effective citizenship in a huge and highly integrated world. Contrary to the author's original intention, the study will remain largely theoretical and macro in focus rather than micro or applied. A more specific and applied study is under way.

The social and economic involvements of American cities in the global community are many and growing: dramatic Japanese investments in our cities; the inflow of foreign-produced drugs; the spread of AIDS; the stock market crash of October 19, 1987, precipitated by trade deficits and slippage of the dollar; the dangerously depleted ozone layer over the Northern Hemisphere; the increasing evidence that the arms race could prove fatal to our urban civilization.

Yet we go on with our lives as though our cities were immune to the risks and cares of the rest of the world. We ignore the fact that the world and not the United States has become our ultimate survival community. But because American cities *are* so inescapably involved, we, as urbanists, have the responsibility to develop ideas on how the political potential of our cities can be enhanced. We need ideas on how cities and their citizens can play a more active role in the new, larger world. It is possible that cities with larger, more effective governments can contribute significantly to a fuller citizenship. A more active citizenship, in turn, might help to guarantee the safety and continued viability of all cities.

Inevitably, a theory of political power involves such concepts as loyalty, obligation, legitimacy, rights, myths and symbols, authority, tradition, and the very meaning of community (Mandelbaum, 1987). This analysis proposes a community-based theory of power which would maximize the chance for cities to become effective political arenas. And new and stronger political arenas are essential to empower cities and citizens.

Specifically, this paper will: i. describe a theory of community-based power, ii. show how such a theory can strengthen cities, and, iii. demonstrate how these stronger cities would be uniquely positioned to help empower a more active and effective citizenship on a global scale.

Community-Based Power

Community-Based Power rests on an awareness that, over the long pull, non-violent power is preferable to and far more durable than power based on threat, and that talking and listening will be increasingly preferable to killing. The whole course of modern political development has been an effort to reduce the need for force and to increase the opportunity for dialogue, framed by constitutional and legal understandings, limitations and divisions of power. A Community-Based Theory of Power tries to take into account the extraordinary size and complexity of the world and the fact that a balance has to be struck between the rights and privileges of individual people living locally and the demands of a very large and diverse world community.

There is no turning back from the global economy no matter how much we might prefer an older way of doing things or a less advanced technology. Yet it is clear that this involvement is jeopardizing citizenship, not just here in America, but all around the world. A certain defensiveness is understandable. How puny we individual Americans are facing the alien values of billions upon billions of foreigners – Iranians, Chinese, Russians, Indians. It is not surprising, therefore, that under President Reagan the emphasis has been on trying to be Number One, to be the most powerful and most feared force the world has ever known. How else could we minimize the possibility that unwanted external change would be forced upon us and, at the same time, maximize the probability that our values will prevail in the rest of the world?

But this misguided and almost certainly doomed effort to control too much already shows definite signs of failure: As professional urbanists, we are acutely aware how American cities have been left to fend for themselves, how the condition of the homeless has become a national scandal, how the national budget has been hopelessly unbalanced, and how we pour our vast but nonetheless limited resources into a national security system that endangers not only our lives but the very values of freedom and self-government we are trying so hard to protect (Peterson, 1986). There are disturbing signs that citizenship is being seriously neglected in favour of other, often more frivolous, activities, and that no one really knows or seems to care very much how the many problems facing our cities are to be overcome.

A Community-Based Theory of Power seeks a safer and more permanent political stability than the Pax Americana and does so through increasing the potential for self-determination. Thinking of power exclusively in terms of force does have a basis in reality. Weapons *are* coercive. The Soviet Union, the Chinese, the Vietnamese, the Nicaraguans have made life more difficult for us as Americans. It is true that the whole system of sovereign, stubbornly independent Nation-States seeking to protect their interests makes the world a more difficult and dangerous place. On the one hand, we fear anarchy will prevail if the United States does nothing which tempts us to be Number One. On the other, we know that we cannot do everything. We know, for example, that no one speaks for the planetary ecosystem, the commons upon which we all depend. Community-Based Power sees that the industrial economy continues to produce too much carbondioxide, to cut down the rain forests and to threaten other severe degradations of the earth's fragile environment. In short, it acknowledges that there is a global community to be built and protected.

Power can be viewed in various ways: coercion can be emphasized or persuasion can be stressed. There is some truth in both views. A certain immediate but limited power comes from the barrel of a gun. All theories of power seem to involve a significant element of getting other people to do things they are not eager to do. But there are a variety of ways to move people. Being politically free means *not* being unduly subject to the arbitrary power of others. Empowerment is giving peoplc a sense that non-violent means can actually be made to work (Arendt, 1970).

A Community-Based Theory of Power sees two communities in special need of empowerment–the urban and the global. The Nation-State system cannot do the job because even the largest sovereign State is far smaller than the world. We need, therefore, new systems of identification and trust, a citizenship capable of intelligent and sensitive governance at *both* the global and local levels. Inescapably, this will involve shifting loyalty and obligation away from the government of the United States downward towards cities (which to a very limited degree Ronald Reagan tried to do and which may be his greatest accomplishment) and outward to the world (which President Reagan made little or no attempt to do) (Peterson, 1986).

A Community-Based Theory of Power calls for abandoning a major portion of our political heritage, or at least that part which rests on violent coercion and separate, sovereign Nation-States. If the generic meaning of power deals with the way in which people influence or have their way with others, the importance of these two communities to our future should be clear. We live in cities. We have only one inhabitable planet; there are no spares, no second chances if we destroy this one.

An inescapable conclusion is that individuals will have to be empowered through these two communities or not at all. We must stop waiving the American flag and expecting others to bend to our will; we must stop saying that "the buck" stops with the President, when, in fact, he has no control over most of the eco-sphere. Similarly, we cannot get along without giving cities new constitutional responsibilities. The empowerment of cities and the empowerment of citizens rests on putting cities into a global constitutional order under a global charter just as soon as we possibly can.

As Americans we are highly respectful of constitutions. The Congressional hearings on nominees for justice for the U.S. Supreme Court are a reminder of this. But it is not so clearly understood or commented upon to what degree *constitutions are now and always have been statements of non-violent intent–agreements to debate rather than kill*. Doubtless constitutions rest in some ultimate way on the coercive power of police and army, but far more significantly constitutions are statements of mutual understanding and agreement. The alternative to a constitutional order is a Hobbesian jungle and a state of perpetual war. Written or not, all stable political regimes have constitutions. The most successful polities enjoy a high degree of support for that all-important underlying political consensus (Friedrich, 1950).

And, of course, that is the rub. The world community lacks the consensus found in the United States or any other State. In dozens of places people are at one another's throats precisely because they cannot agree on basic principles. Too often the fighting is over what the basic principles are to be.

And there are other serious complications. The world community as such cannot produce goods or services–they are produced by and in individual nations. Implementation and enforcement of decisions following debate and discussion is a problem for any international organization. This is why the United States has thought it must go-it-alone in shaping the international community in its own image and to its own tastes.

Finally, there would have to be universal agreement that constitutional violations, such as single-handed, unilateral efforts to apply force are no longer acceptable, because they would adversely affect the rights of all to self-determination and even to physical survival.

It cannot be emphasized too strongly that a Community-Based Theory of Power would have to work constantly to promote non-violent solutions to pressing issues. Rambo-like shoot-outs are infantile solutions that can be outgrown and outlawed. Naturally, Americans, as well as others, carry a lot of mythic baggage about patriotism, loyalty, and obligation to the Nation-State system that will have to be redirected.

To put all this slightly differently, a Community-Based Theory of Power would have to employ and cultivate modified versions of most of the classic political virtues. Loyalties would have to be re-directed to the two communities that have to be built. Loyalty and attachment to the species, to life, *and* to the particular city, are much more important than loyalty to the Nation-State. In the years ahead we will need a sense of obligation and responsibility to *both city and world* much more than we need it to the United States standing alone. We need a way to claim the value of human rights not primarily because we are citizens of any particular country, but because of our citizenship in a less hostile, more participative world (Wagar, 1971).

But what do we do with all the people in the world who, as Lyndon Johnson once said, "want what we've got?" What do we do when the first people start throwing rocks, or thousands of Mexicans begin walking across our borders, or the Soviets or Chinese make a threat, or someone threatens to blow up a whole city with a hidden nuclear device?

Two things seem clear: first, because these threats are real and potentially fatal, we have to see the world clearly and precisely and without illusion, and, second, we have to start doing things quite differently to meet such threats. In other words, we must understand the powers and behaviours of States and the politically aggressive, and then, we must apply our imaginations as never before to figuring out new ways of dealing with that reality. Unfortunately, our imaginations freeze up at any conception of power different than that contained in the prevailing myths of the Nation-State. We have done dismally poorly in seeing beyond the power relationships of today's institutions.

To summarize this first section of the analysis, only a few people have begun to think hard about alternative political means to protect our freedoms in a global setting, of new ways to divide governmental power. As Americans we know about the division spelled out by the national constitution for dealing with power in Washington, D.C. by separations between legislative, executive and judicial branches of the national government. However, we are much less clear about the territorial division of power. At best, American cities have enjoyed something called home rule granted by the separate State Governments. The powers of cities, even under the Constitution of the United States, have been of interest to only a few, for the fact is that the 50 States themselves have often been the de facto governments of regional cities. We have only scratched the surface of what cities might mean to the world as a whole as parts of a larger constitutional order (Frug, 1980, 1986, 1987).

Community-Based Power must be constitutional and non-violent. It has to rest on negotiated agreement rather than force. It also seems likely that the most promising way to proceed is to acknowledge the importance of developing two political communities or arenas as more urgently in need of help than the Nation-State, *neither one of which could be allowed to make claims of sovereign authority*. In short, what we will need to get used to if we are going to have decent cities in a livable world is running two flags up the flag pole: one for the individual city and one for the global human community.

Empowerment of Cities

Thinking in terms of Community-Based Power, utilizing a territorial division of authority and power rather than violent power would help cities immediately in a variety of ways: first, it could lead to a less heavily armed, less belligerent United States straining less hard to be Number One; second, it would help in the transfer of political identification from the United States of America to our most important urban regions; third it would help strengthen the local political arenas needed to design cities in which we will be living; fourth, it could serve as a reminder for the future that no one city can possibly pretend to run the world unilaterally. To be sure, the very idea of empowering cities raises a raft of questions: What size urban regions are we talking about? What would happen to existing constitutional understandings of State and Nation? And, as a practical matter of adoption, who would support giving cities more power? Who would oppose?

Size: Empowerment will be a lot easier if we think of cities as urban regions. Cities of several million people have greater resources, more citizens, and a greater chance to have an impact on the world than smaller places. Given the way in which cities are growing in much of the world, it would seem appropriate to think of city-centred territories with several million people each. At this scale, some people might well prefer to call the new entities urban regions rather than cities.

Constitutional understandings: The basic rules of government for the United States were drawn up over 200 years ago without reference to cities. Thus, for two centuries American cities have been waiting for constitutional recognition, and the need for some kind of constitutional standing remains clear. Over the long term, American cities need to be weaned from their dependence on the government of the United States. Of course, under such a constitutional order the new cities could not even think of being fully independent or sovereign. The constitutional and de facto powers of these new regional cities would have to be considerable to assure survival as parts of a highly integrated world system of cities. In retrospect, it may well be seen that President Reagan contributed to the empowerment of cities by withdrawing federal support (Frug, 1986, 1987; Norman, April, 1987). An additional vital step towards the empowerment of cities would be increasing their capacity for economic planning. Better data, more analytical capability and improved decision-making structures will help make a territorial division of power possible.

In constitutional terms, then, what is required to empower cities is to think along community-based lines of a territorial division of *global* power. The conventional, male-dominated, State-oriented system of power is excessively coercive and rests on the familiar idea that power is violence-based. Recall that in the traditional theory of power the emphasis is on the person with the gun, with the power of the police or the army; that under a non-violent constitutional conception of power the emphasis is on a mutual relationship rather than the possession of weapons or capacity to threaten with violence; the emphasis is on argument and persuasion by an earned and legitimate leadership rather than edict backed by force.

Who would support the empowerment of cities? All who are willing to take chances. Winning sports clubs generate a lot of sound and fury in support of the home team. But could there ever be as much loyalty and enthusiasm for the local city government? What we know about the behaviour of small States and nationalistically inclined provinces in other countries suggests that there could be an abundance of enthusiasm.

Fighting *for* the new City Halls rather than against them here in the United States we would expect to find: the local Chambers of Commerce; the local members of Congress; the locals of the various labour unions; the local educational and cultural elite. Much more importantly, fighting for cities, probably organized by neighbourhoods, suburbs and small towns, would be all those loyal fans, ordinary people who turn out to root for the home team, who also might want to re-establish some small measure of control over their lives.

Who would oppose the empowerment of cities? Who would fight *against* giving new regional cities appreciably more of the governmental load? Enemies of the regional cities would include many who come from white, male elites (those in charge of things as they are), who would fear loss of privilege or position. Large multinational corporations certainly are not happy over the efforts of today's much weaker cities to regulate plant closings–so general corporate support is unlikely, although there might be some support from smaller, local enterprises. Few in the federal government are going to like a shift of attention to the provinces, because they are the least accustomed to opposition. Even so, Senators and Congressmen do have local constituencies. In all probability the military would oppose because a non-violent theory of power and the strategy it supports runs counter to their world-view. Some will put down the idea of a system of power based on debate and discussion as the stuff of wimps, quiche-eaters, and those who are demonstrably less than real men.

It is not possible in the short space of this paper to deal with the questions of international organization, with what the central apparatus for global governance would look like. As urbanists, however, we would expect that cities figure prominently in any international order (Alger, 1977). The main contention to be made here, and it is significant, is that *the task of getting the global community together will be made much easier by eliminating the sovereign and militaristic presumptions of the Nation-State and by thinking in smaller, city terms, as a means to achieving the larger global community.* This is not a totally novel idea to students of international affairs, for, among others, Falk (1975) and Kohr (1957, 1977) have argued elements of the case. This line of thinking is newer to urbanists.

The empowerment of cities, then, can be brought about over time by thinking harder about non-violent, constitutional solutions to problems. Empowerment will come by reducing the attention and resources going to the national government and by retaining them locally or redirecting them to major urban regions. And always there is the hope that people who will have a better chance at citizenship will be less belligerent towards their neighbours.

But in any such planning for the future, it is essential to keep in mind that more than one level of community must be involved. We start with the United States represented today by its single flag. Looking ahead, the world community needs a flag as do the new cities. The two flags would represent a constitutional division of power between the local regional community and the global community each with its own flag. By mutual agreement and understanding, neither level in the new spatial community would have total or absolute.dominion over the other. Even on issues of global security, responsibility could never rest exclusively with the Central Government, for vigorous debate would be expected in every city and by constitutional agreement all cities would be involved in executing global security policy. Keeping the peace and making sure the earth is not destroyed environmentally will be everyone's responsibility, the responsibility of every locality under the constitution. The global community per se would have maximum power over a minimum of functions.

Note how empowered cities differ from the typical force-based Nation-State System in which so much power is concentrated at the national level, in which no claims above those of the national government are seriously entertained, in which claims of sub-national entities are squelched in the interests of national unity, reason-of-state, and national security. So strong is the hold of the Nation-State mythology, which seems to always play up the danger of foreign enemies, that our political imagination has been almost totally defeated. When did you last hear anyone seriously propose an alternative to the United States? It is literally unthinkable to consider the matter because so much of our past, present and future seems to ride with the State, with the historical configuration of State power.

But there is reason for hope. Some of the best minds in the world have spoken up in favour of the city or urban region, many with specific reservations about the Nation-State.

* Plato and Aristotle, who spoke directly of the Political values of their city.
* Alexis De Tocqueville, who argued passionately for powerful sub-national communities.
* Max Weber, who was immensely impressed with the history of the European city, which avoided both slavery and sovereignty in achieving community.
* Manuel Castells, who like Max Weber, admires the way in which cities have defended themselves and pushed for social change.
* Kenneth Boulding, who 20 years ago saw that cities might play a more active role in governing the world.
* Jane Jacobs, who loves cities and wants them to control their own political economies.
* Gerald Frug, who argues that something went wrong when for-profit corporations became more powerful than municipal corporations.
* Hannah Arendt, who while not an urbanist, shares de Tocqueville's enthusiasm for self-government.
* John Friedmann, who has been in the vanguard of those seeing that the 21st century will be a world of cities.
* Lewis Mumford, who last but perhaps most importantly wrote brilliantly for so many years that the idea of city had only begun to be used.

In one way or another all of the above writers have argued that local communities can and should be empowered. Only the earliest (those writing 2000 years ago) wished to see cities be all-powerful. Max Weber (1958) admired "the urban community" of significant but limited power, and Hannah Arendt (1970) offered a non-violent theory of power based on the vigorous use of urban political arenas. All of the above emphasized the need for places to settle political disputes and plan the future.

For the future, cities are needed because, as Boulding (1970) and Dahl (1967, 1970) saw, there is no way that the independent and sovereign Nation-States can be the answer: They are overwhelmingly part of the problem, in that they concentrate power rather than dividing it, rely on violence, and are dominated by too much patriotic mythology. In the short-term we must deal with sovereign Nation-States; in the long run they must go.

Empowering Citizens

To be a citizen of a world of several billion people is an uncertain prospect. Citizenship requires a sense of territory, of place. At best, world citizenship would mean being in tune with the whole of humanity; while at worst world citizenship means not having a country of one's own, to have no vote, no power, no influence. It is to be the ultimate expatriate. We should wish to empower cities as a means to empower citizens in a world so large and diverse that citizenship otherwise would be meaningless. How else are we to have government and protection of local freedoms represented by the flags of each and every city?

This size and diversity of the world implies at least two things. First, that the total number of people to be accommodated in a government for the world all but precludes most direct participation by citizens. Polling everyone in a planetary referendum would be a mammoth undertaking; electronic voting by everyone is mindbog-gling. And then there is the prospect of a global bureaucracy of stag-gering proportions. Second, and closely related, the diversity of the world is such that the only possible way of accommodating that diversity is through large, numerous and equally populous subdivisions–what here are being called cities or urban regions.

We are in severe danger of giving up on global government because we immediately think of the highly centralized Nation-State, which is a totally inappropriate model to copy. It is such a bad model that we would justifiably be tempted to forget about trying to govern the world. Yet we have to think in these terms because of the fact that national security systems can no longer work and the growing awareness of the importance of universal human values. But the global economy is a reality for cities are trading with one another in such a way that global economic regulation is an absolute necessity.

Assisted by a community-based theory of power, empowered cities could serve as local governments for the world. After all, people have not changed all that much since local government was seen as necessary for individual sovereign States. The new regional cities would have to be much more powerful than today's cities. In many cases local citizenship would be enhanced because each city would be closer to the citizen than entire countries the size of the People's Republic of China, India, or the Soviet Union can ever be.

Furthermore, under a two-flag system based on cities, citizenship would be enhanced because the global authority *could not* deal intelligently with most issues. Individual cities would have to carry a much heavier governmental load than they do today. In other words, if cities do more, the possibilities for global law and order could be expected to improve with a territorial division of power (Maass, 1959).

Again a few caveats. Political participation is always a difficult topic, and entrenched leaders are often quite eager to stage participatory events designed to show fraudulent involvement of people the powerful do not wish to empower at all. Similarly elections are often held with no expectation that power will be transferred. Why is there so little interest in political matters in the United States? Consumerism may be the most important reason for the decline of interest in citizenship in the United States. The people in charge of creating our social myths are very effective in keeping the business of the country, business. The Founding Fathers would be shocked at the decline in citizenship. There is absolutely no certainty that even the empowerment of cities would restore citizenship. It does seem likely, however, that without more powerful cities the complexities of the world will discourage the limited urge for active citizenship that survives and perhaps kill forever any interest in self-government.

Because the United States cannot run so large a world unilaterally, the task of empowering cities in the world and the task of empowering citizens come close to being the same.

What of Neighbourhoods: In all this, it seems that neighbourhoods have some role to play, but just what it should be is far from clear. Similarly, it is unclear how much public power can be given to–or taken by–this micro level. Villages and neighbourhoods are very small in the world economy and might appear to be of little help in dealing with any territorial division of power. Their small size would imply the need for several levels of authority between them and the global authority, which gets messy because, there is a distinct limit to how many levels of government even the most alert citizens can keep track of. Because a monolithic, unfederated city without neighbourhoods would be daunting and discouraging to empowerment of citizens, strong neighbourhoods, villages and suburbs would appear to make sense–but only if they are part of the region-wide network. They cannot be expected to make law, but certainly could serve as active political arenas for debate and discussion. Community television and computer networks can empower by connecting the neighbourhoods to one another and to the city.

But should neighbourhoods emphasize heterogeneous or homogeneous populations? There is considerable literature on either side. Who's laws are to be followed? Who's rules? Who's morality is supposed to apply? Some neighbourhoods are highly resistant to change, others are quite flexible and innovative (Mandelbaum, 1987).

People need to be citizens of some place, not of the world exclusively. Increasingly they are living in cities, so it makes sense to look for empowerment in producing more effective places to live, aided by neighbourhoods and suburbs, which individually would have little voice. And always, individual citizens and neighbourhoods need the collective action of powerful local governments to speak for them in the global community.

It is hard to think of a better local government arrangement than cities serving as voluntary associations of free men and women (Weber, 1958). To be sure, there are major questions of right to travel, movement to work, shifting of local citizenship, unequal resources, poverty, and the like. But they can be overcome.

Conclusions

A Community-Based Theory of Power, relying on non-violent action, is required to empower cities and citizens. A Garrison State cannot afford and will not tolerate an outspoken opposition, it needs soldiers to defend it and taxpayers to pay for the soldiers. Garrison States and Self-Government are totally incompatible over the long run. It is safe to say that only a constitutionally non-violent political community can maximize the opportunity for empowerment over time. It is clear, too, that the typical Nation-State has limited tolerance for opposition, territorial or otherwise. Sheldon Wolin of Princeton University has been very blunt about the qualities of the modern State not having much to do with citizenship or self-government (1980). Dwight Waldo, formerly of the University of California and Syracuse University, has been equally outspoken in pointing out that there is no alternative to bureaucracy and that the United States will continue to take Rome as its example rather than Greece (1980).

Cities could be the basic units of a territorial division of power, but there are limitations. In a world grown accustomed to political parties, imperial bureaucracies, multi-national corporations and mass media, not just Thomas Jefferson's "ward" is in trouble, but *any* form of self-government on any scale.

E.F. Schumacher (1973) saw clearly the extent to which peace and permanence are necessary for effective citizenship and vice versa. Earlier, Max Weber (1958) saw the quality of work and craftsmanship as being closely aligned with effective citizenship. Similarly, Hannah Arendt (1970) saw good work and access to tools as essential to effective empowerment. Thus, the economy can greatly help or hinder citizenship.

The United States, a superpower among Nation-States, has been killing itself (and others) to bring a unilateral order and its conception of freedom to the world. This paper has argued the case that there is a major impediment to empowering cities and citizenship–the Nation-State system per se. In its post-World War II, Cold War mode, the United States took on grave new military responsibilities and a new seriousness of purpose. There is reason to believe we have taken our responsibility too seriously. The public has been lied to with great regularity, small countries have been crushed, domestic rights trampled because of the weight of these demands on one country's limited resources. Oliver North saw rather clearly the imperial role of the United States and what was required to maintain it. He was willing to sacrifice traditional values because, as he told us, "it's a dangerous world".

A Community-Based Theory of Power aims to serve individual needs through community; its non-violent practices will be hard to learn, but they are completely essential to the empowerment of cities and citizens. Because a system based on community power would have little need for weapons, either to keep the domestic peace or to fight off enemies, it could get along with a minimum of force. Because it would not be absolute, this model, which is not without historical precedent, would facilitate division of political power territorially. We can feel confident that constitutional means *can* be employed to ensure that cities have a place in the global economic and social order.

To be sure, there are innumerable problems and questions. But it seems clear that there will be no solution if we do not put serious work into a theory of non-violent empowerment of cities. The world is dangerous, but it can be made less so. Political life always requires struggle, but making that struggle constitutional and non-violent will make it a lot safer.

REFERENCES

1. Alger, C. (1977), "The Impact of Cities on International Systems," *Ekistics* 44, 264. (November), pp. 243-53.
2. Arendt, H. (1970), *On Violence*, Harcourt. Brace, World, Inc., New York.
3. Axelrod, R. (1984), *The Evolution of Cooperation,* Basic Books, INc., New York.
4. Barnard, C. (1954), *The Functions of the Executive* Cambridge, Harvard

University Press, Mass.

5. Boulding, K. (1970), "The City as an Element in the International System," in Martin Meyerson (ed.), *The Conscience of the City*, George Braziller, New York.
6. Boyte, H. (1980), *The Backyard Revolution: Understanding the New Citizen Movement*, Temple University Press, Philadelphia.
7. Castells, M. (1983), *The Cities and the Grassroots*, Berkeley, University of California Press, California.
8. Clavel, P. (1986), *The Progressive City: Planning and Participation,* Rutgers University Press, New Brunswick, New Jersey.
9. Cooney, R. and Michalowski, H. eds. (1987), *The Power of the People: Active Nonviolence in the United States,* from an original text by Marty Jezer, New Society Publishers, Philadelphia, Pa.
10. Dahl, R. (1970), *After The Revolution,* Yale University Press, New Haven.
11. Ebenstein, W. (1951), *Great Political Thinkers*, Rinehart & Company, Inc., New York.
12. Eisenstadt, S. and Schachar (1987), *Society, Culture, and Urbanization*, SAGE Publications, Beverly Hills, CA.
13. Falk, R. (1975), *A Study of Future Worlds*, The Free Press, New York.
14. Fischer, L. (1950), *The Life of Mahatma Gandhi*, Harper and Row, New York.
15. Friedmann, J. and Weaver, C. (1980), *Territory and Function,* University of California Press, Berkeley, Calif.
16. Friedrich, C. (1950), *Constitutional Government and Democracy*, Ginn and Company, Rev. Ed. Boston.
17. Friedrich, C. (1963), *Trends of Federalism in Theory and Practice*, Frederick A. Praeger, New York.
18. Frug, G. (1980), "The City As A Legal Concept," *The Harvard Law Review*, Vol. 93, No. 6, April, pp. 1157-1154.
19. Frug, G. (June, 1986), "Cities and the Constitution," published in L. Levy, K. Karst, D. Mahoney, *Encyclopedia of the American Constitution*, pp. 255-57.
20. Frug, G. (Summer, 1986), "The Choice Between Privatization and Publicization," published in American Bar Association, *Urban, State and Local Government Newsletter*, Vol. 9, No. 3, p. 2.
21. Frug, G. (1987), "Empowering Cities in a Federal System" in *The Urban Lawyer* (Spring).
22. Gandhi, M. (1957), *An Autobiography: The Story of My Experiments With Truth*, Beacon Press, Boston.
23. Jacobs, J. (1961), *The Death and Life of Great American Cities,* Random House, Inc., New York.
24. Maass, A. (1959) ed., *Area and Power: A Theory of Local Government*, The Free Press, Glencoe, Illinois.
25. Mandelbaum, S. (1987), "Open Moral Communities:" "Theorizing About Planning Within Myths of Community." A paper presented at the Conference of the Association of the Collegiate Schools of Planning, in Los Angeles, California, on November 7, 1987.
26. Mumford, L. (1961), *The City in History*, Harcourt, Brace, and World, New York.
27. Norman, L. (1987), "Inwit and Outlaw," in *The Acorn: A Gandhian Review*, September, Vol. II, No. 2.
28. Norman, R. (1984), "A Local Government Approach to World Order," *Peace and Change*, Vol. X, No. 1, Spring.
29. Norman, R. (1987), "The Priority of Cities on the National Social Agenda,"

a paper presented at the 17th Annual Meeting of the Urban Affairs Association, Akron, Ohio, April.

30. Norman, R. (1987), "Violence and the Planning of Cities," a paper prepared for the 29th Annual Conference of the ACSP in Los Angeles, November.
31. Peterson, G. and Lewis, C. (1986), *Reagan and the Cities*, The Urban Institute, Washington, D.C.
32. Schumacher, E.F. (1973), *Small is Beautiful*, Harper and Row Publishers, New York. Syed, A. (1966), *The Political Theory of American Local Government*, Random House, New York.
33. De Tocqueville, A. (1956), *Democracy in America*, edited by Richard D. Heffner, New American Library, Inc., New York.
34. Wagar, W. (1963), *The City of Man,* Penguin Books, Baltimore, Md.
35. Waldo, Dwight (1980), *The Enterprise of Public Administration*, Chandler & Sharp Publishers, Inc., Novato, California.
36. Weber, M. (1958), *The City* translated and edited by Don Martindale and Gertrud Neuwirth, Free Press, New York.
37. Williams, J. (1987), *Eyes on the Prize:* America's Civil Rights Years, 1954-1965, with Introduction by Julian Bond, Blackside, Ind., Viking Penguin Inc., New York.
38. Wolin, S. (1980), " Reagan Country," *New York Review of Books*.

19

EDUCATION FOR INTEGRATED DEVELOPMENT

K.M. MUNIANDI

It has been rightly stated that Education is Investment in Man. But in the modern world we have taken to investing money to enhance its values through interest on it and reinvesting it in trade and commerce to make more and more money. This has evidently landed us in a world of disquieting disparities disfiguring the global peace and progress immeasurably. Therefore if we invest in Man, who is our supreme consideration, and educate him in the true sense he will be of more use to his ever developing society. Why the so-called advanced countries do not think along these lines is still a mystery. Let us today ponder over this viewpoint to arrive at solutions for putting us on the road to real development.

Body Development

Who is Man after all? He is the synthesis of body, mind and spirit. He needs an integrated approach for developing these three specific characteristics together in his life. Let us now take his body which is a veritable tool for service. It is the most intricate machine that man, despite his claims for his breath-taking inventions and innovations in the fields of science and technology, has yet to invent. Our students should be made to comprehend this unique fact of life *at all stages of learning*. They should feel proud of having been born as human beings in this ever changing world. They should also be made to understand that such a mighty machine should not be allowed to rust. In fact it should be properly looked after and used for realizing the very purpose of life-integrated development. By involving himself in this realization he will be imperceptibly led to the practice of Science of Nutrition, Agriculture and Agro-industries which account for bodily health and hygiene, besides offering opportunities for perennial employment of millions on a positive note. Agriculture will then become a Way of Life as against the modern trend of making it a lucrative business concern. This latter approach has degraded it into a realm of malpractices ruinous to the very health of man for whom it is intended. If this idea is dinned into the ears of the learners, from early childhood, they will not resort to devious dealings when they grow into personalities of their own. Their regard for their neighbours will make them adopt non-violent techniques to preserve and protect human existence.

Food for Mind

Our educational psychologists aver that ours is a body-mind combination. They mutually effect each other in any learning process. Besides, we cannot limit the boundaries of human mind to time and space. It is so expansive that we can go to any extent of learning the varied and innumerable vistas of knowledge moulding our life accordingly. It is a fact that natural wild streams of water will endanger our very existence if they are not channelized through dams and other proper checks. Similarly we have to be ultra careful in shaping our mind to be of immediate use to society. This is the reason why our forebears insisted on controlling the mind lest it go astray and become destructive. Their fears have been proved to be true in the present context. We are talking of the Computer Era launching us into the Yuga of Space Ship. Where do we stand now? We are ready to commit Harakiri and act in the manner of Bhasmasura Mohini as narrated in our mythology. Can we say that the moderns are sensible and accountable human beings? Certainly not, because we in the name of science and technology have created a situation where Damocles' sword is ever hanging over us. Why? We have failed to understand the simple fact that the very purpose of our birth is Self-Realization. We are born in this world through the mutual understanding and love of our parents. We are nurtured and brought up by the motherly love throughout the unusually expanded years of our childhood. Our father's affectionate guidance has shaped our character and our course of life. Our kith and kin have showered their love on us on many an occasion. Our bosses and colleagues have helped us in our professional growth. In our dotage our children will exhibit their concern for us. Thus from our birth to death we have been in the realm of love and love only. Then why is it that man has, in this Kali Yuga, begun to cultivate hatred for his own kind and spread the cult of violence and discrimination? In order to avoid this self-killing situation we have to follow the path of love, tenderness and mutuality. Out children have to learn the art of loving through undertaking productive labour in their schools and colleges. Even at the university level youths are to discover their vital needs and learning through them. As production is for consumption only, they should be made to understand that anything in excess should go to help the needy. Thus activities that will reveal the cooperative efforts of the participants with the sole aim of fulfilling their daily needs through accredited and intelligent labour will go a longway in engendering the qualities of love, compassion and mutual sharing among the people.

Cultivation of the Spirit

We are in the image of our Creator who is Omniscient, Omnipresent and Omnipotent. He is called *Paramatma* and we are *Jeevatmas*. Just as a drop in the ocean has all the characteristics of that vast expanse of water, so also every atom in us possesses all the qualities of the Paramatma. If everyone is made to understand this significant point, he will not mistake it for his body which is perishable. He will realize that he is the immortal Soul and that his body is only an instrument for service to his neighbours. This fact will make him completely fearless which quality is the sine qua non for successful undertaking of developmental activities on this planet. Only a man of spirit will thus be able to love his neighbours, dedicate himself for their cause and help them in their physical, mental and spiritual development harmoniously without exploiting others. So educational institutions should practise *Sarva Dharmi Samanatva* prayer in their complexes and make their students involve themselves in humanitarian activities both in and out of their premises.

The Efficacy of Nai Talim

The aims of education are manifold based upon the situations. But its general aims are the same. Perhaps, *Sa Vidya ya Vimukteya*, is the best among the lot. For here we want to free ourselves from all bondage. That is the reason why when the Father of the Nation proclaimed Basic Education for India, he defined it as the *Spearhead of a silent social revolution*. Under the aegis of the British rule we became competitive and exploitative in our approach shunning our traditional role of the co-existing peaceful citizens. In order to achieve our selfish aims we became unmindful of the means we wanted to adopt. A man of Truth as Gandhiji was, he recommended completely non-violent techniques to change our existing immoral and decaying society. For that he offered Basic Education as the sole remedy. Through implementing it faithfully, we will be coordinating the physical and social media with the craft medium. Local crafts will become the medium of instruction in bringing out the latent talents of the learners in the most scientific manner. They will not only produce their daily needs but also know the why and the wherefore of them. There will be no cleavage between the physical and mental labour as it is today culminating in the hierarchy of the High and the Low. Education, if practised in this way, will become least expensive but most natural and easy for all, establishing a just, cooperative, non-exploitative, non-violent social order with insistence on manual labour for all its citizens. Naturally the students that pass out of such an institution will take to non-violent occupations like Khadi and Village Industries for their peaceful living without resorting to soul-killing and competitive economy of today. Thus Gandhian education, if taken to comprehensively, will pave the way for an all-round development of all its citizens of all age groups.

What Then Must We Do?

This is a pertinent question which, when cleared, will make us proceed in a systematic way of implementing our developmental programme. Let us, therefore, pinpoint those moves in clearcut terms.

1. Education must be the concern of the community and not of the Government. The Government may suggest a broad curriculum on the basis of its Democratic Socialist Secular Republican Constitution and ask the elders of the villages to implement it successfully with their aid.

2. The village should be told in unmistakable terms that there should not be any illiterates there within a stipulated time, as otherwise they will be deprived of their franchise. This ultimatum together with the finance allotted for the said purpose to every village will certainly goad them to action on a war-footing thereby enabling them to participate actively in the biggest democracy of the world.

3. Every village should have a *Balwadi* with trained local women. This will serve as a creche, too, to the children of working mothers with play materials and nutritive diet. The village should share 25 per cent of the expenses on the feeding of the children. This insistence on their contribution will help them have a say on the proper running of *Balwadis* without external supervisors.

4. There should be a school in every village for the children of the age group 6 to 14 years with five acres of land donated by the village with charkhas and looms for craft work and tools for garden and agricultural work supplied by the State. Every boy and girl should put in manual labour for at least two hours a day in any of the available productive activities.

5. The entire school in any area should be involved in *Safai* every day without fail. The so-called wastes gathered during this activity will be deposited into the manure pits dug for that purpose and decomposed into natural manures.

6. Every school should have a Urea Pit where the pupils should pass their urine to be converted into natural urea once in every five months.

7. Wardha Latrines should be provided to all schools which should transform our excreta into useful manures to be utilized immediately in their garden and agricultural operations. Creation of Wealth from Waste is thus taught to the boys and girls of the school-going age.

8. Students should plant as many trees as possible every year in the school area besides slowly extending this operation to the village. That green vegetation is an antidote to air pollution will then be easily understood by the learners apart from its contribution to copious rains in general.

9. Students should be trained in the art of Self-Government by giving them opportunities to elect their own leaders and work under them in the spheres earmarked for them by the school management.

10. The school should conduct *Sarva Dharmi Samanatva* prayer every day so as to enable the students to understand and practise the essence of all religions in a secular country like ours.

11. Every school should celebrate the National Festivals like August 15, January 26 and October 2, besides one festival belonging to every religion of the land. These *should* not be declared holidays but be Working Days humming with activities involving the staff, students and the public.

12. All children up to 14 years of age must be fed at school through contributions in cash and kind from the villagers as well as the Government. Students should produce vegetables, grains and pulses in the school land and use them in the Meals Centre to have the satisfaction that they too have put in their share in the form of physical labour. This will ultimately desist them from depending on external factors for their subsistence.

13. Field Trips for lower classes and Excursions for upper classes should be a regular annual feature to make students learn effectively through observation and contact and improve their knowledge content with a wider vision and mutuality.

14. At least four *Manuscript Magazines* must be produced in every class in order to provide the students with opportunities to express themselves fully and creatively.

15. The school should become a real Community Centre for the village. It should entertain the parents twice a year with dances, dramas, one-act plays, *Harikathas* exhibitions, reflecting social, cul-

tural and religious values with the help of their wards in order to educate them and others in happy, cooperative and community living.

16. There should be at least five High Schools and one Higher Secondary School in a Block so that those who pass out of High Schools can easily go to the Higher Secondary School without paying Capitation Fee in the form of aid, donation, etc. The staff of the Higher Secondary School should always help their Feeder High Schools to reach the expected academic standards and otherwise.

17. All the items mentioned for eight-year schooling should be practised here with more vigour and purpose. In addition, there should be a variety of vocations available in the Higher Secondary School to provide wide choice to students in their selection of crafts. The goal of the staff in this direction must be to enable the students to stand on their own legs with their acquired skills and to start earning their bread in right earnest from the day they leave the school. They should also be motivated to qualify themselves further and further through study during their leisure hours.

18. The Higher Secondary School should be fully equipped with a laboratory, a library and agricultural farms and function during the Summer Vacation for its old students to come and acquaint themselves with the latest developments in their areas of specialization in life. This annual feature will go a long way in updating their knowledge and skills resulting, sometimes, in their attitudinal changes.

19. The Higher Secondary School in the Block should arrange every year at least two Conferences and two Seminars for the common people to let them have a close liaison with the School and also an Exhibition on Science and Technology to educate them adequately. This will bring to the School Village willing and voluntary support from the local people in all its undertakings.

20. We need no more universities in the country. Instead the existing ones should begin effective Correspondence Courses in all faculties and help the Working Men and Women in furthering their knowledge and skills. There should be constant and continuous

research on the feedback materials gathered from the villages and towns and the universities should always strive to lead the nation through propagating such innovative *technologies as are appropriate to the local situations and skills*. If this is done purposefully, they can stop the exodus from villages to cities and towns thereby improving the standard of life of the villagers. As the educated youths and intelligentsia will not leave their rural hearth and home, the villages will prosper economically paving the way for social equality and peace. As the Gita says, only tranquillity will help us develop a stable and integrated personality and acquire purposeful knowledge. Thus the present universities should strain every nerve to make the findings of their researches reach the common man in their day-to-day life and thus contribute to his harmonious development.

To conclude, I have placed before you a few practical points to be adhered to steadfastly in order to make our education really development-oriented leaving the rest to the Planners and the Rulers to achieve. Let the Almighty grant us the strength and will to realize this objective.

20

NATIONAL INTEGRATION AND EDUCATION – A GANDHIAN PERSPECTIVE

SANDHYA CHAUDHRI

National integration occupies a place of great significance for the survival of any country. It is a practical necessity for a country in its march towards development and progress. The issue of national integration and unity acquires an added importance for India as it is inhabited by a heterogeneous population having a variety of languages, castes, communities and religions. Unity of the country involves not only political unity but unity of mind and heart also which can discipline the narrow urges leading to disharmony and bickerings.

The problem of national integration is not confined to India alone. Almost all nations have to face this challenge in one form or the other, the intensity of which may differ. In the Indian body politic, it is not a new phenomenon. During the freedom struggle, the Muslim separatism posed a serious challenge to the aspirations of the Indian nationalist leaders and ultimately resulted in the division of the country. The problem, however, has not ceased with the creation of Pakistan, rather it has acquired an alarming overtone in independent India. Today, even after 40 years of independence, India finds herself confronted with the problem of disintegration not only under the garb of religion but also caste, community, language and province.

Being conscious of the dangers inherent in these tendencies Jawaharlal Nehru, the first Prime Minister of India, convened the first meeting of the National Integration Conference in October 1961. He said, "We ventured to ask you to attend the Conference not because some sudden catastrophe was over-hanging us or the country was on the verge of disintegration but because we thought that at this moment in our history we should lay some stress on this problem and turn the people's mind in a particular direction.[1] He laid stress on emotional integration and asked the people to guard themselves against momentary passions aroused by communalism, casteism, regionalism and linguism. He considered them as the main disintegrating factors and deplored the narrow-mindedness in the present context when nations cannot live in isolation and have to interact with other nations frequently, more so with the development of science and technology which has made the globe shrunk in size. He further condemned these tendencies at a time when efforts were afoot for the socio-economic development of the country as social and economic disparities are the root cause of the trouble.[2]

Therefore, the need of the moment is to give a fresh thought to this problem and review the philosophy of national integration in its broader perspective. An endeavour has to be made to include the feeling of unity in all the fields, viz. constitutional, political and social. The constitutional unity requires certain uniformity in the pattern of government at the Centre and in the various States and a strong central or federal government. The Constitution envisages a structure tilted in favour of the Union in order to hold the unity and integrity of the country. After 1967, however, the constitutional basis for the governance of India was challenged as the hitherto one-party rule at the Centre and the States had failed to develop healthy conventions. Of late, there has been increasing demand for redefining the Centre-State relations. It is being demanded that more powers should be given to the States. Various committees, both regional and national, have been appointed from time to time to review the demand. Five years ago, the Sarkaria Commission was entrusted with the task of determining the relations between the Centre and the States. The Commission has recently submitted its recommendations comprising 247 suggestions. While upholding the need for a strong Centre, it has pointed out that this does not necessitate further weakening of the States.[3] The Report says, "The concept of federalism is in-built in the Constitution so that with time there should have been a progressive decentralisation of economic and political powers. But, unfortunately, "There was not only inadequate territorial and functional decentralisation in India ... there has been a pervasive trend towards greater centralisation of powers over the years, inter alia, due to the pressure of powerful socio-economic forces."[4] The Report has also suggested enhancement of the financial resources of the states and restraint on the part of the Centre for enacting laws on subjects incorporated in the Concurrent List.[5] The findings of the Commission have mainly laid stress on decentralization of powers which, in turn, would pave the way for constitutional integration.

Political unity is an essential requirement of the philosophy of national integration. It makes it imperative that all the citizens of the country should owe loyalty to India and regard themselves as Indians first and anything else afterwards. The emerging regional tendencies over the issue of State boundaries, water resources, sharing of power, etc., are posing serious challenges to the political unity of the country. During the freedom struggle, the broader vision of independence of India kept these narrow loyalties submerged but now, under the garb of regionalism, these tendencies are raising their head again.

Social Unity no Less Important

Social unity is equally essential for weaving the fabric of unity and is no less important than political and constitutional unity for national integration. It requires a new social order based on social justice and equality among the citizens. This just social order necessitates the abolition of hierarchical structure of society, based on caste and untouchability. Mahatma Gandhi, along with Ambedkar, endeavoured hard to remove the parasite of untouchability which had sapped the vitality of the Hindu society. And their unfailing efforts were rewarded by the constitution which upheld the abolition of untouchability. It was made a penal offence.

Religion is yet another very potent irritant to national integration in India as Indian society is mainly religion oriented. It is not only the birthplace of Hinduism, Budhism, Jainism and Sikhism but other religions like Christianity, Zoroastrianism and *Islam* have also thrived in India. Misunderstanding regarding the tenets of the respective religions and the exclusiveness at times pose a problem to the unity of the country as adherents of different religions tend to give religious colour to their cultures, social customs and practices. Such religious fundamentalists ultimately claim separate nationality and nationhood. The demand for a separate homeland for the Muslims by the Late M.A. Jinah resulting in the division of the country on the basis of religion is recent history. The Sikhs clamouring for a separate homeland in Punjab is again rooted in religious fundamentalism. The riots in Meerut, Aligarh, Delhi, Ayodhya and many cities of the Punjab have their root in religious fanaticism.

India is a multi-lingual country. The linguistic survey of India has recorded 179 languages and 544 dialects prevalent in India. The Indian Constitution has incorporated 14 languages in the Eighth Schedule and has accepted Hindi as the national language. The regional languages have their place and are equally important in the life of a nation but they should not be given precedence over the national language.

The reorganization of States on the basis of a linguistic formula in November, 1957 has given a fillip to the disruptive forces. Almost all the States are giving undue importance to regional languages at the cost of the national language with the result that regional languages are being encouraged to be used in offices for administrative purposes as well as a medium of instruction in schools, colleges and universities. The attitude of exclusiveness towards the regional language and indifference to national language has added to inter-state alienation. Though the Sarkaria Commission in its Report has laid stress on the use of local languages for the work of Union and State Governments yet it has emphasized the fact that effective steps should be taken to uniformly implement the three-language formula in the true spirit in the interest of unity and integrity of the country.[6] National integration cannot be achieved unless and until some steps are taken to curb this tendency so that languages of different regions can serve as a binding rather than a divisive force.

For developing the required spirit of harmony and cohesion, a regular disciplined training of mind is needed which is possible through education, a powerful and effective process for inculcating this consciousness. It requires a new approach to education as the education system of any country reflects its culture. A nation with a heterogeneity of languages, religions, castes, communities and regions needs an education system that imparts training in living in harmony. Proper education requires culturing the mind to adjust in life. Education should be instrumental in bringing about changes in the mentality and outlook of people and help in the development of a harmonious personality. It should impart training that helps to choose the right priorities and in the development of a social sense which will teach the individual to sacrifice his personal interests for the well-being of society. Education aiming at these goals will cultivate attitudes and values essential for fostering national unity. Further, the education system should be such as to build an integrated India binding the country together despite its diversities.

Educational institutions like schools, colleges and universities at all levels can effectively help in the promotion of national solidarity. Education imparted in these institutions form only a part of the formal education. There are various informal institutions and social groups like the family, neighbourhood, peer group, political parties, the media, written and electronic, etc., which play an important role in shaping a man's personality. Family's role in educating the child is indeed very significant as has been rightly pointed out that the child learns the first lesson of citizenship in through his mother's kisses and father's caress. In this paper, however, the role of education has been confined to the institutions of formal education only.

The importance of the role played by schools is tremendous as school age is the most formative period of man's life and the impressions of childhood are not easily erased. It can help so discipline a mind that it can eschew the evils of casteism, linguism, parochialism, etc. The young children can be taught the quintessence of all the religions being practised in the country. The schools can help in inculcating the art of living together and teach the young pupils the process of inter-group relations.[7] Here child develops respect and regard for his fellow beings belonging to different communities, castes, religions and provinces.

Make Student Aware of India's Rich Heritage

Student of today is citizen of tomorrow. Education has a very important role to play in this process. The life of young students can be moulded to bring about integration in diversity of the nation. Students should be given knowledge of the grandeur of Indian geography. Geographical maps should be displayed on the walls of schools and colleges to make the students conscious of the diversity of different regions and the integrity and oneness of the country. Educational tours of students from one part to another part of India can be conducted to acquaint them with and help them have a first-hand knowledge of other regions and cultures. Similarly, inter-State tournaments and competitions can be held to provide them an opportunity to mix with the students of different States. Further, the study and thorough knowledge of history should be made part of the school/college curricula to make the students aware of their rich heritage.

Likewise, the institutions of higher education including colleges and universities can be instrumental in infusing the spirit of national solidarity. The universities act as an important catalyst of social change and play a significant role in the process of national integration including emotional integration by creating proper social and intellectual atmosphere in the country.[8] The institutions of higher learning can establish a new social order based on complete integration in all the fields, viz. constitutional, political and social. In a large democracy like India, these institutions can help individuals have a broader vision and better understanding of the democratic ideals like dignity of individual, equality of opportunity, equal freedom for all, a just social and economic order and mutual respect and toleration. They can impart knowledge of the country's common social and historical heritage, of the unifying culture, and its common political and national aspirations. They can teach the students the wider vision of co-existence, the right ordering of loyalty, service and even self-sacrifice for the national cause.

They can also help in building up a good moral character and provide inspiration to imbibe good qualities required for being an ideal citizen. The institutions of higher learning can effectively promote fellow feeling among the individuals having faith in different religions, speaking different languages and belonging to different parts of the country. A democratic educational approach can help the students transcend the linguistic and sectional interests and rise above the communal prejudices and help in the development of better human relations.

In a country like India having a pluralistic society made up of diverse groups possessing separate identities, an important responsibility of a teacher is to promote inter-cultural understanding and to disseminate knowledge about the cultural contributions of various groups so that the students as members of different groups can know and respect the culture of other communities. They should have a greater knowledge of the dynamics of behaviour and a better understanding of the psychological problems of people. Gandhi emphasized that teachers should establish with their students a real heart contact[9] fashioning their hearts rather than their brain, encourage them in their efforts to lead good lives and build up strong dependable character.

Role of a teacher is very important in the process of imparting education.[10] He should explain the facts effectively and objectively and try to inspire the students to inculcate among themselves creative and constructive thinking. The young creative mind of the student is more amenable to become constructive when chisled by the factual information provided by the teacher.

Education, for Gandhi, is an instrument of socio-economic progress and moral development. Formal literacy for him did not constitute real education. It is neither the end of education nor the beginning. It is only one of the means whereby men and women can be educated.[11]

True education, according to Gandhi, consists of an all-round drawing out of the best in child and man, body, mind and spirit. [12] His main emphasis is on the three H's, i.e. head, heart and hand, rather than on the three R's, i.e reading, writing and 'rithmetic. [13] He laid equal stress on the education of heart, i.e. refinement of emotions and impulses and awakening of deepest feelings of love, sympathy, fellowship.[14] It is a life-long process. It should cultivate the spirit of toleration, cooperation, public spirit and a sense of responsibility.[15]

Gandhi's Philosophy of Education

Gandhi was critical of the existing system of education as he believed it to be wasteful and positively harmful. Under this, he thought, the boys were alienated from their parents and from their parental occupation.[16] Instead, he wanted the education to be given by vocational or manual training. Education, he believed, should be imparted through useful handicrafts in a scientific way[17] so as to enable the child to start producing from the moment he started his training. Gandhi considered that this method led to the highest development of body and soul. This constituted the core of Gandhi's philosophy of education. He wanted the school to teach all the subjects through a vocation, though he was particular that the school may not be turned into a factory. He said "the fact that the whole person in the boys and girls has to be developed through a vocation automatically saves the schools from degenerating into factories.[18] This system would bring into focus the self-supporting aspect of the craft which could help in developing the personality of the child along with making the education self-supporting in his later life.[19]

Gandhi did not want schools to be a store-house of dead, obsolete and bookish knowledge but to provide a platform for work, experimentation and discovery. The school will also help in cultivating character required for becoming a socially useful citizen by providing him opportunity for practising civic virtues, art of discipline and develop a broader vision and the capacity for sacrifice. He gave great importance to the character building aspect of education. To him this was more important than even literacy. For him, schools and colleges are factories for making of character.[20] Further, education, according to him, should aim at producing not only good individuals but socially useful citizens who understand their social responsibilities as an integral element of society.[21]

His political philosophy is also in perfect accord with the idea of national solidarity. He envisaged an ideal society which is a Stateless democracy where social life has become so perfect as to be self-regulated and self-disciplined.[22] According to Gandhi, "National unity consists in having a common purpose, a common goal and common sorrows. It is best promoted by cooperating to reach the common goal by sharing one another's sorrows and by mutual toleration.[23] He added that it must be partnership between equals, each representing the other and the other's way of life.

Gandhi not only aimed at achieving unity but was particular about maintaining it also. He said "the unity we desire will last only if we cultivate a yielding and charitable disposition towards one another.[24] Gandhi wanted his countrymen to adopt non-violence as their creed for regulating the relations among different races. He was conscious of the significance of toleration for a democracy when he said, "Evolution of democracy is not possible if we are not prepared to hear the other side. We shut the door of reason when we refuse to listen to our opponents or having listened if we make fun of them. If intolerance becomes a habit, we run the risk of missing the truth. We must always keep an open mind...."[25]

According to him, nationalism occupies a higher position than sectarianism. He said, "We are Indian first and Hindus, Musalmans, Parsis and Christians afterwards".[26] He firmly believed that multiplicity of religions did not stand in the way of national integration. According to him, various religions can be compared to the branches of a tree which have a common trunk. Different religions have the same root "God". The key to the solution of the tangle, according to him, lies in everyone following the best in his own religion and entertaining equal regard for other religions and their followers.[27]

He added, the need of the moment is not one religion but mutual respect and tolerance of the devotees of different religions. "We want to reach not the dead level but unity in diversity. The soul of religion is one but it is encased in a multitude of forms. The latter will persist to the end of time. Wise men will ignore the outward crust and see the same soul living under a variety of crusts."[28]

Similarly, existence of many languages and provinces did not pose any problem to national solidarity. He even favoured the redistribution of provinces on a linguistic basis,[29] as he considered it conducive to the cultural advancement of the country. But he warned that such redistribution should not endanger the organic unity of India. "Autonomy", he asserted, did not mean disruption. If each province started considering itself as a separate, sovereign unit, India's independence will be lost and with it will disappear the freedom of the various units also,[30] He wanted Indians belonging to different provinces to abjure all separatist inclinations and consider themselves as Indians.

Likewise, Gandhi was emphatic about social and economic equality in society. He also laid stress on achieving a just social order devoid of exploitation as wide economic disparities between the rich and the poor pose a serious challenge to the unity of the country.[31] We may not be able to have absolute equality but attempt at minimisation of inequalities would pave the way to National Unity.

Deviation from the Path Truth and Non-Violence

He believed that unity did not require uniformity. In his view, it is a narrow and irrational approach to life. According to him, it is intolerance and lack of faith in truth and non-violence that stand in the way of national unity. All these ideals which Gandhi perceived decades ago are very much relevant and valid even today. But the trouble erupting in different parts of the country off and on is indicative of the fact that we have deviated from the path shown by the Father of the Nation.

To sum up, national integration can be achieved if we realize the relevance of Gandhi and infuse the spirit of mutual tolerance and brotherhood by curbing the fissiparous tendencies arising out of casteism, communalism, linguism and provincialism. The casteless and classless society can be established if the regional problems are viewed in the national context and education is designed to play its role of creating a psychology of national integration. What we need today is a multi-pronged attack on the various forces of disruption. To keep the monster of disintegration at an arm's length we have not only tackle to problems of religious fundamentalism, casteism, linguism and provincialism but also of social and economic inequality, and defferent levels of development in different regions on a war footing. Our educational processes and the media will have to create a social and silent revolution in the communities constituting this great nation.

REFERENCES

1. *Jawaharlal Nehru's Speeches,* September 1957 to April 1963, Vol. IV , p. 7, Publications Division, New Delhi.
2. Vivek Ranjan Bhattacharya, *Towards National Unity and Integration,* P. 109, Metropolitan Book Co. Ltd., 1985, New Delhi.
3. *The Tribune,* February 1, 1988.
4. *India Today,* February 29, 1988, p. 82.
5. *The Tribune,* January 31, 1988.
6. *The Tribune* February 7, 1988.
7. W.H. Kil-Patrick, 1926, *Educatiion for a changing civilization,* Macmillan Company, New York, pp. 114-115.
   The Rev. P.C. Eapen, 1968, "Education for Emotional Integration" in P.D. Saggi, *We Shall Unite - A Plea For National Integration,* Indian Publications Trading Corporation, New Delhi, pp. 38-44.
8. P.B. Gajendragadkar, 1974 *The Philosophy of National Integration*, National Publishers House, Delhi, pp. 56-57.
9. M.S. Patel, 1953, *The Educational Philosophy of Mahatma Gandhi,* Navajivan Publishing House, Ahmedabad, pp. 90-100.
10. Raksha Saini, "Ronle of Teachers in National Integration," in seminar on *National Integration and Communal Harmony,* Gandhi Darshan Samiti, New Delhi, 1987, pp. 127-131.
11. *Harijan,* July 31, 1937, Vol. V, p. 197, Garland Publishing Inc., NewYork, 1973.
12. Ibid.
13. M.S. Patel, op. cit., p. 32.
14. R.K. Prabhu and U.R. Rao, 1946, *The Mind of Mahatma Gandhi*, Navajivan Publishing House, Ahmedabad, pp. 378-379.
15. Humayun Kabir, 1961, *Education in New India,* George Allen and Unwin Ltd., London, p. 23.
16. *The Collected Works of Mahatma Gandhi,* Vol. LXVI, p. 263, The Publications Division, Government of India 1976.
17. *Harijan,* op. cit., Vol. V, July 31, 1937, pp. 197-198. *Collected Works,* op. cit., Vol. XLVI, p. 263.
18. M.S. Patel, op. cit., pp. 18-19.
19. *Collected Works*, op. cit., Vol. LXVI, pp. 264-265.
   Harijan, Vol. V, July 31, 1937, pp. 197-198.
20. M.S. Patel, op. cit., pp. 35-36.
21. V.T. Patel, "*Gandhi's Concept of Education,*" *Gandhi Marg,* Vol. IV, No. 6, September 1982, pp. 91-92.
22. *Young India,* Vol. XIII, July 2, 1931, pp. 16-17, Navajivan Publishing House, Ahmedabad, 1981.
23. Op. cit., Vol. II, Feb. 25, 1920, p. 3.
24. Op. cit., Vol. III, May 11, 1921, p. 148.
25. *Harijan*, op. cit., Vol. IX, May 31, 1942.
26. *Young India,* op. cit., Vol. IV, January 26, 1922, p. 62.
27. *Harijan,* op. cit., Vol. XI, January 4, 1948, p. 497.
28. *Young India,* op. cit. Vol. VI, Sept. 25, 1924, p. 318.
29. *Harijan,* op. cit., March 29, 1942, Vol. IX, p. 97.
30. *Harijan*, op. cit., February 1, 1948, Vol. XII, p. 14.
31. Op. cit., Vol. X, March 31, 1946, p. 63 and Vol. XI, June, 1, 1947, p. 172.

21

SOME REFLECTIONS ON DEVELOPMENT, PEACE AND EDUCATION IN THE GANDHIAN PERSPECTIVE

MARJARIE FERNANDES

The three important terms which are much used in everyday parlance are development, peace and education. However, the meaning and implications of each of these three terms as well as their interrelationship do not seem to be properly understood by everyone. The present paper is therefore an attempt to contribute to this understanding. Starting with a discussion of the views generally held in both advanced and Third World countries, which are of limited relevance and use in the present-day world context, the paper then goes on to consider the Gandhian perspective which can provide the real meaning of and interrelationship between development, peace and education.

For a long time development was considered as synonymous with economic growth. Maximization of the rates of growth of output and the pursuit of material welfare were given top priority. The emphasis was on the end or objective but no attention was paid to the means adopted to achieve the end. As a result of high rates of investment, especially of physical capital, huge capital-intensive machinery and technology, several countries, which today are regarded as developed or advanced, achieved high rates of economic growth. Impressed by the performance of the developed countries, many Third World countries chose to follow the same path to development. But, unfortunately, the experience of the past two or three decades has shown that this chosen model of development was wrought with serious problems both in the so-called developed countries themselves and even more so, in the Third World countries.

In the advanced countries, the development has resulted in excessive consumption and multiplication of wants. The exploitation of natural resources and pollution of the environment have reached such dangerous levels that the very survival of humanity on this planet is threatened. Increased inequality between the rich and the poor, unemployment and poverty have accompanied the high rates of growth of output. In the Third World countries following the Western model of development, the resulting situation is even worse. Although some Third World countries have experienced considerable rates of economic growth, they are beset with the same problems, but of even greater intensity, as in the advanced countries which they initiated. There is a widening of the gap between the few who have enriched themselves and the multitudes who are steadily getting impoverished. The rate of unemployment has registered a steady rise. Mounting debts have reduced several countries to a condition more dependent than before and exposed them to economic domination and penetration in spite of their political liberation. Also, the policy of blind adoption of Western technology has produced a dual system accentuating the gulf that has divided the city and the countryside from the days of the colonial era. Development as it has taken place in the world is in the nature of mal- and over-development of the North and under-development of the South. People in both the North and the South, i.e. the advanced and Third World countries, are clearly dissatisfied with such development.

Development in the real sense of the term should be a more participatory humane mode of development of all people and the entire society. It should be just or equitous in distribution and conserve natural resources, especially of the non-renewable type. In short, development should be "need-based, endogenous, self-reliant and ecologically sound".

Just as in the case of development, people are also dissatisfied with the pursuit of peace as it has been going on since the days of the Second World War. Earlier, peace was considered in narrow terms to mean absence of war or direct personal violence. This view was sometimes referred to as negative peace. The pursuit of such peace, especially during the days of the Cold War was through the policy of Nuclear Deterrence (sometimes termed as MAD, i.e. Mutually Assured Destruction) which resulted in the build-up of nuclear arms and armament industries absorbing huge amounts of scarce resources both in developed and Third World countries. The consequences of such a policy were even worse for the latter as the resources siphoned off for purchase of arms were not available for urgent programmes to ameliorate the living conditions of the masses.

Besides the narrow viewpoint on peace, the idea of positive peace to refer to the absence of structural violence has been considered to be increasingly relevant in more recent times. This term is used to refer to the violence which is endemic in the system being built into its structure. Such violence shows up in the distribution of unequal life-chances in society and socio-economic injustice. For many people in the Third World countries, the implications of war are less significant than the abject poverty and injustice they suffer from. So, positive peace is more relevant to them than negative peace. A country wherein there is no war cannot be said to have peace if its people are suffering from various types of socio-economic injustices. Positive peace cannot exist in conditions where income and wealth are concentrated in the hands of a few people who are exploiting the masses or if poverty and unemployment are on the increase. In other words, those very aspects which are found lacking in the development process are also seen to contribute to the lack of peace. Achieving development in the real sense of the term would thus result in peace in its complete sense as well.

Human Capital Approach

In terms of education too, dissatisfaction has been expressed just as it was in the case of development and peace. Earlier, the Human Capital approach to development gave tremendous importance to education resulting in large amounts of resources being invested in education. However, education was considered as synonymous with schooling to be undergone for a certain period before joining the world of work. Both in content and process, the education system was developed in consonance with the model of development that was followed by various countries. Skilled people were required for increasing output of goods and services and education enabled people to acquire the skills demanded by their jobs. Gradually, however, education came to be identified virtually with certification or credentialism. Instead of learning how to do a job, people learnt how to get a job using the certificate/credential which was taken as a proxy for the skills abilities required for the job. Irrelevant and useless knowledge was transmitted from the teacher to the taught and if the latter were able to reproduce it in the examination, they were certified as being educated. Apart from being wasteful in terms of the resources required for its provision, such education resulted in making the majority of the people subservient to the fulfilment of the interests of the dominant class in society which benefited from the development process as well. Promotion of peace could hardly be achieved through an education system which was founded in terms of Paulo Friere's "banking" concept of education. Such education promoted values contrary to the principles of peace, e.g. killing initiative and opinion on the part of students, keeping discipline through punishment and compulsion, provoking envy and rivalry through the marking system, etc. If instead, education involved a process of Friere's "conscientization", it would promote both positive and negative peace as well as development in the real sense of the term.

This, a meaningful approach to development, peace and education should be a holistic one. Considering that the three are intimately inter-connected, it is not possible to merely achieve one in isolation. Gandhi's approach provides a viable alternative and a holistic approach to development, peace and education. His basic tenets which are of relevance to us here are: Swadeshi, Bread Labour, Aparigraha or Non-possession, Trusteeship, Non-exploitation, Equality, Restricted Use of Machinery, Satyagraha and Basic Education. There is no hierarchy presumed amongst the various elements. They are inter-dependent so that taken together they form a coherent system.

The Swadeshi concept suggests that the individual consumer will reduce his wants and reorder the preference function so that it is made up of mostly goods produced in the neighbourhood (defined in terms of a community) and also that producer and consumer neighbours cooperate to produce efficiently through avoidance of wasteful competition and overmechanization.

Bread Labour refers to the work performed in the service of other human beings by expenditure of energy through body-work and resulting in ethical production which has value in use and not mere exchange. (Thus war goods would find no place here.)

Aparigraha or Non-possession means "possession by all". It ensures a minimum level of consumption to all irrespective of income and is based on the principle of "contentment" as against the principle of greed or "more and more". This is linked to Gandhi's view on Want Limitation which would result in social justice and conservation of resources.

Trusteeship is based on the highest moral principle of service to others and results in an egalitarian society. The endowments of better abilities and larger resources do not allow a person the privilege of using these for personal gains; rather they impose an obligation of using them for the benefit of all Trusteeship implies decentralization of the economic and administrative structure and thus poses a limit to power and its use.

Non-exploitation involves the reduction of and eventual elimination of privileges arising out of non-accountability or easy opportunity or due to any other economic privilege. It thus involves the reduction in the elite-mass contradiction based on exploitation which is the "essence of violence as well". Hence Non-Exploitation approach to both development and peace.

Equality involves reduction in economic inequalities through redistribution of assets in favour of the poor and raising their income levels and by changing the attitude and motivation of the rich. As a result there will be lowering of the prices of necessities consumed by both elite and mass society and raising of the prices of luxuries consumed only by the elite society.

Restricted Use of Machinery implied that Gandhi did not rule out the use of machinery or large-scale industries in the economy. They would be permitted where individuals cannot function. Thus, electricity, ship-building, iron-works, machine-making, etc., were visualized to exist side by side with village handicrafts but the former were to subserve the interests of the village and its crafts. However, "machinery which helps a few to ride on the backs of millions" is not desirable. Gandhi felt that in an over-populated backward, the deteriorating living conditions of the masses could be improved only by solving the problem of growing structural unemployment through revitalizing the labour-intensive occupations of the traditional sector.

Satyagraha Weapon of the Strongest: Satyagraha is considered as a relevant alternative to tackle the problem of violence. This term was coined by Gandhi in South Africa to express the force that the Indians there used. It is conceived as a weapon of the strongest and excludes the use of violence and hatred in any shape or form. Satyagraha is a relentless search for truth and a determination to reach truth not by infliction of suffering on the opponent but on one's self. It literally means holding on to truth and is also referred to as "soul-force". Satyagraha is a very powerful non-violent method of direct action. A Satyagrahi exhauts all other possibilities like persuasion and conciliation before he resorts to Satyagraha. Four basic ideas are stressed in Satyagraha: (a) it is essentially the use of soul-force; (b) it excludes the use of physical force; (c) through the suffering of the Satyagraha, it appeals to the heart and thus seeks to convert the wrong-doer; and (d) means and ends are convertible terms – "as the means, so the end", good results can be produced only by good means.

Basic Education is founded on the fundamental principle of learning by doing. It is primarily a method of correlation of book-learning, craft and life-situations and involves an intimate interaction between the teacher and the student. Such education aims at the all-round development of human personality and is value-centric. It involves values like cooperation, discipline, fearlessness, sacrifice, etc. Although the young would mostly be catered to through Basic Education, older people are not ruled out from the benefits of education. For Gandhi, education was co-terminus with life and should not be compartmentalized into water-tight categories.

Educating adults from the Gandhian perspective involves the additional task of removing the undesirable elements from the existing social ethos that have been imbibed and internalized by adults before imparting to them "the literacy of the whole personality", not merely reading and writing ability.

All these Gandhian principles are based on two central notions, viz. the nature of the cosmos or world and the nature of man. Gandhi believed that the cosmos is governed by a Moral Law referred to as God, Truth, Dharma, etc. Only a seeker after truth guided by this Moral Law in all spheres of activity is a man in the real sense of the term. Development, peace and education should be man-centered and thereby promote both his spiritual and material welfare.

tend will to continue a minimal urge for active enlistment in the lives and political affairs of any interest in self-preservation.

Because the United States cannot run on their own a world unilaterally, the task of empowering cities in the world and the task of empowering citizens come close to being the same.

What of Neighbourhoods: In all this, it seems that neighbourhoods have some role to play, but just what it should be is far from clear. Similarly, it is unclear how much public power can be given to or taken by this microlevel. Villages and neighbourhoods are very small in the world economy and might appear to be of little help in dealing with the territorial division of power. Their small size would imply the need for several levels of authority between them and the global authority, which gets messy because there is a distinct limit to how many levels of government even the most alert citizens can keep track of. Because a monolithic, unfederated city without neighbourhoods would be daunting and discouraging to empowerment of citizens, strong neighbourhoods, villages and suburbs would appear to make sense—but only if they are part of the region-wide network. They cannot be expected to make law, but certainly could serve as active political arenas for debate and discussion. Community television and computer networks can empower by connecting the neighbourhoods to one another and to the city.

But should neighbourhoods emphasize heterogeneous or homogeneous populations? There is considerable literature on either side. Who's laws are to be followed? Who's rules? Who's morality is supposed to apply? Some neighbourhoods are highly resistant to change; others are quite flexible and innovative (Mandelbaum, 1987).

People need to be citizens of some place, not of the world exclusively. Increasingly they are living in cities, so it makes sense to look for empowerment in producing more effective places to live, aided by neighbourhoods and suburbs, which individually would have little voice. And always, individual citizens and neighbourhoods need the collective action of powerful local governments to speak for them in the global community.

22

INDIAN TRADITION – PERENNIAL PRINCIPLES AND ETERNAL ELEMENTS

D. B. KERUR

We often talk of history and discuss concepts of heritage, tradition and culture. History is broadly understood as a record of past events involving human affairs. Usually, it has been an account of political activities of a nation. We get an account of conquests and conquerors, wars and victories. Historians have been occupied more with tales of kings and heroes, their strategies and techniques.

Recently, however, the coverage of history is significantly widened. It is now a story of total human affairs – political, economic and social. We now have history of ideas, and of thoughts. Growth of science and its impact is a new development. We have [illegible] Science of History.

In science and scientific investigation, we normally have three stages. We need precisely to identify the situation we intend to study. We observe the situation, gather information, collect the data. This is the first stage – Identification. The data has to be classified separating different parts and elements that compose and constitute the situation. This is the second stage – Classification. Next in the process, we need to discover elements which are relatively stable and constant and elements which are variable. Even here, we can identify dependent variables and independent variables. This is the third stage – Analysis.

With the help of such an analysis, we infer laws that explain the behaviour of the situation. Laws that explain how the situation functions. Discovery of these laws in terms of cause-and-effect relation is the purpose of all scientific investigation. An understanding of these laws enables us to devise ways and methods, design weapons and instruments which help us control and master the situation. In other words, Science and Technology endow us with power.

Finally, we have the Time element. We observe a situation at a point of time. We now have to examine the situation through a period of time. Precisely, we have to discover the Laws of Movement and the Laws of Change.

This entire methodology has to be applied to history, to the study of society. We are aware of Hegel and Marx – master thinkers in the field. Hegel interprets social change in terms of changing ideas and ideals. He gives an idealistic interpretation of society. Marx gives an economic or materialistic interpretation. Changing technique of production, changing production relations, Marx holds, determine the course of social change.

When we observe a situation changing through a period of time, we have to note what elements have remained unchanged; what elements have changed; what precisely is the core character of the situation – the core that has stood the test of time, the core that has withstood the upheavels – political, economic and social.

Culture and Tradition

Here, we come to the concept of tradition. The concept of culture is close to tradition. Arnold Toynbee holds culture as a social heritage transmitted from generation to generation through education. He makes a distinction between instinct and culture, and states that the role of instinct is subordinate to the role of culture. Culture includes all human activities that do not spring from instincts. In-all human activities that do not spring from instincts. Instinctual activities, e.g. impulse to satisfy hunger, sex are governed and modified by customs, which are clearly manifestation of culture. In so far as instincts escape the cultural control, man becomes less than human.

Tradition can now be defined as the transmission of knowledge, doctrines, customs from earlier generation to later generation.

Society is basically a biological group. Existence, survival and continuity constitute the fundamental urge of any being or creature. Man's concern with security has resulted in the emergence of the State. His concern to protect culture and tradition gives us the concept of Nation. His anxiety to exist has led to the development of economic institutions. Through time, the institutions of war and slavery—in some forms—have dominated the scene of history. And it needs to be noted that war—as Toynbee states—is a product of culture and not of instinct. War is manifestly an evil.

In a sense, culture is ethically ambivalent—a mixture of good and evil. The relative proportion would differ at different times, in different regions, and in different classes. One thing more—culture, good or evil, is always a product of economic surplus. Neither class differentiation, nor slavery nor war is possible and practicable before society begins to produce an economic surplus beyond the requirements for meeting its day-to-day needs.

Life, any living organism and, therefore, society, is a dynamic phenomenon with growth and change as its basic characteristics. Yet in the process, society retains and preserves certain distinctive elements that account for continuity. And precisely these elements constitute the Tradition—heritage transmitted from generation to generation.

Indian Society, Indian Nation

While pondering over Indian Tradition, let us concentrate on those distinctive basic elements conspicuous with Indian way of life. Those elements which emerged as historical categories and evince tendencies to wither away in the course of history need not detain us. One is often tempted to refer to the caste system in this respect. But it is necessary to note that caste as a social institution is positively a historical category relevant only to a given period and given situation. With the development of science, technology, emergence of new economic institutions, changing production relations, etc., the caste system will wither away.

Further at any point of time inequalities do exist in any community. These may refer to property, power, status, race, educational attainment or mere physical strength. With the passage of time, development of science and technology tend to perpetuate – even accentuate these inequalities. This is so, for the simple reason that fruits of development and accruing benefits remain confined to those who already hold the positions and enjoy the privileges.

With inequalities going deeper and getting harder, the social structure groans under strain and tension. Solution is sought either through peaceful reforms of violent revolutions. In any way, the society moves on – evolving a new structure relevant to the new needs.

History of Indian society is no exception. Caste system or any social structure is but a historical category subject to change in the course of history. However, while discussing Indian Tradition. let us take up only those basic elements that have stood the test of time and have encountered the upheavals – political, economic and social.

A modern historian often asks whether India was ever a Nation. Sometimes, he seems inclined to hold that Indian Culture and Civilization is a by-product of foreign conquests – be it Muslim or British. This is clearly unhistorical. India is an ancient land with a distinct civilization and a distinct culture. Dr. D.D. Kosambi, in his classic *Culture and Civilization of Ancient India*, refers to the conquest of Alexander. And he rightly points out that Alexander was drawn to the East by the magic name of India, when England and France were barely coming into the Iron Age. Arabs – intellectually progressive and active people – took their treatises on medicine and a good deal of their mathematics from Indian sources.

Indian Nationalism, it is true, is linked up with our freedom struggle – waged against the British. However, it needs to be clearly acknowledged that we owe our Nationhood to the divine souls like Ramakrishna Paramhansa and Swami Vivekananda.

The State as the key social institution emerges at a stage when a community emotionally integrated with a capacity to govern its own affairs comes to be endowed with Sovereignty. In political science, State is equated with Nation plus Sovereignty. A people aspiring to be the State has to discover its identity, build up its image and develop a strong rational emotional base. Precisely, this process was initiated in India by Swami Vivekananda.

The British impact was being intensely felt. The educated elite and even the high caste Hindus were entertaining a feeling of inferiority complex. There was a wave of social reforms which consisted in only aping Western ways of living with scant regard for Indian traditions.

Narendra, - a restless, educated youth, met Shri Ramakrishna Paramhansa and saw in him a living incarnation of crystallized Indian Tradition. It was a discovery of India's identity. India in her own way can now be a Nation and aspire to be the State. Narendra, now Swami Vivekananda, descended as the apostle of Indian Nationalism. Yogi Arvind, Lokmanya Tilak and Mahatma Gandhi – all stood for this Nationalism, which originated in the Indian Tradition.

Ramakrishna Paramhansa, a great mystic of Dakshineshwar, taught the fundamental unity underlying all religions. Perception of Unity in the Universe is our supreme tradition. Swami Vivekananda carried the message to the world at large. Gandhiji preached the same principles.

Swami Vivekananda was aware of the immediate social problems. Throughout his career, the great patriot-monk had pleaded passionately for the removal of poverty and ignorance of the masses and for the emancipation of Indian Womanhood. The Swami was clear in his mind as to the passing phase of the caste system. He stated in unequivocal terms, "The days of exclusive privileges and exclusive claims are gone and gone for ever from the soil of India." He even held the Muslim conquests as salvation to the downtrodden.

With the Brahmin at the one end and the Chandal at the other, the task is, he said, to raise the Chandal up to the Brahmin.

India's lifeblood, Swamiji declared, is spirituality. If it flows clear every thing will be right. Appreciating the role of Saints and Prophets in the early Maratha period, Great Justice Ranade writes, "National idea of Spiritual Excellence was shaped by these realised mystics."

In the context of Indian Tradition Gandhiji's contribution consists in "Spiritualisation of Politics". He raised politics to the level of religion. He took over, as it were, from Swami Vivekananda his social programme. Truth and Non-Violence in place of propaganda were the keynotes of Gandhiji's programme. Dr. Ambedkar is another evidence of the vital element in the Indian Tradition. All his life Dr. Ambedkar fought for the eradication of untouchability and found solution in Buddhism and the Great Buddha – a gracious product of Indian Tradition.

Timeless Panorama

We can now identify the eternal elements of Indian Tradition that have stood the test of Time, test of Science and Conscience.

Perception of the substance of Universe – the Brahma — is the core of Indian Tradition. A rational investigation, an intellectual inquiry to discover what this World is about.

A moving universe, a changing society, a dynamic existence is basically a Timeless Panorama. Indian Tradition insists on viewing the phenomenon at a point of time, through a period of time and perceive the cosmos beyond time. Lord Krishna in his celestial song – Gita – says HE is Time. *Kavyah Kavyatamaham*. In the morning, the Sun is in the East, in the evening, in the West: we say 12 hours have gone. We indeed measure Time, yet we hardly realize what Time is. If at all we move at the speed of the Sun, for us the Sun will never set.

Perception of Time and an urge to know the Absolute Reality beyond Time is the essence of Indian Tradition. Quest for the

Reality which is comprehensive and coherent, that category which accounts for every aspect of the Universe.

Science and Reality

Science has attempted to look at the periphery of the world, the outside things, the variety and the multiplicity of the universe. But the centre of Being from which all these things emerage, from which these arise is the Eternal Reality – Absolute Truth.

The Gita sings brilliantly about the Knowledge of the Reality , and shows the Pathway too. *Nahi jyanen Sadrisham paritramih vidyate. Tat swayam yogsansiddhih aatmenatmani vindati*. Knowledge is the End, Yoga is the Means. Yoga is another significant aspect of Indian Tradition.

Here again, the Gita in its colophon says "*Brahmvidyayam yog-shashtre*" – Yoga is practical discipline – which converts an intellectual proposition into life's conviction. Yoga is the assured pathway to self-realization.

Knowledge of the material things that are means to the satisfaction of wants, and the knowledge of the technique of acquiring these things positively impart security to life. Security in turn leads to pleasure and happiness. The aspect of life implied here is obviously physical, i.e material one. It refers to the comforts of physical existence.

The basic thing in physical existence is the Body – which is itself perishable. This hard truth at once brings out an apparent contradiction, an obvious inconsistency in our labours of life. We aim at security and certainty in a situation which is basically insecure and uncertain. Clearly an impossible situation. Indian Tradition shows a way out here.

Mortal Existence and Immortal Consciousness

Indian Tradition exhorts us to transcend the material aspect of life. It tells us to raise the question, "who am I" – a favourite question with Raman Maharshi. We do perceive the Body, feel the Mind and are often conscious of the Reason. However, in the course of life, we do get an awareness of our existence distinct from physical existence. Indian Tradition aspires and inspires to discover the inter-relation between one's existence and the infinity that permeates the Universe around. This is verily a basic quest – into the very basis of existence. The knowledge that will dawn is verily Realization.

End-result of Realization

Realization at once lifts one to the highest plane and ushers in eternal security. The thing now known is imperishable beyond mortal body.

Indian Tradition accords supreme significance to the End-result of Realization. Realization – being a part of Infinity – would make once at one humble. Infinity is greater than the greatest. A part is a micro unit. Humility – Namrata is the first end-result. Realization of being an integral part of the Infinity is bound to create a sense of eternal security. Infinity is endless. A feeling of eternal security makes one fearless – Nirbhay. This is the second end-result. And when one is fearless, one is happy and blissful – Anandmaya. This is the third end-result.

Thus, Humility, Fearlessness and Bliss constitute the end-result of Realization. A mortal verily becomes immortal.

Glory of Realized Souls

Indian Tradition sings the glory of such realized souls. In *Vivek Chudamani*, Shankara mentions three rarest facts of life *Manushyatva, Mumukshutva* and *Mahapurush Sanshraya*. To be born a human being is itself a rare phenomenon. As aspirant individual is anothyer rare event. And finally and conclusively the grace of Mahapurusha is the rarest fortune.

Mahapurusha – Self-Realized Soul – showers his grace on and transmits his eternal knowledge to the deserving disciple. Divine teachers – Gurus, with effective power of transmission – are indeed rare but are not altogether extinct.

Shankara himself was a Mahapurusha. Besides, he provides an excellent evidence of India's deep respect for democratic ways. History records the famous debates between Shankara and the distinguished Buddhist scholars. In all the sessions and seminbars, Shankara had the last word. His was a conqueror – Uttara Digvijaya – not through arms or armies, bullets or battles, weapons or wars.

It was a victory of reason, intellect and logic. It was a victory realized through dialogue and discussion, argument and acceptance, reasoning and response. Shankara was a Guru in the highest Indian Tradition.

We do discuss the concept of Education. The root verb – to Educe – means to bring out. Education is training of mind, development of capabilities. Understood in this sense, education will only manifest the potential – either good or bad. Good may become better, even best and bad, worse or worst.

Indian Tradition conceives education in a far different way. Indian Tradition regards Education as a way not only of training the mind and developing the faculty, but a positive process of transformation – the Light of Liberation. *Sa Vidya Ya Vimuktaye*. The taught, emerges a totally changed person with a passiom for the Eternal Truth.

This is possible only at the feet of the divine teacher - a Guru, the supreme symbol of the Indian Tradition.

Rebirth and Incarnation

Concepts of Rebirth and Incarnation are further distinctive elements in the Indian Tradition. Possibly these very concepts account for the vitality of Indian Tradition.

As to the concept of Rebirth, one may question its validity on the ground of modern science. Science deals with matter. Matter may change the form but basically is an imperishable substance. Science has discovered co-existence of Matter and Energy. Science takes cognizance of Consciousness. However, it has yet to establish a cor relation between Energy and Consciousness. Consciousness, aware ness has been the eternal theme in the Indian Tradition.

Nothing in the Universe is perishable. In an ever moving, ever existing Universe; change and transformation are ever experienced features. The concept of Rebirth, therefore, is indeed logical. A being is bound to be reborn in one form or the other. The only uncertainty would be memory of the earlier life. For that matter, even in one single life, we do not – possibly, we need not – remember every detail of our concept of rebirth at once generates a conviction of continuity, and holds an assurance of future opportunity.

The concept of Incarnation is another remarkable element in Indian Tradition. Indian Tradition stresses the concept of Eternal Truth, of Impersonal and Personal God.

Our Vedas – Shrutis – are perfectly impersonal. Persons, Avatars, Incarnations, God, Prophets all come from the Smritis and Puranas. Indian Tradition holds all human creation as a reflection of the ultimate Divinity. Every being is heading towards attainment of that Perfection. What is required is the guidance from time to time according to different times and places, according to different circumstances and environments. People had to be guided along the path leading to unity with the Infinity.

It is just for this that the great Gurus, great Sages, Avatars and Incarnations come in all ages. The Lord so promises in the Gita. He says, "For the protection of the good, for the destruction of the wicked and for the establishment of righteousness, I come into being from age to age." (4,8)

Again, in the Gita itself, the Lord declares, "Whenever an extraordinary spiritual power is manifested by external man, know that I am there. It is from ME that manifestation comes".

Even in normal parlance, we refer to Merits and Morals, Character and Chastity, Virtues and Values. But these are abstract concepts. We experience and realize them through the behaviour of an individual. Jesus Christ personified Pure Love, Gandhiji stood for Non-Violence, Meera was Silent Suffering.

Concept of Incarnation is in a similar category.

INDEX